STAKES AND KIDNEYS

LIVE QUESTIONS IN ETHICS AND
MORAL PHILOSOPHY

Tom Sorell, University of Essex, UK
Norman Bowie, University of Minnesota, USA
and London Business School, UK

The series offers short, accessible studies addressing some of the most topical questions shared by moral philosophy and the social sciences. Written by leading figures who have published extensively in the chosen area, single-author volumes in the series review the most recent literature and identify what the author thinks are the most promising approaches to the live questions selected. The authors are philosophers who appreciate the importance and relevance of empirical work in their area. In addition to single-author volumes, the series will include collections of contributions on live questions. The collections will consist of important published literature and freshly commissioned pieces, with introductions explaining why the contributions represent progress in the treatment of the live questions selected.

Topic areas of focus in this series include: Inequality; Ageing; Minorities; Refugees; Health Care; Childhood; Globalization; Genocide; Civil Society; Privacy, Secrecy; Sustainability; Public Office; Harm and Offence.

Other titles in the series:

Children, Family and the State
David William Archard

Is it Rape?
On Acquaintance Rape and Taking Women's Consent
Seriously
Joan McGregor

Stakes and Kidneys

Why Markets in Human Body Parts are Morally Imperative

JAMES STACEY TAYLOR
Louisiana State University, USA

ASHGATE

Published by
Ashgate Publishing Limited
Gower House
Croft Road
Aldershot
Hampshire GU11 3HR
England

Ashgate Publishing Company
Suite 420
101 Cherry Street
Burlington, VT 05401-4405
USA

Ashgate website: http://www.ashgate.com

British Library Cataloguing in Publication Data
Taylor, James Stacey
　　Stakes and kidneys : why markets in human body parts are morally imperative. – (Live questions in ethics and moral philosophy)
　　1. Sale of organs, tissues, etc. – Moral and ethical aspects 2. Kidneys – Transplantation – Moral and ethical aspects
　　I. Title
　　174.2′97954

Library of Congress Cataloging-in-Publication Data
Taylor, James Stacey, 1970–
　　Stakes and kidneys : why markets in human body parts are morally imperative / James Stacey Taylor.
　　　　p. cm. — (Live questions in ethics and moral philosophy)
　　Includes index.
　　ISBN 0-7546-4109-0 (hardcover : alk. paper) — ISBN 0-7546-4110-4 (pbk. : alk. paper) 1. Procurement of organs, tissues, etc.—Economic aspects. 2. Procurement of organs, tissues, etc.—Law and legislation. 3. Procurement of organs, tissues, etc.—Moral and ethical aspects. 4. Kidneys—Transplantation. I. Title. II. Series.

　　RD129.5.T395 2004
　　362.17′83—dc22

2004006838

ISBN 0 7546 4109 0 (Hbk)
　　　0 7546 4110 4 (Pbk)

Printed on acid-free paper

Typeset by Tradespools, Frome, Somerset
Printed and bound in Great Britain by Antony Rowe Ltd, Chippenham

To Margaret

Contents

Acknowledgements

I first became interested in the ethical issues surrounding markets in human body parts while working as Jeremy Shearmur's graduate research assistant at the Social Philosophy and Policy Center at Bowling Green State University. At the time, Jeremy was criticizing Richard Titmuss's arguments against a commercial blood supply, and was generous enough to discuss his work with me at length. I am still reaping the benefits of these discussions, and I thank both Jeremy and the Social Philosophy and Policy Center for them.

My interest in the ethics of markets in body parts was later rekindled by reading Paul Hughes's article 'Exploitation, Autonomy, and the Case for Organ Sales,' published in the *International Journal of Applied Philosophy*. I wrote a response to this paper (entitled 'Autonomy, Constraining Options, and Organ Sales') that Paul very generously and constructively critiqued, and that subsequently appeared in the *Journal of Applied Philosophy*. This paper was an early ancestor of Chapter 4 of this volume, and I thank the editors of the *Journal* and Blackwell Publishers for granting me permission to reprint sections of it here.

Early ancestors of sections of this volume have been presented at the University of Wisconsin – Stevens Point, the University of Texas – San Antonio, Central Michigan University, and a meeting of the Society for Business Ethics. I thank my audiences of those occasions for their excellent – and often trenchant – criticisms. I have also greatly benefited from comments that I have received on sections of this manuscript from Michael Almeida, Sam Bruton, Austin Dacey, Jason Grinnell, Gary Hardcastle, John Hernandez, Paul Hughes, Bill Kline, Mark LeBar, Dan Palmer, Robert Noggle, Marina Oshana, James Spence, Margaret Taylor-Ulizio and Paul Tudico. I especially thank Mark Brady, whose extensive written comments on Chapters 5 and 9 saved me from many economic mistakes and stylistic infelicities. I also thank Dr B. Broumand and Dr R.R. Kishore for clarifying for me the legal status of the Iranian and Indian kidney markets respectively, and Joseph Shapiro for kindly providing me with a copy of his Stanford University Honors Thesis on the ethics of the kidney trade. More generally, I also thank both Christine Blundell and Walter Grinder for encouraging my interest in ethical issues related to market transactions. Given the topic of this volume it is, perhaps, more than usually important for me to note that I alone am responsible for its contents, and for any flaws that it might possess.

I am also grateful for the institutional support that I have received both prior to and during my work on the project. First, I thank my colleagues in the Department of Philosophy and Religious Studies at Louisiana State University for providing me with an academic environment supportive of writing and research. I also thank the Institute for Humane Studies at George Mason University (especially in the persons of Damon Chetson, Elaine Hawley and Nigel Ashford), both for its financial support and also for introducing me to many people outside of philosophy whose work bears on my own.

I am also grateful to R.G. Frey, my PhD supervisor at Bowling Green State University, for encouraging me to pursue my arguments (both on my PhD work and on this separate project) to their logical conclusions (no matter how repugnant these might at first appear), and to Paul Coulam at Ashgate for his support and encouragement during this project. I also thank Liz Greasby, at Ashgate, and Maria Morgan for their editorial advice and assistance.

Finally, I thank my wife, Margaret Taylor-Ulizio, not only for her exceptionally helpful comments on various drafts of the manuscript of this volume, but also for her patience during its genesis, and my parents, Tom and Betty, without whose support I would not have entered philosophy at all.

Author's note

Throughout the text, 'he', 'his', 'him' and 'himself' shall stand for 'he or she', 'his or her', 'him or her' and 'himself or herself'.

Chapter 1

The Problem – and Some Proposed Solutions

It is well known that the number of human organs that become available for transplantation each year falls far short of the number that are required.[1] It is also well known that because of this thousands of people die each year as a result of the failure of one or more of their organs, and thousands more continue to suffer. What is not so well known, however, is that there is a simple solution to this shortage of organs. This solution would, if implemented, save the lives of thousands of people waiting for transplant organs who would otherwise die. It would also vastly improve the quality of life of thousands of others who would otherwise have to continue to undergo debilitating and painful procedures to stay alive. Moreover, this solution to the current shortage of human transplant organs would have significant beneficial side effects, helping to end the abuse and suffering of yet thousands more people who, although not in need of transplant organs, live in poverty. This solution to the organ shortage is also both inexpensive and practical, and could be implemented with ease.

This solution is to legalize current markets in human organs.[2] And there's the rub. To many persons markets have a whiff of sulphur about them. Market systems are, in the view of many, mechanisms that enable the strong to prosper at the expense of the weak, where everything is reduced to the lowest common cash denominator, and from which human feeling, sentiment and spirituality is absent. And markets in human organs are, in these persons' eyes, the very worst face of this morally bankrupt system. Such markets are frequently described in terms of the greedy rich and the exploited poor, so much so that a cursory glance at discussions of them might lead the casual reader to think that 'the rich, tired of gold plating their bathrooms and surfeited with larks' tongues, had now idly turned to collecting kidneys to display with their Fabergé eggs and Leonardo drawings.'[3] And an international market for human organs is held to be even worse, since it is held to reinforce other forms of exploitation, with kidneys moving 'from East to West ... from black and brown bodies to white ones, from female to male or from poor, low status men to more affluent men.'[4] Indeed, so abhorrent is such a trade held to be that those who advocate it have been compared to Nazis in the correspondence pages of the respectable British medical journal *The Lancet*.[5] One author has even noted that his arguments might support the view that 'the state could justifiably bar publication of a book that advocates the sale of body parts,' on the grounds that even the mere discussion of such markets is harmful.[6] And at least one journal article has been rejected as its 'publication would imply approval of commercial unrelated kidney transplants from living donors.'[7]

The view that markets in human organs are beyond the moral pale is not only held by those whom one would expect to oppose the expansion of the market into a new area, such as neo-Marxists and those opposed to increasing commodification and consumerism. Even persons who are ideologically committed to the promotion of markets are opposed to this trade. Margaret Thatcher, for example, arguably the most pro-market Prime Minister that Britain had in the 20th century, stated that any trade in human organs was 'morally repugnant' after hearing in 1988 that several Turkish citizens had travelled to Britain to sell their kidneys to British citizens.[8] Even members of the medical profession, who might be expected to welcome a way to alleviate the chronic and severe shortage of organs and the suffering that this causes, believe that there is something special about a market in human body parts that justifies its condemnation.[9] The reasons that persons within these diverse groups give for their opposition to trading in human organs are very similar. It is generally believed by persons of all political and theoretical stripes that markets in human organs are likely to compromise the autonomy and well-being of those who participate in them as vendors, that they are likely to undermine the well-being of those who receive the body parts thus procured, that they commodify what should not be commodified, that they are demeaning to the vendors and, most simply, that such markets are simply viscerally repugnant.[10]

But all these objections are flawed. Indeed, I will argue in this volume that not only do these objections to a current market in human organs fail to withstand critical scrutiny, but concern for the core values that they appeal to – personal autonomy, well-being and human dignity – *supports* the view that it is morally permissible to trade in human organs. Rather then being the most morally repugnant approach to organ procurement, then, I will argue that a legal trade in human organs is the best solution to the organ shortage, and that its implementation is morally imperative.

Alternative Methods of Organ Procurement

To argue that it is morally imperative to legalize the trade in human body parts is not to argue that other methods of organ procurement should be abandoned. Since one of the main reasons for advocating that such a market be legalized is to increase the supply of transplant organs, it is clear that any ethical means of achieving this should be encouraged. To advocate the legalization of markets in human organs is thus an *inclusive* approach to organ procurement rather than an *exclusive* one, for such markets could operate alongside other approaches to procuring transplant organs. Of course, instituting a market for human organs might adversely affect the number of organs that will be procured through other means. (It is likely, for example, that giving transplant organs a market value will decrease the number that are procured through voluntary donation.) However, even if this is so it does not necessarily tell against legalizing such a market, for (as I will discuss in Chapter 8) both experience and economics tell us that the additional number of organs that would be procured through the market would be greater than the resulting drop in the number of organs that would be procured by more traditional, non-market, methods.

Since the proposed current market for human transplant organs is not an exclusionary method of procurement it would be sensible to outline some of the methods that rival it. This will not only provide a better background to the debate over the moral legitimacy of markets for human organs. It will also show that many of these other approaches to increasing the supply of organs are subject to serious ethical objections, and so it is not the case that a market for human organs is the only approach that is considered (albeit mistakenly) to be ethically problematic. Furthermore, outlining these alternative approaches to increasing the supply of transplant organs will also demonstrate that they have been proposed on the basis that they exhibit respect for autonomy and concern for human well-being. Since these are the same values that undergird my arguments that a current market in human organs is morally permissible and should be legalized, my proposal of such a market comes from within the ethical mainstream of the debate over how to increase the supply of transplant organs – something that is not always acknowledged by those who oppose the commercial procurement of organs. Finally, outlining the four primary approaches to organ procurement will also show that they all suffer from a certain flaw that the market system is immune to – a flaw that results in their being suboptimal means of increasing the supply of transplant organs.

Donation

The most widely accepted method of procuring transplant organs is that of post-mortem donation, with the donation of the organs being performed either by the decedent prior to his death, or by his relatives post-mortem. This system of donation was formalized in England, Scotland and Wales with the Human Tissue Act of 1961, and in Northern Ireland with the Human Tissue Act of 1962.

Such donation of body parts was similarly formalized in the United States in 1968, when the Commissioners on Uniform State laws announced the Uniform Anatomical Gift Act. This was subsequently adopted (with some minor amendments) by all states and the District of Columbia by

1973. The assumption behind this method of organ procurement was (and is) that a person's organs were of no value to him after his death, and, recognizing both this and the fact that they were of enormous value to their potential recipients, persons would be moved by (consequentialist) moral considerations to donate them.

The most significant aspect of this method of procuring transplant organs is its clear failure to secure anywhere near the number of organs that are required. This method fails (and continues to fail) for three primary (and predictable) reasons. First, very few people are motivated to agree to have their organs removed from their bodies after their deaths for transplantation into others. Some people have religious objections to the intentional dismembering of the body (either before death or after it) and so will not consent to having their organs removed.[11] More typically, people might fear that if the staff of the emergency room found a signed donor card on them after they had been brought in with serious injuries they would be less likely to receive life-saving treatments, since their attending medical personnel would prefer to harvest their organs to save a greater number of lives.[12] Furthermore, even if these two concerns could be allayed this system of organ procurement offers no incentive to sign a donor card beyond the feeling of 'acting virtuously.' Since potential donors incur costs in signing a donor card (such as having to confront their own mortality and subsequent dismemberment, and the time spent in getting and signing the card) for most potential donors (that is, those for whom the satisfaction of 'doing the right thing' is low) this system provides a net *disincentive* to donate.[13] Second, even if a person does decide to donate his organs after his death this does not guarantee that his wishes would be carried out, even if his organs were needed and viable for transplantation. This is because there is no fail-safe method in place for ensuring that a willing donor could be readily identified in time for his organs to be harvested. (A person might not, for example, be carrying his organ donor card when he was brought into the emergency room.) Moreover, even if the decedent *was* identified as a donor his family could still object to the retrieval of his organs. Third, this system also imposes considerable costs on the medical personnel responsible for approaching the decedent's relatives and requesting his organs. As Lloyd Cohen notes, it is difficult for a physician 'who only moments before was caring for an injured young man, to approach the man's mother and suggest that she donate her son's liver ... .'[14] This difficulty is made more acute by the need to maintain potential organ donors on life-support to preserve the oxygenated organs (that is, the liver, kidneys, heart and lungs) so that they will be suitable for transplantation. (Once an oxygenated blood supply is removed from these organs they will degenerate rapidly.) In such cases the physician will be requesting organs from the relatives of a person who appears still to be sentient. Moreover, maintaining a person on life-support for the express purpose of preserving his organs before the request for them was made is itself psychologically burdensome for the medical personnel involved.[15]

This system of post-mortem donation is supplemented by the donation of organs to others (usually family members) by live donors.[16] Unfortunately, even under ideal conditions this method of procuring organs could never provide enough organs to meet the current need for them. Not everybody who needs a transplant organ (or organs) will have a relative who could provide an organ for them, and the relatives of those who do might not agree to this procedure. Furthermore, this method of organ procurement cannot procure all the organs that are needed, for live donors obviously cannot provide some organs (such as hearts or pairs of lungs) without dying. At best, then, the system of procuring transplantation organs from live donors must be seen as a supplementary, rather than a primary, method of procurement.

Required Request

In 1984, in an attempt to enhance the numbers of organs that are procured for transplantation by voluntary donation, Arthur Caplan proposed that hospitals be required to request organs and tissues from the next of kin of a person who had recently died and whose bodily parts were suitable for transplantation.[17] The British Medical Association has rejected this method of increasing the supply of transplant organs.[18] However, in the United States on 1 October 1987 the federal government instituted a version of this policy, pursuant to a provision of the 1986 Omnibus Budget Reconciliation Act and Section 1138 of the Social Security Act, such that hospitals must have in place some form of required request procedure in order to continue to be eligible to participate in the government-sponsored health programmes of Medicare and Medicaid.[19]

Like the system of procuring organs through voluntary donation, there is no obvious secular ethical barrier to the Required Request approach to increasing the supply of organs available for transplantation. However, there is an ethical difficulty with this approach that is not obvious: that it will lead to clinical conflicts of interest. In particular, Required Request legislation requires healthcare providers to switch their primary focus from the care of those of their patients they have identified as being potential organ sources (for example, those who have been the victims of accident trauma, sudden acute illness or self-inflicted injury) to securing organs for another recipient.[20]

The implementation of Required Request policies has also encountered practical difficulties. A study concerning Required Request policies that was conducted between 1991 and 1994 in 23 hospitals in the United States discovered that, although compliance with the Required Request laws was high, healthcare professionals did not always know what their legal responsibilities were under these laws.[21] Moreover, since no positive or negative incentives have been put in place to encourage the medical personnel charged with requesting the organs actually to request them, and such requests are psychologically burdensome to those who are charged with making them, the typical medical practitioner is faced with a net *disincentive* to make these requests.

Presumed Consent

Recognizing that neither a system of voluntary donation nor a system of Required Request (nor even both together) is likely to procure the numbers of organs that are currently needed for transplantation, some medical ethicists argue that if a decedent has not *specifically stated* that he *does not* want his organs to be used for transplantation after his death, then they *should* be so used if they are viable and there is a need for them. This system of 'presumed consent' has gathered much support. The British Medical Association voted at its annual meeting in 1999 to implement this system, although the British government immediately rejected this proposed policy change.[22] Presumed consent systems operate in many European countries,[23] and (in a limited fashion) in several American states that permit coroners or medical examiners to remove corneas, pituitary glands and other specified tissues from cadavers where there is no knowledge of the decedent objecting to this.[24]

The systems of presumed consent that are both proposed and in place have faced serious legal and ethical challenges. In the United States presumed consent policies have been legally challenged on constitutional grounds. In each case the plaintiff argued that the state's taking of the decedent's tissues or organs without any explicit permission to do so violated the Fifth Amendment's prohibition on the taking of private property without due process and just compensation. These legal objections have been upheld to an extent, with the courts ruling that the constitutionality of this method of organ procurement is doubtful in the absence of any effective system for recording and respecting objections to having one's organs and tissues harvested post-mortem. If, however, there is an effective system in place whereby persons can opt out of having their organs removed, and such requests are honoured, then this method of procuring organs is held to be constitutional.[25]

The primary *ethical* objection to procuring organs through a system of presumed consent is similar to the legal argument against it: that it will enable the state to take a person's property without his consent.[26] Although the proponents of this objection to using presumed consent to increase rates of organ and tissue procurement assign a property right to persons with respect to their organs and tissues, this does not commit them to the view that it is ethical to trade in organs and tissues, for they might hold that this property right concerns *noncommodifiable* property that cannot be traded legitimately. If so, the proponents of this objection to presumed consent would not be mollified by an argument to the effect that the state should recognize the decedent's property right in the organs or tissues that it removed by paying his relatives just compensation for them.

There is also concern that systems of presumed consent presume too much. As Veatch and Pitt note, to presume consent is to make a particular empirical claim, namely, that the decedent *would have* consented to having his organs and tissues removed for transplant had he been asked when he was competent to respond.[27] But the evidence garnered from surveys into attitudes towards donation does not support this empirical claim. Instead, it makes it clear that not all persons would actually give their consent to have their organs removed post-mortem if they were asked, with only 55 per cent of Americans being willing to grant formal permission for this to occur.[28] Thus, the presumption on which this method of organ retrieval operates will be mistaken in a significant minority of the times it is made. Since this is so, this method of procuring organs is not as respectful of personal autonomy as one might hope.

There is also a practical concern that the use of a presumed consent policy will not secure a sufficient number of transplantable organs and tissues. One might be concerned that the method of presumed consent would be undermined by the public's distrust of the organ harvesters. Moreover, a presumed consent regime will not provide any incentives to medical personnel to harvest organs and tissues, for this method of organ procurement does not adequately address 'the obligation that doctors feel to obtain the consent of the decedent, his next of kin, or both.'[29]

Concerns about the effectiveness of a presumed consent policy are well founded. Although it seems intuitive that there would be a greater number of organs secured for transplantation in countries that had adopted a policy of presumed consent when compared with those that had not, it is not clear that this is so, for there are a number of difficulties that prevent easy comparisons between the donation rates of different countries. In addition to the form of consent that is

required before organs are taken for transplantation, several
other factors will affect the relative donation rates of different
countries. These include, but are not limited to, the number
of transplant surgeons who are available and the number of
transplant centres, the ways in which persons in each country
die (for example, countries with higher numbers of road
traffic accidents might have a higher rate of cadaver
donation) and the number and characteristics of persons on
the waiting list for organs (for instance, what sort of organs
they need).[30]

Yet even if these factors are held constant it is not easy to
prove that there is a causal relationship between an opt-out
system and an increase in organ procurement. For example,
comparisons are often made between two transplant centres
in Belgium in which the incidence of the above variables
was similar. In the Antwerp centre, in which a voluntary
donation system was in effect, the rates of organ donation
remained the same; while in the Leuven centre, in which a
system of presumed consent was instituted, the rate of
donation rose from 15 to 40 organ donors per year over a
three-year period.[31] Although these figures seem to indicate a
causal relationship between the institution of an opt-out law
and an increased rate of organ procurement the British
Medical Association notes that it is possible that other
factors contributed to the increase in Leuven. For example,
the introduction of a presumed consent policy in Spain in
1989 correlated with an increase in the donation of viable
organs for transplantation, but this increase was owed
largely (if not completely) to the simultaneous introduction
of a national transplantation organization in that country
that coordinated donors and recipients.[32] Similarly, although
Belgium experienced a 140 per cent increase in the total
number of organs that became available for transplantation
following its move from a system of voluntary donation to a
system of presumed consent, much of this increase could be
explained by the simultaneous increase in the number of
Belgian hospitals participating in organ procurement rather
than to a change in the type of organ procurement system
used.[33]

Mandated Choice

As Veatch and Pitt noted, one of the ethical problems that the proponents of presumed consent regimes face is that such regimes might presume too much, for many of the persons who will be presumed to have consented to having their organs or tissues removed under this system would not *actually* consent. This problem does not affect an alternative method of organ procurement: mandated choice. This method requires that all persons must explicitly state whether they consent to have their organs and tissues (or some combination thereof) removed from their bodies after death. This might be accomplished by requiring persons to indicate their wishes when they have certain dealings with the state that most persons have at some point in their lives, such as filing a tax return or applying for a driver's licence. This information would then be recorded in a central database that would be accessible by all organ procurement and distribution agencies.

A system of mandated choice was approved by the American Medical Association in 1994, although it has not yet been put into practice. The advocates of mandated choice claim that it has several advantages, both practical and ethical, over other methods of organ procurement. Mandated choice is held to have a practical advantage over a purely voluntary system of donation in that, by requiring that persons indicate whether they choose to have their organs and tissues removed for transplantation, those who claim in surveys that they are willing to grant permission but who have not yet done so would make their wishes known.[34] It is also claimed that mandated choice would allow persons to make their choices about organ donation in a more relaxed setting, in which favourable public attitudes towards organ donation are likely to be considered and are thus likely to spur persons to decide to donate. Moreover, because all competent adults would be forced by a policy of mandated choice to consider donating their organs this system would enhance public awareness of the need for organs. Finally, 'mandated choice would eliminate occasional delays resulting from the need to obtain family consent that can jeopardize the quality of organs.'[35] As well as these practical benefits that are claimed for a system of mandated choice its proponents also claim that it has many ethical advantages over its rivals. The most often cited of these is that this system of organ procurement will avoid subjecting the decedents' families to additional stress by asking them to consider donating their organs soon after their death.[36] This consideration for the families is, claim the proponents of mandated choice, supplemented by consideration for the autonomy of the decedent, whose wishes would become known (and respected) under this system.[37]

The opponents of mandated choice hold that, rather than enhancing the autonomy of potential donors, such a system is instead likely to compromise it, for it would coerce them into deciding whether to donate their organs – and coercion is inimical to autonomy.[38] Furthermore, in coercing persons to decide whether to donate their organs a system of mandated choice is coercing them to perform the unpleasant task of confronting their own mortality. This system is thus not only likely to compromise the autonomy of the potential organ donor, but is also likely adversely to affect their well-being.[39]

Markets in Human Body Parts

All four of the above methods for increasing the supply of transplant organs and tissues suffer from the same difficulty: they provide no incentive to persons to donate, and so their implementation is unlikely to result in a drastic increase in the number of organs and tissues procured. To rectify this a few writers have suggested that persons be given a financial incentive to choose to have their organs transplanted, either pre- or (more usually) post-mortem.[40] That is, they have suggested that a market mechanism be used to procure human transplant organs.[41]

Markets for human organs are currently illegal in almost all countries.[42] In Britain, the making or receiving of payment for the supply or offer of any organ (whether from a live donor or from a cadaver) is illegal under the Human Organ Transplants Act of 1989.[43] In the United States, such markets are prohibited at state level by the standard interpretation of the Uniform Anatomical Gift Act[44] and, at federal level, by the National Organ Transplant Act of 1984, in which the purchase of human organs for transplantation carries a fine of $50 000 and/or five years in gaol.[45]

These legal prohibitions of markets in human organs directly reflect the moral opprobrium that they are subject to. The passing of the Human Organ Transplants Act in Britain was spurred by the moral outrage that attended the discovery in 1988 that a British citizen, Colin Benton, had purchased a kidney (for £2000) from a Turkish citizen who had travelled to Britain for the express purpose of selling it.[46] Similarly, when persons were testifying before the United States Congress in 1983, urging the trade in human organs to be criminalized through the National Organ Transplant Act, the members of the subcommittee appointed to oversee the drafting of this Act were inclined to view this as a phantom side issue that was not worth addressing.[47] However, in September 1983, during the hearings on this Act, a Virginia physician, H. Barry Jacobs, founded the International Kidney Exchange. Jacobs planned to bring in poor persons from outside the United States who were willing to sell a kidney to a United States citizen who wanted a transplant, for which service he would charge a brokerage fee of between $2000 and $5000.[48] Jacobs's proposal had the same effect on the members of the United States Congress as the Benton case had on the British Parliament, and the trade that he proposed was banned.

The opprobrium that the Jacobs and Benton cases attracted reflects the almost universal moral condemnation of the use of markets to procure human organs. As well as being prohibited by almost every country, markets in human organs have also been condemned by the British Medical Association,[49] the American Medical Association,[50] the Transplantation Society,[51] UNESCO,[52] the World Health Organization,[53] the Nuffield Council on Bioethics,[54] the US Task Force on Organ Transplantation[55] and the Catholic Church.[56] Inside the ivory tower of academia opposition to legalizing a market in human organs was, and is, just as pronounced. Of the thousands of articles, books, newspaper op-ed pieces, official statements, legal bills and encyclicals that professional ethicists, theologians, philosophers and economists have authored addressing this issue, only a very few have opposed the dominant anti-market position. Moreover, few of the publications that do not explicitly condemn trading in human organs offer arguments in favour of allowing such trading to occur. Instead, most merely argue for the far weaker conclusion that the case against this trade is, in the words of cautious Scottish courts, 'not proven.'[57]

In addition to this almost unanimous moral condemnation of markets in human parts, two other aspects of this debate are immediately striking. The first is that, although a vast amount of ink has been spilt in voicing opposition to allowing such markets, little of this has been spent in developing new anti-market arguments. Instead, most has been spent on reiterating and developing a series of arguments that are commonly offered against such markets. The first of these holds that markets in human body parts would compromise the autonomy of those economically impoverished persons who would participate in them as vendors, since they would be coerced into selling by their poverty. Thus, respect for the autonomy of the potential vendors in a market for human organs requires that such markets be prohibited.[58] A less common (but more sophisticated) autonomy-based anti-market argument holds that, while an impoverished person might be autonomous with respect to the *act* of selling an organ, the *option* to sell an organ is an autonomy-impairing 'constraining option.' That is, it is an option that is likely to lead to the future diminution of either the vendor's own autonomy, or the autonomy of other persons who are economically impoverished.[59]

These autonomy-based arguments have become the mainstays of the anti-market position. This can be explained partly by their simplicity, elegance and persuasiveness, and partly by the rise of autonomy to its current position as the preeminent value in bioethics.[60] If one accepts that personal autonomy is (and should be) the primary value in contemporary bioethics, and if it can be shown that respect for autonomy requires that markets in human organs be prohibited, then this provides a strong prima facie case against such markets.

Before continuing I must note that the conception of autonomy that I draw on in this volume is not the Kantian conception, whereby a person is autonomous if he acts out of respect for the impersonal moral law, and is heteronomous to the extent that he is moved to act by his contingent 'motives, preferences and desires.'[61] Instead, here I draw on the non-Kantian approach that is dominant within medical ethics and which has been developed and refined by, among others, Harry Frankfurt and Gerald Dworkin, whereby a person is autonomous if he governs himself in accordance with his contingent 'preferences and desires.' Precisely what is required for a person to be autonomous with respect to their desires and actions in this non-Kantian sense is a vexed question.[62] For the purposes of the arguments in this volume, then, I adopt a very broad account of this sense of autonomy. Here, someone is autonomous with respect to their desires if they arise from the self in some way – they are not implanted by another – and the person in some way reflectively accepts them, and is autonomous with respect to their actions if it is they, and not another, that controls the performance of them. This account of autonomy is both acceptable to all parties in the debate over the denotation of this term, and captures how this term is used in the debate over the moral permissibility of markets in human body parts.

Of course, not all laud the recent shift in bioethics' primary focus from the Principle of Benevolence to the Principle of Respect for Autonomy, and so not all would agree that the primary rationale for prohibiting markets in human organs is that they might compromise the autonomy of the poor.[63] Instead, some argue that the primary rationale for prohibiting such markets is that they will undermine the altruistic donation of transplantable body parts. This, it is variously argued, would be bad because it would undermine community feeling, or because organs donated altruistically are likely to be of better quality than those procured commercially or because if organs are commodified in this way then fewer will be procured. Finally, it is argued (most notably by Richard Titmuss) that if organs were commodified persons would lose the option of being able to donate organs in a situation where these could not be bought.[64] Thus, the proponents of this argument conclude, commodifying organs would remove an important option from persons' choice sets, which would compromise their autonomy.

Related to these anti-market arguments about autonomy and altruism are a series of arguments that markets in human organs would illegitimately commodify the human body and thus undermine human dignity. At one extreme of this anti-market position lies the claim that allowing markets in human organs would be a return to chattel slavery.[65] Less drastically, opponents of such markets follow Kant in arguing that the commodification of the human body is an affront to human dignity, or, in a more consequentialist vein, that such markets would erode respect for persons, and so would eventually lead to them being seen as no more than bundles of spare parts.[66]

Finally, it is argued that markets in human organs are unjust.[67] The appeal of this argument is immediate. If organs are bought and sold on the free market, it is believed, then it is likely that the desperate poor will be the sellers, with the rich and middle class being the purchasers, for the poor who need transplant organs will be unable to compete financially with wealthier persons.

As well as both the almost unanimous opposition to allowing markets in human body parts and the limited number of arguments offered against them, it is also striking that very few of the opponents to 'the market in human body parts' recognize that there is no such thing as *the* market for human body parts. Instead, there are many different ways in which markets for human organs might be organized, and a proponent of one type of market for organs is not necessarily committed to being a proponent of any other type. For example, a person who believes that a market for cadaveric organs (that is, organs that are removed from a cadaver to be sold by its legal possessors) is morally acceptable is not thereby committed to the view that a current market in human organs (whereby someone sells their own organs for removal while they are alive) is also morally acceptable.[68] Similarly, a person who is in favour of offering small, fixed financial incentives to the relatives of a recently deceased person to encourage them to agree to the harvesting of their organs is not committed to an unbridled free market in which transplant organs are bought from live vendors and sold to the highest bidder without regulatory oversight.

Recognizing that there are many different ways of arranging markets in human organs is extremely important, for the moral objections that might apply to one type of market will not necessarily apply to them all. For example, the claim that markets for human organs should be prohibited because they are unjust would not apply to a system whereby there is only one purchaser (such as the state or a charitable body), which then distributes the organs on the basis of the recipients' need. In a related vein, concerns that markets in human body parts would compromise the autonomy of the poor by allowing their economic situation to coerce them into selling could be eliminated by limiting participation in the market to those in the top 60 per cent of median income distribution.[69] Similarly, one could allay fears that the poor would be drawn irresistibly to sell their organs, and so have their autonomy compromised by the lure of filthy lucre, by capping the price at a less than irresistible level.[70]

Once it is recognized that an objection to one type of market for human organs is not an objection to them all, both the proponents and the opponents of such markets have to be very clear about precisely what sort of market they are proposing or criticizing. First, one must determine whether it is morally permissible for persons to sell their organs for removal and transplantation into another while they (the vendors) are still alive (a *current* market), to sell their organs for harvesting after their death (a *futures* market) or whether it is impermissible for persons to sell their organs at all. One must also decide whether it is morally permissible for someone's relatives (or other legal possessors of a cadaver) to sell their organs after that person dies (a *cadaveric* market). All of these decisions may be made independently of each other – although if one views a current market in human organs to be morally permissible one is unlikely to have moral objections to any other type of organ market. Second, one must determine whether it is morally permissible to use market mechanisms to both procure and allocate organs, or whether it is morally permissible to use such mechanisms only to procure organs and to leave their allocation to non-market mechanisms. Similarly, one must also determine if it is morally permissible to leave only the allocation of organs to market mechanisms and to use other means (such as altruistic donation or presumed consent) for their procurement. Finally, one must determine whether it is morally required to regulate whatever market for human transplant organs is instituted (by, for example, fixing minimum prices for the organs that are purchased, or by requiring post-operative care be provided to, and/or informed consent be secured from, the vendors or the purchasers, or both) or whether such regulation is morally impermissible.

In Praise of a *Current* Market for Human Kidneys

In this volume I argue for what is usually considered the most morally repugnant solution to the growing shortage of organs: the market solution. In particular, I argue that concern for personal autonomy and human well-being morally supports the use of a regulated, *current* market to secure human organs. That is, I argue that concern for these two moral values supports the use of a market for the procurement of human organs in which the organs that the vendors sell are removed from their bodies while the vendors are still alive. I also argue that concern for these two moral values supports the use of market mechanisms for both the procurement of transplant organs *and* for the distribution of the organs thus procured.[71] Moreover, the regulation that such a market would require would be fairly minimal, limited only to ensuring that the vendors are afforded adequate protection against being abused by those who directly purchase their organs.

In arguing for a minimally regulated current market in human organs that would serve both to procure and to allocate human organs I am arguing for the type of market that is considered to be (almost) the most morally objectionable.[72] This type of market is subject to all of the objections that all of the other types of markets for human organs are subject to (with the exception of an *unregulated* current market for the procurement and distribution of organs).[73] Since this is so, once I have argued that all of the objections to this form of organizing a market for human body parts can be met and that this type of market is not only morally permissible but is morally *required*, I will also have argued that all other, less objectionable, types of markets for human body parts are also morally permissible.

Given that any type of market for human organs is currently subject to almost universal moral condemnation, a person with my view on this subject is likely to be greeted by the same reaction that the main characters in H.M. Bateman's cartoons met when they committed their social gaffes.[74] To alleviate some of the mistrust that my arguments will (at least initially) be greeted with I should mention that none of them are based on what might be considered dubious premises acceptable only to doctrinaire libertarians. Instead, my arguments in this volume appeal *only* to those values that are shared by the majority of contemporary bioethicists, namely, personal autonomy and human well-being. If I can show that these values morally support a minimally regulated, current market in human organs, then the legalization of such a market should be accepted prima facie by all who accept these values. Of course, one might object that autonomy and well-being are trumped when considering markets for human organs if respecting such values would violate the values of justice or undermine human dignity. I accept the legitimacy of these objections and, to meet them, will show that the sort of market for human body parts that I propose will not lead to either of these deleterious consequences – nor will it lead to other adverse consequences that might morally justify its prohibition.

The arguments that I offer to support my view that a minimally regulated current market in human organs is morally imperative are thus located firmly within the mainstream of contemporary bioethical debate. Furthermore, they are also supported by a wealth of empirical evidence concerning the effects that markets in human body parts have on their participants – including evidence that might at first sight support increasing efforts to prohibit such markets.[75] However, to mitigate further the likely initial adverse reaction to the eventual conclusion of my argument in this volume I do not begin by directly arguing for a current market in human organs. Instead, I begin (in Chapters 2, 3 and 4) by arguing for the weaker conclusion that none of the arguments that have been offered to show that markets in human organs will compromise the autonomy of those who participate in them as vendors are successful. I develop this further in Chapter 5, arguing that a current market for human organs should be regulated to protect the autonomy and well-being of those who would participate in it. I then argue (in Chapter 6) that allowing persons to sell their kidneys in such a regulated market is morally comparable to allowing them to engage in other dangerous and unpleasant activities that are also morally permissible. I then move (in Chapters 7 and 8) to defend such a market against the objection that it would illegitimately commodify human body parts, and against the altruism-based objections that I outlined above. Up to this point I will have argued only that it is morally permissible to use a current market to procure human transplant organs. This position is compatible with the view that it would be moral only to use a non-market mechanism to distribute the organs thus procured. It is also compatible with the view that, even if such a market is *morally* acceptable for reasons of public policy, it should still be legally prohibited. In Chapter 9 I conclude by arguing further that using market mechanisms to distribute as well as to procure human transplant organs is not unjust and, since this would not lead to other adverse consequences – such as the stimulation of an unregulated black market in human organs – such a market should be legal.

Before I begin, three important caveats must be noted. First, my arguments in this volume are based on the assumption that it is morally permissible to donate certain body parts, such as kidneys and blood. I thus do not address in this volume any religious objections to current markets in human body parts that hold that such donation is immoral on the grounds that any such dismemberment of the body is a sin.

Second, I intend only to establish that allowing a regulated, current market in (some) human body parts would make things better both for those who would receive an organ but who would not have done so if such a market continues to be prohibited, and also for those of the poor who would be able to improve their economic standing by selling a marketable organ. I am thus not endorsing Richard Cobden's dubious claim that 'commerce is the grand panacea.'[76] A regulated current market in human organs is not a miracle cure that would both save or improve the lives of all those who need transplant organs while simultaneously improving the lives of those desperate poor who decide to sell.[77] But such a market would, I argue, certainly make things considerably better for both groups of people, as well as for all who are affected by their situation.

Third, although in this Introduction I have been outlining the current discussion concerning the moral permissibility of markets in human organs (and have noted that I will be arguing that a certain type of market should be legalized both to procure and to distribute them), the bulk of this volume will be focused more narrowly on the question of whether such a market should be used to procure and distribute human kidneys. This is so for several reasons. First, kidneys are both paired and nonrenewable. As such, they fall somewhere on the moral scale between single, nonrenewable organs (such as hearts and livers) on the one hand, and renewable (or plentiful) body parts (such as blood, semen and ova) on the other.[78] Focusing on kidneys thus enables me to address the core issue of whether persons should be allowed to sell their body parts without also addressing the separate issue of whether they should be allowed to sell body parts that are vital to their lives (although I will address this issue in Chapter 9, which outlines the implications of my arguments). Moreover, focusing on kidneys will also enable me to gain more ground from my arguments in this volume than I would have been able to gain had I addressed the issue of whether blood, semen, ova and skin should be traded prior to the issue of whether kidneys should be traded. Once I have demonstrated that a minimally regulated market should be used for the procurement and distribution of human kidneys, I will have gone a long way towards demonstrating that such a market should also be used for the procurement and distribution of renewable body parts. This is because, owing to the renewability (or plentifulness) of these body parts, there are fewer moral qualms associated with persons selling them for profit than are associated with persons selling their (nonrenewable) kidneys.

There is also a practical reason why this volume focuses on the kidneys: the stakes in the debate over the moral permissibility of markets in them are high, for it is possible that such markets will be legalized. A legal, regulated market in human kidneys is already operating in Iran[79] and, until recently, a similar market operated in Iraq.[80] Israel now tolerates an unofficial trade in transplant kidneys from live vendors, with both private Israeli insurance companies and the Israeli Ministry of Defence (the body responsible for the healthcare of Israeli veterans) refunding the costs of such transplants.[81] Closer to home (at least culturally) a legal *barter-based* market for human kidneys in which no money changes hands between the providers of the kidneys and the recipients already exists in the United States.[82] In such a market altruistic donors who want to donate to particular individuals but who cannot do so because of tissue incompatibility seek out similar donor–recipient pairs in which the donor in the first pair is compatible with the recipient in the second pair, and the donor in the second pair is compatible with the recipient in the first. Once such pairs have been matched both kidney transplants are performed simultaneously. Calls to legalize a current market for the procurement of human kidneys have also appeared in such respectable (and influential) publications as *The Lancet*[83] and the *British Medical Journal*,[84] and the British National Health Service recently held a closed meeting to discuss the possibility of paying for human transplant kidneys.[85] Once a regulated, current market in human transplant kidneys has been shown to be morally permissible, the chances of such legalization occurring will increase. And since such a market would increase the number of kidneys available, and so both save the lives of persons who would otherwise die and alleviate the suffering of those currently suffering from debilitating dialysis, its legalization is morally imperative.

Notes

1   As of 31 May 2003 there was a total of 5708 patients on the United Kingdom's national transplant waiting list, with only 315 transplants having been performed from 1 January 2003 to 31 May 2003. At the end of December 2001 there were 6842 patients on the waiting list, with 2717 solid organ transplants performed that year; in December 2000 there were 6779 patients on the waiting list, with 2708 solid organ transplants performed that year. For kidneys alone there were 4846 patients on the waiting list for a transplant at the end of 2001, and 4822 at the end of 2000, with a total of 1691 kidney transplants having been performed in 2001 and 1689 in 2000. These statistics were prepared by the UK Transplant Support Service Authority (UKTSSA) from the National Transplant Database maintained on behalf of the UK transplant community. In the United States, as of 31 May 2003 there was a total of 81 736 patients on the Organ Procurement and Transplantation's National (OPTN) waiting list, with 24 888 transplants performed in 2002 and 24 165 performed in 2001. The US statistics are based on OPTN data as of 31 May 2003.

2   In Britain the Human Organ Transplants Act of 1989 expressly prohibits markets for the procurement of human organs. In the United States sales of human organs are prohibited at state level by the standard interpretation of the Uniform Anatomical Gift Act (with the exception of Mississippi; see *Mississippi Code*, 1972 and Supp. 1988, 41-39-9) and at federal level by the National Organ Transplant Act of 1984.

3   This caricature of the kidney trade was noted by Radcliffe Richards, Janet (1996).

4   These concerns were noted by Scheper-Hughes, Nancy (2003), p. 1645.

5   This *ad hominem* attack was levelled at Janet Radcliffe Richards et al. (1998), who were writing for the International Forum for Transplant Ethics – a body that is not usually regarded as a cabal of Nazi apologists. The article that aroused such ire was 'The Case for Allowing Kidney Sales,' *The Lancet*, 351, 27 June pp. 1950–51. The critic was N. Velasco, whose letter was published in *The Lancet*, 352, 8 August 1998, p. 483.

6   Munzer, Stephen R. (1994), p. 278. Munzer does not endorse such a restriction on free speech. He was merely noting an objection to his position whose proponent held that his arguments could be expanded to justify such a prohibition.

7   The article in question was Frishberg, Y. et al. (1998), 'Living (unrelated) commercial renal transplantation in children,' which was eventually published in the *Journal of the American*

  Society of Nephrology. Its rejection on ideological grounds was noted in *The Lancet* by Friedlander, Michael M. (2002), p. 972.

8 Cited in Munson, Ronald (2002), p. 112.

9 All major professional medical associations have condemned trading in human organs. See notes 48–54 in this chapter.

10 Stephen Wilkinson and Eve Garrard suggest that the repugnance felt towards sales of human organs can be explained (although not, perhaps, justified) by attributing the view that bodily integrity is intrinsically valuable to those who are so repelled. They also suggest that similar repugnance is not felt towards organ donation because the violation of bodily integrity is outweighed by the altruism involved. Wilkinson and Garrard (1996), 334–9.

11 Orthodox Judaism is frequently cited as being opposed to organ donation (either pre- or post-mortem) on the grounds that it will compromise the integrity of the body. In fact, Orthodox reasoning on this issue is both less restrictive and more complex that this simple characterization recognizes. For a discussion of this see Mackler, Aaron L. (2001), 420–9. For a general overview of religious approaches to the moral permissibility of disintegrating the body for organ transplantation see Childress, James (1989), pp. 215–40.

12 See British Medical Association (2000), p. 8.

13 This was argued by Cohen, Lloyd R. (1995), pp. 49–50.

14 Ibid., p. 26.

15 See Martyn, Susan et al. (1988), p. 29.

16 Many countries restrict who can act as a live donor, often requiring that the donor be genetically related to the recipient. See Garwood-Gowers, Austen (1999), Chapters 4, 5 and 6.

17 Caplan, Arthur L. (1984), pp. 981–3.

18 British Medical Association, p. 20.

19 Cohen, Lloyd R., p. 15.

20 Martyn et al., pp. 27–9.

21 Siminoff, Laura A. and Mercer, Mary Beth (2001), pp. 377–86.

22 Noted in Erin, Charles A. and Harris, John (2003), pp. 137–8.

23 These include Austria, Denmark, the Czech Republic, the Slovak Republic, Finland, France, Greece, Hungary, Italy, Norway, Poland, Spain, Sweden, Switzerland, Belgium and Portugal. See Cohen, Lloyd R., p. 32, n. 72; British Medical Association, p. 14; Pena, J.R., Pena, R. and da Costa, A. Gomes (1991), pp. 277–9. Although these countries are held to have 'presumed consent' laws the actual legislation to support this claim does not mention that decedents are held to have consented to the retrieval of their body parts. Thus, although such laws might operate as though the decedent has consented, for the sake of accuracy they might better be termed 'routine salvage' laws. For a discussion of this see Veatch, R.M. and Pitt, J.B. (1998), pp. 174–5.

24 See Mehlman, M.J. (1991) and Menzel, P.T. (1991).
25 Council on Ethical and Judicial Affairs (1994).
26 Cohen, Lloyd R., p. 38.
27 Veatch and Pitt, p. 176.
28 Ibid.
29 Ibid., p. 39.
30 British Medical Association, pp. 13–14.
31 For a discussion of this example see Kennedy, I. et al. (1998).
32 British Medical Association, p. 14.
33 Ibid.
34 Noted by Veatch and Pitt, p. 177.
35 Spital, Aaron (1998), p. 149.
36 Ibid.
37 Ibid., p. 148.
38 See Veatch, R.M. (1991).
39 Cohen, Lloyd R., p. 30.
40 Markets for organs from persons unrelated to the recipient have been made possible by the development of new immunosuppressive drugs such as cyclosporin and mycophenolate mofetil. See Andrews, Peter A. (2002).
41 Of these writers most have been economists rather than ethicists, and to my knowledge only very few of them have argued that a current market (that is, a market where organs are sold by, and removed from, live vendors) should be used for both the procurement and distribution of organs. Moreover, most proponents of markets in human body parts content themselves with arguing for either a futures market or a market in cadaveric organs. If they do argue for a current market, they typically restrict its use to the procurement of organs and not to their distribution. Proponents of a current market for both procurement and distribution include Clay, Megan and Block, Walter (2002), and William Barnett II, Saliba, Michael and Walker, Deborah (2001). A less radical suggestion is that a current market could be used to procure organs, with non-market mechanisms used for their distribution. Those who argue for this position include Dworkin, Gerald (1994), Harris, John and Erin, Charles A. (2002) and (1994), Beauchamp, Tom L. (2003) and Hoffenberg, Raymond (2001). (Hoffenberg mainly argues that the case against a current market for the procurement of human kidneys is weak, making it clear that his arguments here are borrowed from Radcliffe Richards, 1996.) Persons who endorse a market for procurement but who do not address the issue of distribution (or whose views here are unclear) include Friedlander, Michael M. (2002), Wilkinson, Stephen (2003), Chapter 7, Radcliffe Richards, Janet, Gill, Michael B. and Sade, Robert M. (2000); Jeffries, David E. (1998), Epstein, Richard (1997), pp. 253–61; Reddy, K.C. (1993) and Pattison, Shaun D. (2003).

Less radically still, a futures market in human kidneys is argued for by Lloyd R. Cohen, Barnett, Blair and Kaserman (2002), pp. 89–111; de Castro, L.D. (2003), Schwindt, R. and Vining, A. (1986) and Love, Andrew J. (1997). A market for cadaveric organs is argued for by Harris, Curtis E. and Alcorn, Stephen P. (2001), Arnold, R. et al. (2002) and Perry, Clifton (1980).

Schemes akin to futures markets in human organs where 'donors' receive some form of benefit for agreeing to act as future donors if they are killed (such as a reduction in insurance premiums, waivers of driving licence or motor vehicle registration fees or a reduced income tax bill) have been respectively suggested by Hansmann, Henry (1989), Trebilcock, Michael J. (1993), p. 36 and Oswald, Andrew (2001). An even weaker conclusion is argued for by Savulescu, J. (2003), who holds that persons have the right to sell their body parts – a position that falls short of endorsing the use of markets for their procurement.

42   World Health Organization (1992), pp. 12–28.

43   British Medical Association, p. 4.

44   Although Mississippi does allow a limited futures market in body parts, with its citizens being allowed to sell these to hospitals for collection after their death. See *Mississippi Code 1972* and Supp. 1988.

45   In fact, the National Organ Transplant Act only prohibits the purchase of human organs for transplantation insofar as this 'affects interstate commerce.' However, the term 'interstate commerce' admits very broad construal, after the United States Supreme Court ruling in the 1942 case *Wickard v. Filburn* (317 U.S. 111, 63 S. Ct. 82) that a farmer growing wheat on his own land for use by his own family was affecting interstate commerce. Given this, as Lloyd R. Cohen notes, 'it is doubtful that intra-state sales of organs would escape federal jurisdiction.' Cohen, p. 14.

46   The Benton case is reported in Munson, p. 112.

47   Cohen, Lloyd R., p. 14.

48   Munson, pp. 109–10.

49   British Medical Association, p. 20.

50   Council on Ethical and Judicial Affairs (1994/95), p. 9. However, the American Medical Association accepts that it might be morally possible to remunerate a person's family for organs removed after their death; ibid., pp. 26–7.

51   The Transplantation Society Council (1986).

52   UNESCO, (1989).

53   The World Health Organization, pp. 12–28.

54   Nuffield Council on Bioethics (1995).

55   United States Task Force on Organ Transplantation (1986).

56   As Pope John Paul II made clear '... any procedure which tends to commercialize human organs or to consider them as

items of exchange or trade must be considered morally unacceptable ... ' John Paul II, Pope (2001), p. 90. See also Directive 30 of the National Conference of Catholic Bishops (1995), which states that although the transplantation of organs from living donors is morally permissible, the donor should not reap any economic advantages from the donation. For a discussion of the Catholic Church's views concerning organ donation see Stempsey, William E., S.J. (2002). For an alternative Catholic view see Cherry, Mark J. (2000a). See also Pope Pius XII (1960).

57   See, for example, Radcliffe Richards (1996), Cherry (2000b), Nelson, Mark T. (1991) and Harvey, J. (1990).

58   See, for example, Dossetor, John B. and Manickavel, V. (1992), p. 63.

59   Hughes, Paul M. (1998) and Zutlevics, T.L. (2001a).

60   Noted by Smith, Janet (1997).

61   This distinction between the Kantian conception and the conception of autonomy as *personal* autonomy is outlined in Frankfurt, Harry G. (1999b), p. 132.

62   For an overview of recent work on the concept of autonomy see Taylor, James Stacey (2005).

63   These principles are outlined in Beauchamp, Tom L. and Childress, James (2001), Chapters 3 and 5.

64   Titmuss, Richard (1997), pp. 307–308. The original edition of Titmuss's book was published in 1970.

65   Abouna, G.M. et al. (1991), p. 169. See also Scheper-Hughes, p. 1645.

66   This fear was noted in Rothman, David J. (1998), p. 16.

67   See, for example, Dickens, B.M. (1990).

68   Arguments in favour of cadaveric markets in human organs are more frequently presented in the United States than in Britain because of a long-standing common law tradition in Britain that 'there are no property rights in a corpse.' For a discussion of this, and of how US common law has diverged from this British principle, see Scott, Russell (1981), pp. 186–90.

69   This was rhetorically proposed by Hansmann, p. 14.

70   Rhetorically proposed by Radcliffe Richards, p. 384.

71   These arguments will be 'sufficient to establish in general secular terms ... whether it is good or bad to have a market in which one can ... buy human body parts.' For doubts concerning the efficacy of such secular moral argument see Engelhardt, Tristam H., Jr. (1999), p. 295.

72   Harris and Erin (1994, p. 135) note that 'Arguing for commerce in the context of organs obtained from cadavers is less morally problematic than in the case of the living.' Similarly, Lysaght, M.J. and Mason, J. (2000) accept that their argument against trading in organs is 'admittedly stronger' when directed at a current rather than a cadaveric market. McConnell notes that

some proponents of future markets in human organs take pains to distinguish themselves from proponents of a current market on the grounds that 'the latter is wrong.' McConnell, Terence C. (2000), p. 129.

73   Such a market has been proposed by Kervorkian, Jack (2001).

74   The Australian cartoonist was famed for his *Punch* comic strips and 'The Man Who ...' drawings of embarrassing situations. Were Bateman alive today he would undoubtedly produce a cartoon entitled 'The man who suggested to the British Medical Association that he should be allowed to sell a kidney.'

75   In particular, I will address evidence concerning the black market in kidneys provided by Goyal, Madhav et al. (2002).

76   Cobden, Richard (1878), p. 20.

77   For an account of some of the negative effects of the legal Iranian market in kidneys see Zargooshi, Javaad (2001). Many of the negative effects that Zargooshi cites are the result of fraudulent promises made by official kidney procurers or the kidney recipients, inadequate post-operative healthcare or simply continued poverty. None are intrinsic to a current market for human kidneys.

78   The strategy has also been adopted by Radcliffe Richards, p. 376, and Gill and Sade, p. 20.

79   This trade is legal in that there is no law in Iran that prohibits it, and the trade is controlled and paid for by two Non-Government Organizations (NGOs), the Charity Foundation for Special Diseases (CFSD) and the Charity Association for the Support of Kidney Patients (CASKP) that are endorsed by the Iranian government. (I thank Dr Behrooz Broumand for clarifying the legal status of this trade for me.) The CASKP puts potential vendors and recipients in touch with each other, and after the transplant the CFSD pays the vendor the equivalent of approximately $1219 from government funds. See Zargooshi (2001a) and (2001b), p. 1795. See also Ram, Vidya (2002). I discuss the Iranian situation further in Chapter 8.

80   Michael Friedlander discusses this market in an interview. See Finkel, Michael (2001).

81   Friedlander, p. 972. Israel is considering paying persons to donate a kidney. See Siegel-Itzkovich, Judy (2003).

82   Meinkoff, Jerry (1999).

83   Radcliffe Richards et al. (1998).

84   Harris and Erin (2002).

85   This meeting was reported in the Leader, *The Guardian*, 4 December 2003.

Chapter 2
Dworkin on Autonomy, Fear and Kidney Sales

The most famous (or, perhaps, most notorious) argument that has recently been offered in favour of allowing a current market in human organs is that which has been developed by Gerald Dworkin in 'Markets and Morals: The Case for Organ Sales.'[1] Dworkin's argument is both simple and powerful. He first notes that since 'noncommercial solid organ donations' and 'the sale of blood, semen, ova, hair and tissue' are held to be morally legitimate 'we accept the idea that individuals have the right to dispose of their organs and other bodily parts if they so choose.'[2] This being so, Dworkin continues, we recognize that individuals are sovereign over their own bodies, and so should be allowed to engage in voluntary market transactions with others. Thus, since respect for a person's bodily autonomy requires that they be allowed to engage in voluntary market transactions, and since this respect is already manifested in the fact that 'we accept the idea that individuals have the right to dispose of their organs and other bodily parts if they so choose,' Dworkin concludes that respect for a person's autonomy requires that persons be allowed to engage in market transactions with their bodily organs. According to Dworkin, then, respect for personal autonomy requires that persons be allowed to sell their organs if they so choose.[3]

If Dworkin is correct that respect for personal autonomy supports allowing persons to sell their organs this will be a significant point in favour of allowing a current market in human kidneys, for it is widely accepted by medical ethicists, policy makers and healthcare professionals that personal autonomy both is, and should be, the preeminent value in contemporary bioethics.[4] However, Dworkin's autonomy-based argument for allowing a current market in human organs faces an immediate objection. The crucial premise of Dworkin's argument is that a market transaction in which someone sells one of their organs will be (at least typically) a *voluntary* transaction, in which they exercise their personal autonomy. But this premise is challenged by many of those who hold that current markets in human organs are morally impermissible. (Although Dworkin writes of organ markets *per se*, for the reasons outlined in Chapter 1 I will now simply address my arguments to the narrower question of whether or not a current market in human *kidneys* is morally permissible.) Rather than the sale of a kidney being a *voluntary* transaction some opponents of a current market in human kidneys argue that such a sale is (at least typically) an *involuntary* transaction – one in which the seller suffers from *impaired* autonomy when he engages in it. In their view this is because the typical vendor would be coerced into selling the kidney through economic desperation – and actions that persons are coerced into performing are not fully autonomous. Therefore, these opponents of a current market in human kidneys argue that, instead of requiring that persons be allowed to sell their kidneys in a current market for them, as Dworkin claims, respect for personal autonomy requires that people continue to be *prohibited* from engaging in such transactions to protect their autonomy from being compromised in this way. If the opponents of a current market in human kidneys are right in that respect for autonomy requires the prohibition of such markets, this will be a serious blow to the pro-market position. In this chapter and the next, however, I argue that Dworkin's opponents are wrong here and that Dworkin is right to regard such transactions as (typically) voluntary.

Unfortunately, like the course of true love, philosophical arguments rarely run smooth. This is especially true of the debate over whether allowing a current market in human kidneys is required out of respect for the autonomy of potential vendors, or if it would be likely to lead to the impairment of their autonomy. This debate is complicated by the fact that, although Dworkin is well known for arguing that allowing persons to sell their kidneys is required out of respect for their autonomy because such sales would be voluntary, he is even *more* well known for arguing (in his paper 'Acting Freely') that personal autonomy would be *impaired* if someone performs an action that they would prefer not to do out of fear of the consequences if they do not.[5] As the opponents of Dworkin's pro-market argument note, it is likely that the typical kidney vendor would prefer *not* to sell a kidney but only does so from fear of the consequences if they did not.[6] Since this is so, Dworkin's own account of the relationship between fear and impaired autonomy appears to commit him to the view that a current market in human kidneys *would* be likely to impair the autonomy of the typical kidney vendor. Therefore, he appears committed to the view that such sales would *not* be performed voluntarily – and it is this view that is the basis for the position that respect for autonomy militates *against* such markets.

My defence of Dworkin's autonomy-based, pro-market argument must thus come in two parts. In the first part (which is the subject of this chapter) I show that Dworkin's view in 'Acting Freely' that commits him to the claim that the typical kidney vendor would be forced into the *involuntary* sale of a kidney, and so would suffer from impaired autonomy, is mistaken. Of course, showing that Dworkin's argument here is mistaken does not preclude the possibility of there being an alternative argument with the same anti-market conclusion that *is* sound. Since this is so, the second part of my defence of Dworkin's pro-market position (in the next chapter) shows that typical kidney vendors in a legal, regulated current market would sell their kidneys *voluntarily*, and so would *not* suffer from impaired autonomy in that respect. Thus, since the sale of a kidney would (typically) be a voluntary act Dworkin's original pro-market argument holds. Respect for autonomy does indeed require that persons be allowed to sell their kidneys if they so wish.

Before moving to the first part of my defence of Dworkin's pro-market argument from 'Markets and Morals' I should clarify my reasons for devoting this chapter to a discussion of his views on autonomy, coercion and kidney sales, rather than moving directly to oppose the anti-market argument from economic coercion. First, unlike many philosophical arguments, the practical stakes in this one are high, for the outcome of the debate over whether to allow a current market in human kidneys could conceivably affect the autonomy and well-being of thousands of people. It is thus essential that all of the pertinent arguments are considered carefully, otherwise the conclusion reached might not be the right one. And so if this debate reaches the wrong conclusion, which is then implemented (that is, the market is allowed when it should not have been, or banned when it should not have been) this will have serious consequences. Thus, even though Dworkin's arguments in 'Acting Freely' do not *directly* address the issue of whether a current market in human kidneys should be allowed, since they seriously affect this debate they must be addressed within it. My second reason for addressing Dworkin's views on autonomy, coercion and kidney sales is related to the first. Since Dworkin's view of how personal autonomy is impaired with respect to actions performed out of fear of the alternatives is both well known and highly influential, any pro-market argument that claims that the typical vendor would be fully autonomous in selling a kidney – even if he does so out of fear of the consequences if he does not – will be greeted with scepticism until Dworkin's views on this matter are rebutted.

The Argument from Economic Coercion

Dworkin's argument that favours allowing persons to sell their organs in a current market rests on the premise that such a market transaction is *voluntary*, and the vendor is autonomous with respect to it. Yet it is a moot point whether most persons who would sell their kidneys in such a market would do so voluntarily. On the face of it, it appears that they would. After all, the typical vendor would choose to sell after weighing up the available options and deciding which was the most appealing. This is the view that Dworkin implicitly accepts in 'Markets and Morals.' His opponents, however, challenge the assumption that the sale of a kidney will be a voluntary transaction on the part of the vendor through the

'argument from economic coercion.' The anti-market proponents first point out that given the pain, suffering and risks
that are involved in selling a kidney, the typical vendor is
likely to be extremely poor and selling the organ out of
economic desperation. Therefore, they continue, the typical
kidney vendor would only choose to sell if they believed that
this was their only chance of avoiding a fate they considered
to be even worse. The motivation of the typical kidney
vendor would thus be very similar to that of any typical
victim of coercion who is also forced by his coercer to act out
of a desire to prevent his situation from becoming worse – for
example, to prevent himself from being shot if he refuses to
hand over his wallet to a highwayman. Thus, the proponents
of the argument from economic coercion continue, the agents
concerned are required by their situations to perform actions
that they would not otherwise perform, and that they resent
performing, but which they do anyway from fear of the
consequences if they do not.[7] Moreover, it is generally
accepted that anyone coerced into performing an action will
suffer from a diminution in autonomy with respect to that
action.[8] If this is true – and if it is also true that the typical
kidney vendor would be coerced into selling the kidney by
their economic situation – then they would suffer from
impaired autonomy with respect to the sale, despite
Dworkin's claims to the contrary. Thus, the proponents of
the argument from economic coercion conclude, respect for
the personal autonomy of potential vendors requires that
such markets be prohibited, not allowed.

Why Dworkin's Views in 'Acting Freely' Support the Argument from Economic Coercion

The argument from economic coercion is simple, elegant and
highly persuasive, both as a counter to Dworkin's pro-market
argument and as an autonomy-based, anti-market argument
in its own right. Because of this, it is widely cited by medical
ethicists, policy makers and professional bodies as a reason
why a current market in human transplant kidneys should
continue to be prohibited. The medical ethicists John B.

Dossetor and V. Manickavel, for example, rhetorically ask 'Surely abject poverty ... can have no equal when it comes to coercion of people to ... take risks ... which their affluent fellow citizens would not want to take?' – a point that is echoed almost ad infinitum by other academic opponents of current markets in human kidneys.[9]

As I noted above, the argument from economic coercion also appears to be supported by Dworkin's own account of how personal autonomy is impaired when someone performs an action out of fear of the consequences of not performing it – an important point that has been overlooked not only by Dworkin, but also by all the other participants in this debate. Here, Dworkin focuses on a standard case of coercion: that of a traveller who surrenders his money to a highwayman to avoid being shot. In such cases, Dworkin claims, 'What [the victim] doesn't want to do when faced with the highwayman is to hand money over in these circumstances, for these reasons.' More generally, he suggests that

> ... it is the attitude a man takes toward the reasons for which he acts, whether or not he identifies himself with these reasons, assimilates them to himself, which is crucial for determining whether or not he acts freely [autonomously]. Men resent acting for certain reasons; they would not choose to be motivated in certain ways ... They resent acting simply in order to avoid unpleasant consequences with no attendant promotion of their own interests and welfare.[10]

Later, after noting that 'There must be part of the human personality which takes up an "attitude" toward the reasons, desires, and motives which determine the conduct of the agent,' Dworkin outlines his thesis succinctly: 'We consider ourselves compelled because we find it painful to act for these reasons' (that is, those that move the person concerned to act in a way that cannot improve his situation, but only prevent it from getting worse), and goes on to claim that 'A does X freely [that is, autonomously] if A does X for reasons he doesn't mind acting from.'[11]

In 'Acting Freely,' then, Dworkin holds that people will suffer from diminished autonomy when coerced into performing a certain action (such as giving up their wallet to a highwayman) because they resent acting for the reasons they did. For Dworkin, this is only a particular example of a general point: that a person suffers from impaired autonomy with respect to an action if they resent having to satisfy their desire to perform this action because they recognize that they are performing it solely to prevent their situation from becoming worse. Since this is so, Dworkin's arguments support the anti-market argument from economic coercion. It is likely that the typical vendor in a current market for human kidneys would be poor, and would be selling a kidney because this is the only way available to them to secure desperately needed money. The typical vendor thus would be likely to resent having to sell an organ because they would resent the fact that (in their view) such a sale would be the only way to prevent their dire economic situation from becoming worse.[12] The typical kidney vendor is thus likely to meet both of the conditions that Dworkin outlines for a person to suffer from impaired autonomy with respect to an action that he performs, and so it is likely that they would (if Dworkin's views in 'Acting Freely' are correct) suffer from impaired autonomy with respect to the sale. Since this is so, it seems that the argument from economic coercion holds: the typical vendor is likely to be coerced by poverty into selling a kidney, and so is likely to suffer from impaired autonomy with respect to this sale. Respect for autonomy thus requires that a current market in human kidneys should continue to be prohibited – *not* that it should be allowed.

Distinguishing between Global and Local Autonomy

Dworkin is thus faced with the dilemma that if he sticks to his views in 'Acting Freely' then it seems he must repudiate his pro-market argument developed in 'Markets and Morals' and vice versa. However, he has two possible ways to escape this dilemma, the first of which I will discuss in this section, and the second in the next. The first way in which Dworkin might resolve the conflicting views in these two essays draws on his more recent work on autonomy, which focuses primarily on autonomy as a *global*, rather than a *local*, phenomenon, such that the question of whether a person is autonomous 'can only be assessed over extended portions of ... [his] ... life.'[13] The question of why a person who acts out of a certain type of fear might thereby suffer from impaired autonomy, however, only addresses the question of how a person will suffer from a *local* impairment of his autonomy when he is so moved to act. (That is, it only addresses the question of how autonomy is impaired with respect to those particular actions performed out of fear.) Since this is so, one might argue that there is no necessary contradiction between Dworkin's view that respect for autonomy requires that people should be allowed to be vendors in a current market for human transplant kidneys, and his view that most of these people would suffer from impaired autonomy with respect to their vending actions. Holding that someone's autonomy would suffer with respect to their act of selling a kidney (a local impairment) is compatible with claiming that selling their kidney enables them better to exercise autonomy overall (a global enhancement.) That is to say, the financial resources secured from the sale of a kidney could provide the vendor with a greater variety of options. Although this would not in itself make the vendor more autonomous, it would make their autonomy more instrumentally valuable in that they could now better use it to pursue their goals.[14] Even though persons might be coerced economically into selling a kidney and suffer from impaired autonomy as a result, then, respect for the value of their autonomy might still require that they be allowed to sell on the grounds that such sales would enhance the overall value of their autonomy to them. Moreover, the idea that the value of personal autonomy might be enhanced in this way is not just speculation to allow Dworkin to reconcile his various theoretical commitments. Instead, the use of money acquired through the sale of a kidney to, for example, set the vendor up in business is a very real phenomenon noted in both India and the Philippines.[15]

At first sight this way of rescuing Dworkin from the dilemma of having to choose between his autonomy-based pro-market argument and his view of why a person who acts out of fear thereby suffers from impaired autonomy looks

extremely promising. Not only does it reconcile his conflicting views, it does so by making them consistent with some of
his more recent work on autonomy. However, this attempt to
extricate Dworkin from this apparent impasse does not show
that the *original* form of his autonomy-based pro-market
argument can be reconciled with his views on fear and
autonomy. In his original argument Dworkin held that
allowing a person to sell their kidney is required by respect
for their autonomy, for this would allow them to act
voluntarily. But the way of alleviating the tension between
Dworkin's views that is suggested here requires him to accept
that the typical kidney vendor would *not* sell their kidney
voluntarily, as Dworkin originally claimed, but would suffer
from a diminution in autonomy with respect to the sale. To
reconcile Dworkin's autonomy-based pro-market argument
with his views in 'Acting Freely' in the way suggested here,
then, his original pro-market argument must be altered.
Rather than arguing that respect for autonomy *directly*
requires allowing persons to sell their kidneys, Dworkin
should instead argue that it *indirectly* requires that they be
allowed to sell their kidneys. Even though such sales would
not be fully voluntary their consequences would have positive
effects on the instrumental value of the autonomy of those
making them.

Yet even once Dworkin's pro-market argument has been
revised in this way this attempt to reconcile his views in
'Markets and Morals' with his views in 'Acting Freely' fails,
for both practical and theoretical reasons. Although there is
some evidence of kidney vendors in India and the
Philippines using the money from the sale of their organs
to start small businesses (and so enhancing the instrumental
value of their autonomy) the evidence from the most
comprehensive study of the economic consequences of
selling a kidney shows that most vendors in India use the
money to pay off their debts.[16] Since these (typical and
non-entrepreneurial) kidney vendors satisfy Dworkin's conditions to have acted out of fear (see p. 35), he is committed
to holding that they suffer from a local impairment of their
autonomy with respect to their actions. However, since
these non-entrepreneurial vendors did *not* use the money

from the sales of their kidneys to escape from their autonomy-inhibiting poverty, they did *not* enjoy any consequent global enhancement of their autonomy. There is thus evidence that allowing the poor to sell their kidneys would instead only serve to impair their autonomy, and not to enhance its value.

Moreover, the fact that some entrepreneurs *do* sell their kidneys to raise capital and thus globally enhance the instrumental value of their autonomy cannot be used as evidence that Dworkin's autonomy-based pro-market argument can be reconciled with his views on coercion and autonomy. Even if such entrepreneurial vendors might resent having to sell their kidneys in order to raise business capital, their resentment does *not* stem from the belief that they cannot act to improve their situation, but only to prevent it from getting worse. (Indeed, such vendors are selling their kidneys in an attempt to make their situations *better*.) These vendors do not, therefore, meet Dworkin's conditions for economic coercion (that is, they do not sell their kidneys out of fear that if they do not their situations will worsen). Thus, in Dworkin's view, they do not suffer from any impairment in their autonomy with respect to their vending actions. In this case there is no set of persons who both suffer from a local impairment of their autonomy as a result of being coerced into selling their kidneys on Dworkin's account of how coercion impairs autonomy, *and* for whom this loss is offset by a global enhancement of their autonomy's instrumental value as a result of the sale.[17] Those who *are* economically coerced into selling their kidneys (and consequently suffer from impaired autonomy) do *not* enjoy any post-sale global enhancement of the instrumental value of their autonomy because the money gained from the sale goes towards paying off their debts. Furthermore, people who *do* enjoy a post-sale global enhancement of their autonomy do not suffer from impaired autonomy with respect to their vending actions as they are *not* coerced into them. This attempt to reconcile Dworkin's views in 'Acting Freely' with his (revised) autonomy-based pro-market argument, then, fails.[18]

A Different Construal of Dworkin's View in 'Acting Freely'

The above attempt to reconcile Dworkin's autonomy-based pro-market argument with his account of how being moved to act out of a certain type of fear impairs a person's autonomy with respect to that act accepts my construal of Dworkin's view of the relationship between autonomy and actions performed from fear at face value. The second approach instead provides a construal of his view in 'Acting Freely' that differs significantly from that which I provide above. And, if this alternative construal is correct, it can be shown that Dworkin's views here are not at odds with those in 'Markets and Morals.'

This approach to reconciling Dworkin's two views begins by outlining his hierarchical analysis of personal autonomy.[19] Asserting that an 'autonomous person is one who does *his own* thing,' and stating that he was concerned with providing an account of what it was for a person to be autonomous with respect to his motivations, Dworkin claimed that he needed both to characterize what it was for a person's motivations to be *his* (that is, *authentic*) and what it was for them to be his *own* – for him to possess them *independently* of controlling influences.[20]

Thus, using the formula 'autonomy = authenticity + independence,'[21] Dworkin outlines what is required for a person to enjoy both authenticity and independence with respect to their motivations. For a person's motivations to be authentic, Dworkin states that it is 'the attitude that ... [the] ... person takes towards the influences motivating him ... [that] determines whether or not they are to be considered "his." '[22] That is, for a person to be autonomous with respect to his motivations it is necessary that he endorse his being moved to act by them. For Dworkin, then, a person's autonomy will be impaired if he is moved to act by a desire that he has a second-order desire (that is, a desire *about* a first-order desire) *not* to be moved by. For example, if a person is subject to a neurotic compulsion constantly to wash their hands (a first-order desire) from which they desire to be free – they have a second-order desire to be free from this first-order desire – their autonomy will be impaired if they act on this repudiated desire. Yet even though a person's motivations might be authentic (that is, they endorse their being moved to act by them) this will not suffice for autonomy with respect to them in Dworkin's account. Dworkin also required that the person's endorsement of their motivations should be independent of any autonomy-undermining factors such as 'manipulation, deception, the withholding of relevant information, and so on.'[23] In this case, Dworkin held that the person enjoyed procedural independence with respect to the endorsement. In addition, Dworkin held that a person would enjoy substantive independence with respect to his motivations if he did not come to have them as a result of his commitment to anything outside himself (such as 'a lover, a goal, or a group').[24]

Dworkin recognized that this account of what it was for a person to enjoy procedural and substantive independence required refinement.[25] Fortunately, that is not an issue here because this second approach to reconciling Dworkin's views in his two articles focuses on his claim that a person's motivations must be *authentically* his for him to be autonomous with respect to them. Recall that in Dworkin's account a person will fail to be autonomous with respect to his motivations if he fails to endorse them. Since a person who is motivated by fear would resent being moved to act solely to preserve his current level of well-being, he would 'not choose to be motivated' to act in this way. Drawing on Dworkin's hierarchical analysis of autonomy one could hold that his claim that a person who acts out of fear 'would not choose to be motivated' to so act *should be construed as indicating that this person would be moved to act by a desire that was not authentically their own*. That is, someone acting out of fear would *repudiate* at the level of their second-order desires their first-order desire to perform that action. On this construal of Dworkin's view that a desire must be authentically a person's own for them to be autonomous with respect to it, people who act out of fear would *not* be autonomous with respect to their effective first-order desire *because they have repudiated it* – and so they would not be autonomous with respect to the actions that this desire moved them to perform.

If this interpretation of Dworkin's view is correct there is no discord between his views in 'Acting Freely' and his autonomy-based pro-market argument in 'Markets and Morals' because it is unlikely that typical vendors would repudiate their effective first-order desire to sell a kidney, even if they are selling out of economic desperation. Indeed, given the gravity of such a sale vendors are likely to have thought long and hard before deciding on this act, and thus would fully *endorse* their first-order desire to sell. In this case typical kidney vendors would *not* suffer from impaired autonomy with respect to the sale, as such impairment would only transpire (on this construal of Dworkin's view) if the person concerned does *not* endorse their effective first-order desire. Thus, Dworkin can escape from his apparent dilemma. Since the typical kidney vendor would endorse his first-order desire to sell, his action would be fully voluntary. He would thus not suffer from any impairment in his autonomy, and so respect for his autonomy requires that he should be allowed to sell a kidney if he so chooses.

Two Competing Accounts of Dworkin's Views in 'Acting Freely'

Before arguing that this second attempt to reconcile Dworkin's views fails I must first make clear how the construal of Dworkin's view in 'Acting Freely' that this attempt is based on differs from my original construal of Dworkin's view in 'Acting Freely' that I outlined above. Understanding the differences between these two interpretations of Dworkin's view is important not only to understand fully this second attempt at reconciliation, but also to understand its flaws. Note also that it is *this* construal of Dworkin's view (developed by Irving Thalberg) and *not* the one I developed above that is generally accepted within the philosophical literature.[26]

Unlike my construal of Dworkin's views of the relationship between autonomy and acts performed from fear, this latter 'standard construal' is explicitly grounded in his hierarchical analysis of autonomy. This standard construal of Dworkin's view focuses on whether the person who is motivated to act by fear *endorses* the *actual* desire that moved him to act, since this is at the core of Dworkin's analysis of autonomy. By contrast, my construal of Dworkin's view focuses on whether the person who acts out of fear would prefer to be moved to act by a desire *other than* his actual effective first-order desire. Unlike the standard construal of Dworkin's view, then, my construal focuses on a question whose answer will leave *open* the question of whether the person who acts out of fear endorses his *actual* effective first-order desire. In my interpretation it is possible for someone to *endorse* their effective first-order desire to perform an action from fear while at the same time preferring not to act on this desire. This is because in my construal a person might endorse a desire as he realizes that *given the situation* this is the best (most prudent) desire for him to act on, but would still prefer to be in another situation where they could act on *another* desire entirely (that is, one which they would act on had they not been faced with the current consequences).

Failings of the Second Approach to Reconciling Dworkin's Views

The second approach, above, to rescuing Dworkin from having to choose between his views in 'Acting Freely' and in 'Markets and Morals' has three advantages. It ensures that his views in these papers are consistent. It ties Dworkin's view of autonomy as expressed in 'Acting Freely' to his influential hierarchical analysis of autonomy. And, finally, it is based on a construal of Dworkin's views in 'Acting Freely' that is generally accepted within the philosophical literature.

Yet, despite its advantages, this second approach comes at a very heavy price, for it commits Dworkin to a mistaken view of why persons who act from the fear of the consequences of their failing so to act thereby suffer from impaired autonomy.

The standard construal of Dworkin's position in 'Acting Freely' holds that, according to Dworkin, a person will suffer from impaired autonomy with respect to an action performed out of fear of the consequences of its nonperformance because he will not endorse his effective first-order desire to perform this action. But this understanding has highly counterintuitive implications. As Irving Thalberg has observed in criticism of this construal of Dworkin's position, most people who act out of fear of the consequences of their inaction 'would, at the time and later, give second-order endorsement to their cautious [and compliant] motives. They are unlikely to yearn, from their elevated tribune, for more defiant ground-floor urges.'[27] Focusing on people who are coerced by others, Thalberg notes that Dworkin is committed to the claim that they do *not* suffer from impaired autonomy with respect to their coerced acts because they are *not* motivated to perform them by first-order desires they do not endorse. This, notes Thalberg, is counterintuitive because we typically think that successfully coercing someone impairs their autonomy. (Indeed, this intuition lies at the heart of the anti-market argument from economic coercion.) However, Thalberg continues, if Dworkin wishes to avoid this counter-intuitive result he must claim that when most people are subject to coercion they do *not* endorse their prudent first-order desires to perform the actions they are being coerced into doing. This seems to be empirically false. Thus, Thalberg concludes, Dworkin's views in 'Acting Freely' lead him into another dilemma: he must either commit himself to the counterintuitive claim that the autonomy of (most) persons under coercion is not impaired; or else he must attempt to salvage his position by implausibly claiming that most people who are coerced do not endorse their effective first-order desires to perform the acts they are forced into.

My Construal of Dworkin's View in 'Acting Freely' as Preferable to the Standard

It is important to note that this dilemma that Thalberg poses for Dworkin is only a fatal objection to his view in 'Acting Freely' if the standard construal of it is correct. It is *not* a fatal objection if *my* construal of it is correct. This is because, as stated above, in my construal of Dworkin's view it is possible that someone could both endorse their effective first-order desire to comply with the coercer's threat, and yet still prefer to be moved to act by a desire other than this desire to comply.

Of course, the fact that my construal of Dworkin's view avoids Thalberg's objection to it as it is usually construed is no reason to hold that it should be adopted, for the question of what Dworkin's views *are* is distinct from the question of whether they are *right*. However, the fact that the standard construal of Dworkin's views in 'Acting Freely' left it vulnerable to such a simple objection should invite suspicion. This might then lead one to question whether this standard construal should have been accepted so readily – and, if not, whether my construal of Dworkin's views outlined above should be accepted in its stead.

In fact, there are three reasons why my interpretation should be accepted in place of the standard construal. First, there is nothing in Dworkin's discussion in 'Acting Freely' that commits him to the claim that a person will *only* suffer from impaired autonomy with respect to their actions if they do not endorse the effective first-order desire that led them to perform the acts in question. Since this is so, the principle of charity requires that another construal of Dworkin's position be sought before Thalberg's criticism is accepted. And, as I outlined above, since my construal is not only plausible but also avoids Thalberg's criticism it is, other things being equal, to be preferred to the standard construal. Second, it is plausible to assume that if Dworkin's view really was that personal autonomy is only impaired if someone is moved to act by a desire that they do not endorse, he would have written this directly rather than using such convoluted locutions such as 'would not choose to be motivated' to convey his point. Third, Dworkin's hierarchical analysis of autonomy is very similar to that developed by Harry Frankfurt who, in discussing the relationship between coercion and autonomy, explicitly *denies* the implicit claim that underlies the standard construal of Dworkin's view.[28] This standard construal, then, is based on the *mistaken* view that a person who offers a hierarchical analysis of autonomy is committed to holding that if a person is autonomous with respect to his effective first-order desire then he is *also* autonomous with respect to those actions that this desire moves him to perform. Once this mistake it recognized it is apparent that Dworkin's view in 'Acting Freely' *could* be understood differently from the standard construal of it. When these three points are taken in conjunction it is clear that my *non*-standard construal of Dworkin's position is preferable to its standard rival and should thus be accepted in its place. Since the standard construal was the basis of the second attempt made above to reconcile Dworkin's views in 'Acting Freely' and 'Markets and Morals,' this attempt should be rejected along with the standard construal of his views in 'Acting Freely' on which it is based.

Why Dworkin's Account of the Relationship between Fear and Autonomy is Mistaken

Dworkin's view in 'Acting Freely' is now clear. Here, a person will suffer from impaired autonomy with respect to an action A if

1. He is motivated to perform A by a first-order desire that he is not autonomous with respect to (this is required by Dworkin's hierarchical analysis of personal autonomy)[29] or

2. He is motivated to perform A by a desire that he is autonomous with respect to, but this desire is one that he would prefer not to be moved to act by because he would prefer to be in a situation other than the one he is actually in, where this preference for a different situation stems from his belief that in his current situation he cannot act to improve his condition but only to prevent it from becoming worse.

It is also clear that Dworkin's view in 'Acting Freely' *does* support the argument from economic coercion, and thus that it *does* conflict with his autonomy-based pro-market position in 'Markets and Morals.' As I noted above, typical (non-entrepreneurial) vendors in a current market for human kidneys would be autonomous with respect to their effective first-order desire to sell. In other words, they would volitionally endorse it, be satisfied with it, it would be authentically theirs in that they would be both substantively and procedurally independent with respect to it and so on.[30] However, they would still prefer *not* to be moved to act by this desire, thus meeting Dworkin's condition for suffering impaired autonomy with respect to the act of selling their kidney. Thus, if Dworkin's view of how motivation out of fear undermines autonomy is correct, the proponents of the argument from economic coercion are correct to claim that the typical kidney vendor will be coerced into selling, and would suffer from impaired autonomy as a result. If so, then respect for autonomy would require that current markets in human kidneys not be allowed.

With this in mind, it is clear that to show that respect for autonomy requires *allowing* a current market in human kidneys, I must first show that Dworkin's account is mistaken. Fortunately, now that his view is clear, it is also clear how it is mistaken. First, Dworkin never explains *why* a person who acts out of fear thereby suffers from impaired autonomy with respect to that act. Instead, he appears merely to rely on the intuition (that he shares with the proponents of the argument from economic coercion) that such persons would act unwillingly, and so would therefore suffer from impairment to their autonomy.

Dworkin's account also fails to be judgementally relevant. That is to say, it does not satisfy the requirement (that Dworkin himself imposed on theoretical discussions of personal autonomy) that accounts of what autonomy is and how it might be impaired be 'in general accord with particular judgments we make about autonomy.'[31] This is so for three reasons. First, this account cannot accommodate the judgement that autonomy might be impaired to different degrees, depending, for example, on the type of coercion. For instance, Dworkin cannot accommodate the intuitively correct view that a person who is told by a highwayman to perform a series of actions to avoid being shot would have their autonomy impaired to a greater degree than would a victim of blackmail, who is told merely to have a certain amount of money ready at a certain time. But it seems that the former's autonomy would suffer greater impairment because they would have less leeway to comply with the demands, and so would be able to exercise less autonomy. Second, Dworkin's account cannot accommodate the judgement that autonomy would be impaired when someone is coerced into performing a certain action *even if* they do not resent being moved to act by an effective first-order desire whose satisfaction can only prevent their situation from getting worse. For example, a veteran teller in a much-robbed bank might not resent being moved to act by his desire to comply with the robber's demands because he has become used to this, but this does not mean that he suffers less impairment to his autonomy as a result of this coercion than his novice colleague who resents having to comply. Just as in the case of the highwayman's victim and the blackmailer's victim, the view that these tellers suffer from the same degree of impaired autonomy with respect to their compliant actions rests on the degree to which they cede control over their actions to another. Finally, Dworkin's view is implausibly broad because it commits him to holding that personal autonomy will be impaired in many situations when this is implausible. A person who steps out of the way of an oncoming car, for example, or a person who tries to recover an imprudent note that he sent to his boss in a fit of pique both act to prevent their situations from becoming worse, and might also resent having to act in this way, but their autonomy with respect to their actions is not impaired.

Conclusion

Once it is properly understood, Dworkin's view in 'Acting Freely' about the relationship between autonomy and fear clearly supports the anti-market argument from economic coercion. It thus contradicts the essential premise of his autonomy-based pro-market argument of 'Markets and Morals.' However, this does not show that respect for autonomy favours the prohibition of a current market in human kidneys. This is because Dworkin's account of how a person who performs actions out of a certain type of fear thereby suffers from impaired autonomy with respect to them should be rejected because it neither provides an explanation of why this is so, nor does it satisfy Dworkin's own requirement of judgemental relevance.

Of course, showing that Dworkin's view in 'Acting Freely' should be rejected does not show that his autonomy-based pro-market argument should be accepted, for the argument from economic coercion might be supported by an *alternative* account of how a person who acts out of fear of the consequences of not so acting thereby suffers impaired autonomy. To preclude this possibility I must show that the typical kidney seller would not suffer from impaired autonomy even if he sold the organ out of fear of the consequences of not doing so. To achieve this I will first explain why coercing a person into performing an action impairs their autonomy with respect to that action, and then show, contra the proponents of the argument from economic coercion, that persons cannot be coerced by their economic circumstances. I will then show that other ways of under-standing the argument from economic coercion – economic necessity or irresistible offers – also fail to establish that the typical kidney vendor would suffer from impaired autonomy.

Notes

1   Gerald Dworkin (1994), 155–61.
2   Ibid., p. 156.
3   Ibid.
4   Even a cursory glance at the literature supports the view that autonomy is the preeminent value within contemporary bioethics, as noted by Janet Smith (1997). However, this claim is subject to increasing criticism. Contemporary feminists, for example, criticize this view on the grounds value that current accounts of autonomy are based on an unrealistic ideal of personhood. See for example, Ells, Carolyn (2001). Similarly, communitarians are starting to react against what they perceive as excessive respect accorded to autonomy in recent bioethics. See Gaylin, Willard and Jennings, Bruce (1996). In a less ideological vein Schneider has argued that medical ethicists accept the primacy of autonomy too uncritically in the face of empirical evidence that patient rights and welfare could be better promoted by a return to a more paternalistic approach.

See Schneider, Carl (1998). Of course, simply because one does not accept that autonomy should be preeminent in medical ethics does not mean that one must thereby oppose a regulated current market in human kidneys if such a market would respect personal autonomy.

5   Dworkin, Gerald (1970).

6   The term 'kidney vendor' was introduced into the literature in Morden, Michael (1988), p. 38.

7   It makes no difference to proponents of the anti-market argument from economic coercion that the highwayman's victim is coerced by another agent and the kidney vendor is coerced by his situation, since in both cases they regard the person concerned as being forced to act in some way. I consider this point in the next chapter.

8   See Frankfurt, Harry G. (1988c); Dworkin (1970).

9   Dossetor and Manickavel (1992), p. 63. This argument is repeated so frequently that it would be tedious to list all of its exponents. However, the most prominent include Titmuss, p. 307; Manga, Pranlal (1987), p. 327; Marshall, Patricia A., Thomasma, David C. and Daar, Abdallah S. (1996), p. 13; Siminoff and Mercer, p. 382 and Joralemon, Donald and Cox, Phil (2003), pp. 27–33.

10 Dworkin (1970), p. 377. Although Dworkin here writes of 'acting freely' rather than 'acting autonomously' there is only a semantic difference between these two terms as he uses them in his work on autonomy. For an argument that supports this exegetical point see Taylor, James Stacey (2003), p. 129, n. 6.

11 Dworkin (1970), pp. 379, 381.

12 There is considerable evidence that this is indeed the mental state of the typical kidney vendor. See, for example, Scheper-Hughes (2003), p. 1647 and Chengappa, Raj (1990), pp. 60–67.

13 Dworkin, Gerald (1988a), pp. 15–16.

14 Recall that the conception of autonomy here is not that of Kant, but the more contemporary conception in which a person is autonomous to the extent that they direct their own life. It is thus no bar to this attempt to rescue Dworkin from his dilemma that it accepts that it is morally legitimate for typical kidney vendors to use autonomy as a mere means to the furtherance of their goals.

15 Cases in which people use the money from the sale of a kidney to help them escape their poverty have been reported in the Philippines by Tiong, Daniloi C. (2001), p. 89. Apocryphal evidence of similar cases in India is noted by Marshall et al., p. 10. However, overwhelming evidence shows that the sale of a kidney does not usually provide an easy route out of poverty. This will be discussed more fully below, and in the next chapter.

16 Goyal et al., p. 1591.

17   It is possible that there are persons who unwillingly sold their kidneys to pay off debts and then (luckily and unexpectedly) had money left over to start a business. But even if such people exist their numbers will be too few to provide anything more than cold comfort for Dworkin.

18   Although this discussion shows that some persons (that is, the kidney-selling entrepreneurs) would enhance the instrumental value of their autonomy through the sale of their kidneys this does not undermine the anti-market argument from economic coercion, for its proponents do not deny this. Instead, they simply deny that the majority of people will benefit in this way. Thus, the fact that some poor people do benefit from selling their kidneys does not blunt the force of this argument.

19   Note that I am not here endorsing Dworkin's account of autonomy.

20   Dworkin, Gerald (1976), p. 24.

21   Ibid.

22   Ibid., p. 25.

23   Ibid.

24   Ibid., p. 26.

25   Ibid.

26   The two most prominent papers that discuss Dworkin's views in 'Acting Freely' are Thalberg, Irving (1989) and Christman, John (1989), pp. 8–9. Both papers give what I term below 'the standard construal' of Dworkin's views. For an argument that shows that this 'standard construal' is mistaken, see Taylor (2003), pp. 133–8.

27   Thalberg, p. 126.

28   Frankfurt (1988c), p. 43.

29   Dworkin (1976), p. 25.

30   These accounts of what it is to be autonomous with respect to one's effective first-order desires are, respectively, those of Frankfurt (1988d) and (1999a), Dworkin (1976) and Bratman, Michael E. (1996).

31   Gerald Dworkin (1988a), p. 9.

Chapter 3

Is the Typical Kidney Vendor Forced to Sell?

I concluded the last chapter by noting that, even though the view that Dworkin expressed in 'Acting Freely' and that supported the argument from economic coercion was mistaken, this does not show that the anti-market argument is itself flawed. In this chapter I move directly to criticize this anti-market argument, arguing that, once the relationship between coercion and autonomy is correctly understood, it is clear that no kidney vendor would suffer from impaired autonomy with respect to their action as a result of being coerced into selling by economic circumstances. I shall then show that the other two primary autonomy-based objections to a current market for human kidneys (the argument from economic necessity and the argument from irresistible offers) are also mistaken. Since this is so, and since Dworkin is correct to note in 'Markets and Morals' that allowing a person to sell a kidney if they so choose will expand the ways in which they can freely exercise autonomy, this will provide a strong prima facie case for holding that respect for personal autonomy requires that a current market for human transplant kidneys be allowed.

The Argument from Economic Coercion – and a Misguided Objection to it

As shown in the previous chapter the argument from economic coercion is simple, elegant, persuasive and widely accepted. Its proponents hold that rather than the sale of a kidney being a *voluntary* transaction in which the seller exercises autonomy such a sale would typically be *involuntary* – the seller would suffer *impaired* autonomy when he engages in it. The typical kidney seller would have been coerced into selling by economic desperation, and coerced actions are not fully autonomous. The proponents of this argument conclude therefore that respect for autonomy requires that persons continue to be *prohibited* from selling in a current market to protect their autonomy from possible impairment.

Despite its simplicity the argument from economic coercion has occasionally been misunderstood, which has sometimes led to its too-swift dismissal. Janet Radcliffe Richards, for example, claims that a 'defender of autonomy' would regard being subject to coercion as 'intrinsically undesirable' because

> Coercion is a matter of reducing the range of options that there would otherwise be. Deliberate coercers come and take away options until the best available is what they want you to choose; circumstances like poverty can, by extension, be regarded as coercive because they are also constrictors of options that make you choose what you otherwise would not.[1]

With this claim in place Radcliffe Richards argues that once one recognizes that coercion works by constricting a person's options, one cannot regard allowing persons to sell their kidneys as subjecting them to coercion because it would *broaden* rather than *constrict* their options. Thus, even though one might agree that a person who is coerced into performing an action would suffer from impaired autonomy with respect to that action, a current market in human kidneys would not be coercive. Therefore, Radcliffe Richards concludes, the argument from economic coercion is mistaken.

Yet although Radcliffe Richards shows that a current market in human kidneys is not itself coercive, she does *not* show that the argument from economic coercion is mistaken. The proponents of this argument do not hold that a current market for human transplant kidneys would itself coerce potential vendors, which is what leads to their autonomy being impaired. Rather (and as Radcliffe Richards recognized earlier) its proponents claim that it is the vendors' *poverty* that would coerce them into selling their kidneys were a current market for human kidneys allowed.[2] The argument from economic coercion, then, is based on the claim that allowing such a market is a *necessary condition* for the economic situation of the desperate poor to coerce them into selling their kidneys. The proponents of this argument thus hold that the institution of such a market *in combination with* their preexisting poverty would provide the jointly necessary and sufficient conditions for the poor to be coerced into selling their kidneys. This argument is thus *not* based on the view that such a market itself coerces the poor into selling their kidneys, as Radcliffe Richards's response to it implies. Rather, it is based on the view that allowing a current market in human transplant kidneys will *enable* coercion to take place. Once this is recognized one can reconstruct the argument from economic coercion in a manner that avoids Radcliffe Richards's objection. A current market in human kidneys would enable the poverty of destitute people to coerce them into selling their kidneys, and would provide the necessary conditions for the poor to suffer from impaired autonomy in a way that they would not have otherwise suffered. Therefore, from the point of view of one who values personal autonomy, a current market in human kidneys should be prohibited in order to protect the poor from an additional way in which their autonomy might be subject to impairment.

Given the failure of Radcliffe Richards's objection to the argument from economic coercion it is clear that a successful refutation of this anti-market view requires more than simply (and falsely) claiming that removing prohibitions that prevent persons from pursuing options that are harmless to others is required by respect for their autonomy.[3] Instead, to refute the argument from economic coercion decisively I must show that even if the typical vendor in a current market for human kidneys would be motivated by poverty, this does not constitute *coercion*, and so autonomy is not impaired in the way that the proponents of the argument from economic coercion claim. To show this I must explain why coercing someone into performing an action will impair their autonomy with respect to that action. I must then show that on this account of how coercion impairs autonomy the typical kidney vendor would not be forced to sell, and so would not suffer impaired autonomy as a result of coercion.

But before that I must make three important points. First, since I am only providing an explanation of why *coercing* a person into acting will impair autonomy with respect to the coerced act my focus in this chapter is much narrower than Dworkin's in 'Acting Freely' – namely, why personal autonomy would be impaired with respect to acts that a person performed out of the fear that if they did not perform that act their situation would become worse; and coerced acts are only one type performed out of such fear. This difference in focus between Dworkin's discussion and my discussion here is important, for one of the reasons why Dworkin's account had to be rejected was because its breadth committed him to holding that some people (for example, those who moved out of the way of an oncoming car) would suffer impaired autonomy with respect to their actions when this was clearly not true. Since the focus of my account is much narrower than Dworkin's it is not subject to these objections. Second, a proponent of the argument from economic coercion might object that my focus is *too* narrow, and that this anti-market argument is not committed to claiming that the typical vendor is coerced into selling a kidney, but merely that they are in some way forced to sell. This is certainly a legitimate concern, and it would be both unfair and unwise to reject this argument outright on the grounds that the typical kidney vendor is not, strictly speaking, *coerced* into selling (although this is how this argument is typically presented). Such a rejection would place too much weight on the semantics of the argument and too little on the intuition that underlies it – that is, that the typical kidney vendor is in some way forced to sell by their economic situation, and that it is this force, whether characterized as coercion or not, that impairs autonomy. To meet this concern, I will argue that the variant arguments that the typical kidney vendor is somehow forced to sell from economic necessity and from irresistible offers are also mistaken. Finally, my explanation of how coercion impairs autonomy is normatively neutral with respect to the debate over whether a current market in human kidneys should be allowed. That is to say, it has not been developed specifically to support any particular position within this debate.

How Coercion Impairs Autonomy

Drawing from Dworkin's example of the highwayman's 'Your money or your life!' it is clear that any explanation of how coercion will impair autonomy must satisfy several requirements, including two apparently conflicting intuitions. First, the highwayman's victim *chose* to hand over the purse after deciding that this was the least unattractive option from a set of unpalatable alternatives. Since the victim thus desired to perform this action and this desire moved them to act, it is prima facie plausible to claim that their autonomy was unimpaired. Yet to claim that a person who has been *forced* to hand over their money to avoid being killed is a paradigm of someone who is engaged in autonomous self-direction seems clearly mistaken. The most obvious way of dissolving this difficulty is to deny one or the other of the intuitions that these claims express. However, it would be far more satisfying to provide an account of the relationship between autonomy and coercion that is able to respond to *both* of these tugs of intuition.

Second, a satisfactory account of how successfully coercing a person impairs their autonomy cannot presuppose that it is legitimate to redescribe the intentional object of a coerced person's effective first-order desire. It cannot, for example, be presupposed that the intentional object of the effective first-order desire of the highwayman's victim that would most naturally be described as 'handing over my money to avoid being shot,' can be redescribed legitimately as 'performing an action that will preserve my well-being' – a move that is often made by those who claim that a coerced person suffers from no impairment to autonomy. Such redescription is not always justified, for, as Dworkin has argued, it is not true that 'we can always replace "doing x in order to do y" by "doing x, in these circumstances, is doing y." '[4] For example, it is not the case that practising parking a car to pass a driving test *is*, in these circumstances, passing the driving test. A further bar to presupposing that it is legitimate to redescribe the intentional object of a coerced person's effective first-order desire is the fact that such a desire will make essential reference to the particular act that the victim of coercion is being required to perform. The victim of Dworkin's highwayman, for example, is not simply moved by a desire 'to save his life,' but by a more *specific* desire 'to save his life *by handing over his wallet.*'[5]

Finally, a successful account of the relationship between coercion and autonomy should recognize that persons who are coerced would not perform *any* act that their coercer requires of them. Instead, they would assess whether they were willing to perform the particular act required in order to avoid the penalty that they are threatened with, where the severity of the penalty might be sufficient to move them to perform some actions but not others.[6]

With these requirements in place I will now develop an analysis of how successfully coercing a person into performing an action impairs their autonomy with respect to that action that satisfies them all. The first point to note in developing this analysis is drawn from the final condition above: that persons who are coerced into acting deliberate as to whether they should resist. It is important to emphasize that this point is *not* that a person who is coerced into an action assesses whether to perform the required act, for to view a coerced person's deliberative process in this way is to misunderstand their situation. When a person who is being coerced deliberates about whether to perform the action that his threatener requires they are not deliberating about whether they should *perform* this action, but whether they should *resist being forced* to do it. This distinction points to the different default positions of people who are being coerced and people who are not. The default conclusion of the deliberative process of the person who is coerced is (typically) that they *will* perform the action under consideration (that is, unless they believe that there is a reason to resist doing so). The default conclusion of the person who is not coerced is (typically) that they *will not* perform the action under deliberation unless they believe they have a reason to do so. Thus, if a person who is subjected to coercion decides that they should perform the act required by the threatener to avoid the penalty, they will not be moved to act by the desire to perform this action *simpliciter*. Instead, they will be moved to act by the desire not to resist another's attempt to exercise control over me such that I do act *x* at his behest.

Once it is recognized that it is *this* desire that is the effective first-order desire of a person who has been coerced into acting a satisfactory analysis of the relationship between coercion and autonomy can be developed. On this analysis a person who is coerced into performing action A *is* autonomous with respect to their effective first-order desire to fail to resist their threatener – that is, they satisfy the relevant criteria outlined in the previous chapter for them to be autonomous with respect to this desire. However, since the satisfaction of this desire involves relinquishing a degree of control to the threatener over what action is performed and when, a person suffers from impaired autonomy with respect to the coerced action.

This analysis of why a person who is coerced into performing a certain action would thereby suffer from a diminution in autonomy satisfies the first condition that such an analysis must meet, as outlined above: it satisfies both of the apparently contradictory intuitions concerning whether a person who is coerced into performing an act is autonomous with respect to that act. The intuition that such a compliant victim of coercion retains *full* autonomy because they *chose* to act as they did is satisfied, insofar as this intuition is understood to refer to retaining autonomy over the *choice* as to whether to submit. This is because, on this analysis, the compliant victim of coercion *is* autonomous with respect to their effective first-order desire not to resist. Similarly, the intuition that such a compliant victim of coercion suffers from *impaired* autonomy because they are *forced* to act as they did is also satisfied, insofar as this intuition is understood to refer to a loss of autonomy with respect to a compliant *action*. This account also satisfies the other two requirements that must be met by a correct account of the relationship between coercion and autonomy. The effective first-order desire that the compliant victim of coercion is posited to have includes as part of its intentional object a reference to the specific act that they are required to perform, and it is the case that the victim decides whether they should resist performing the act that the threatener requires.

Coercion, Autonomy and a Current Market in Human Kidneys

This analysis of the relationship between coercion and autonomy is not a radical departure from Dworkin's account of how acting from fear will impair autonomy with respect to consequent actions. This is because this account is based on Dworkin's crucial (if implicit) insight that, although a person's being autonomous with respect to their effective first-order desire is *necessary* for them to be autonomous with respect to the acts that it moved them to perform, it is not *sufficient* for this.

However, although the theoretical origins of this analysis can be traced back to Dworkin's discussion in 'Acting Freely' it is superior to his because (unlike Dworkin's analysis) it explains why it is that a person's autonomy will be impaired when they are coerced into acting. This analysis also meets Dworkin's requirement of judgemental relevance, for it is able to accommodate both the judgement that the victims of successful coercion will suffer from differing degrees of impaired autonomy, and the judgement that a person might have their autonomy impaired even if they do not resent being moved to act by their desire not to resist their coercer's demands. It accommodates the first judgement because different coercers will submit their victims to different degrees of control. And it accommodates the second judgement because the degree to which a person will suffer from impaired autonomy as a result of being coerced will depend on the degree of control that they have relinquished to their coercer, and not on their attitude towards their situation.

With this account in hand of how personal autonomy is impaired by coercion I can now show why the anti-market argument from economic coercion is mistaken. This argument, recall, was that if a current market for human transplant kidneys was allowed then the (typical) vendor would be coerced into selling by dire economic circumstances. Since a person's autonomy is impaired when they are coerced, then allowing people to sell their kidneys in a current market would result in the impairment of the typical vendor's autonomy. Thus, the proponents of this anti-market argument conclude, respect for the autonomy of potential vendors in such a market requires that it continue to be prohibited. Yet, despite its elegance and plausibility, this argument is mistaken. From the above account it is clear that for a person's autonomy to be impaired through coercion they must act to satisfy a desire to relinquish *control* over their actions to their coercer. Control, however, is an intentionally characterized concept. That is, for A to control B it is necessary that A *intends* to control B. Since only agents can exercise control over others, only agents can coerce (and thus control) persons. It is thus impossible for a person's economic situation to coerce them, since this is not an intentional agent. Therefore, the argument from economic coercion fails.

This is a very rapid dismissal of the argument from economic coercion. Given the importance of this argument within the debate over the moral permissibility of a current market in human kidneys it would be sensible to go over this dismissal of it more carefully. The first point to establish is that only intentional agents can exert control, whether over other agents, animals or inanimate objects. Since this is not intuitively obvious it is helpful to demonstrate it through example. In Shakespeare's *Othello* Iago controlled (some of) Othello's actions by controlling the information that Othello received. Given Iago's intimate knowledge of Othello's desires, values and goals he was able to ensure that Othello's beliefs were such that, when combined with his desires, Othello would perform the actions that Iago wished him to perform. Since it was thus Iago, and not Othello, who was making the decisions as to which actions Othello should perform, Othello was reduced to the status of a marionette, with Iago as his controlling puppeteer – and to the extent that this was so Othello's autonomy with respect to his actions was impaired.

In the original play Iago certainly intended to control Othello. However, it is possible to imagine an alternative version in which Othello's fate is tragic simply because he himself misconstrued such innocent details as his lieutenant Cassio's possession of Othello's wife Desdemona's handkerchief. In this alternative version Iago presents Othello with precisely the same information that he gave him in the original play. However, *unlike* in the original play, Iago now presents this information without having any interest in how Othello will react to it. Unfortunately, just as in the original play, Othello again wrongly comes to believe that Desdemona is committing adultery, and again he smothers her. Yet, despite both Iago and Othello still performing precisely the same actions in the alternative version of *Othello* as they did in Shakespeare's original, in the alternative version it was not Iago but Othello who decided what actions he should perform. Unlike the Othello of Shakespeare's play, then, in this alternative version Othello's autonomy with respect to his actions was *not* impaired because Iago did not control them.[7] This is important, for the only difference between the two versions is that in the original version Iago presented Othello with the information that he did *with the intent* that Othello would perform the actions that he did. With all other factors held constant, then, it is Iago's *intention* to control Othello in the original play that accounts for why Othello's autonomy was impaired there but not in the alternative version.[8] It is thus a necessary (but not sufficient) condition for person A to control person B in such a way that B's autonomy with respect to their consequent actions is undermined that A must *intend* to control B.

In addition to this it has been established above that coercing a person to act will impair their autonomy with respect to that act to the extent that they relinquish control over their actions to their coercer. It is clear then that for a person's autonomy to be impaired through coercion their coercer must *intend* to exercise control over them. If this condition is *not* met (that is, the alleged coercer either cannot or does not intend to exercise control) then the person's (alleged) coercer will *not* exercise control over them – and so this person's autonomy with respect to their actions will be unimpaired. This is fatal to the anti-market argument from economic coercion. As I noted above, a person's economic situation is not an intentional entity, and so it makes no sense to claim that it intends to exercise control over those persons who find themselves within it. Impoverished people thus cannot give up any degree of control over their actions to that which is allegedly coercing them, that is, their economic situation. Given that the impoverished person would thus retain full control over their actions even as they (desperately) sell a kidney there is nothing in their economic situation that bars them from being fully autonomous with respect to this sale. The proponents of the argument from economic coercion are thus mistaken when they claim that persons are coerced into selling their kidneys – and Dworkin is right to hold that the sale of a kidney would be a voluntary transaction.

Kidney Sales and Interpersonal Coercion

Before moving to consider further autonomy-based arguments against allowing a current market in human transplant kidneys another argument from coercion must be addressed. This second argument is based on the recognition that 'the fact that one has new possibilities for choice opens the possibility of social ... sanctions being brought to bear on the maker of the choice.'[9] The proponents of this argument recognize that if a current market in human kidneys is allowed this will open up the possibility of some persons being coerced into selling their kidneys, perhaps by creditors or by family members who want the money that could be raised.[10] Since *interpersonal* coercion would impair the autonomy of the person thus coerced, the fact that a current market for human kidneys would allow such coercion to take place indicates that respect for autonomy would not support the view that such a market is morally permissible.

Yet this anti-market argument from interpersonal coercion should not be accepted, for it is at once too weak and too strong. It is too weak because, although it is true that allowing a current market in human transplant kidneys is likely to result in some persons being coerced into selling their kidneys, it is also likely that the majority of the vendors in such a market would not have been so coerced, but, instead, would sell their kidneys autonomously. (This would be especially true in a regulated current market for kidneys of the sort I propose in Chapter 5.) Since this is so, respect for autonomy seems to require that a current market for human kidneys be recognized as morally permissible, even if a minority of vendors might suffer from impaired autonomy as a result. This second argument from coercion is also too strong because, if accepted, it will show not only that a current market in human kidneys should be held to be morally impermissible, but also that a current market in *any* commodity (or commodifiable good) is morally impermissible. This is because, just as someone might coerce someone else into selling one of their kidneys, they might also coerce them into selling *anything else* that they own. Thus, if this argument is taken to work against a current market in human kidneys it should also be taken to work against any type of market in any good whatsoever, which is a clear *reductio ad absurdum* of this anti-market position.

The Argument from Economic Necessity

Although opponents of a current market in human kidneys might be persuaded that economically desperate persons would not be *coerced* into selling their kidneys, they might still object to allowing such a market on the grounds that the economic situation of the poor would *necessitate* the sale of their kidneys. Thus, since it would not be the poor who were directing themselves to sell their kidneys, but their economic situation necessitating this, they would not be fully autonomous with respect to the sales of their kidneys. Moreover, canny opponents of kidney sales might point out that necessity is distinct from coercion in that, whereas coercion might require the presence of an intentional agent to do the coercing, necessity does not – although forcing a person to act out of necessity seems to impair their autonomy with respect to that act just as much as subjecting them to coercion would. Thus, proponents of this anti-market argument from necessity conclude, even though the above coercion-based anti-market arguments might not be persuasive, if one is really concerned with personal autonomy one should still consider a current market in human transplant kidneys to be morally impermissible.[11]

This anti-market argument from necessity avoids the philosophical difficulties that are associated with the claim that the destitute will be coerced by economic circumstances into selling their kidneys. It also has considerable rhetorical force, for it is based on the common intuition that the poor are merely the unfortunate pawns of forces beyond their control, such that if current markets in human kidneys are allowed then they would be *forced* or *driven* to sell their kidneys by their poverty. This argument thus draws on the same intuition that lay behind the argument from economic coercion: that as soon as a current market for human kidneys is allowed the destitute would be driven to sell by the economic pressures they are subject to, rather as water is forced by the pressure it is under to pour through a dam once it is breached. Yet, despite its rhetorical force, there is a clear difficulty with this anti-market argument: when a person decides to sell one of their kidneys, unlike the water in the burst dam, they *choose* to do so. Thus, even if vendors wish not to be motivated by their desire to sell a kidney because they want to be in a different economic situation from the one they are actually in, they are still directing their own actions within this situation. As such, vendors would not necessarily suffer any impairment in autonomy when selling a kidney, even if they do so out of desperation.

The Argument from Irresistible Offers

Despite its failure, however, this anti-market argument from necessity captures an important intuition that seems to be shared by those who hold that current markets in human kidneys are impermissible – namely, that the options possessed by the destitute are so constrained that they would be forced to sell a kidney to raise money, and therefore their autonomy with respect to their vending actions would be impaired. To put this intuition another way, prior to the introduction of a current market for human kidneys the desperate poor had a series of options of roughly equal unpalatability from which they could choose how to eke out a living. Faced with these options they could direct themselves to pursue that which they thought was best for them. They were thus autonomously choosing from their range of options, and were also autonomous with respect to their performance of their actions. The introduction of a current market for human transplant kidneys, however, introduces an option into the choice set of the poor that (for some of them at least) is so clearly preferable to any of the other available options that it silences any alternative. The introduction of the option to sell a kidney would thus reduce the number of eligible options that they have to one. This, one might think, results in these poor people being *forced* to sell a kidney as this is now their only eligible option. Thus, insofar as they are now forced to sell a kidney by the combination of their economic situation and the introduction of a current market, they are *being directed* to do so by their situations, rather than *directing themselves* to do so, and so suffer impaired autonomy with respect to their actions.

Once this intuition behind both the argument from necessity and the original argument from economic coercion has been brought into the open it is clear that it is the same intuition that lies behind another standard anti-market view – the argument from irresistible offers. This is also based on the intuition that the introduction of a current market in human transplant kidneys would provide an option for some destitute people that was so attractive, so 'irresistible,' that it would supersede all previous options. The desperately poor person to whom the option of selling a kidney is irresistible would thus be unable to refuse it, and so it would not be the vendor, *but the person making them the offer*, who would be directing the sale. In this case the vendor's autonomy would be compromised, and so concern for autonomy requires that such offers (and so current markets in human kidneys) be prohibited.

Against this argument from irresistible offers Radcliffe Richards claims that offers such as payment for a transplant kidney cannot impair the autonomy of those receiving the offers because they broaden rather than constrict their options.[12] This response is unconvincing because Radcliffe Richards fails to recognize that certain options that might be added to a person's choice-set are *constraining* options which, if chosen, are likely to result in the overall impairment of that person's autonomy.[13] Although I will discuss the option of selling a kidney as a constraining option in the next chapter it would be useful here to provide examples of constraining options to illustrate briefly Radcliffe Richards's mistake. The best-known example is the option of selling oneself into slavery. As J.S. Mill famously argued, if one is concerned with liberty (and, by implication, autonomy) one should prohibit persons from having the option to sell themselves into slavery, on the grounds that their choosing this option would defeat 'the very purpose which is the justification of allowing him to dispose of himself.'[14] Similarly, an addict's option to take the drugs that they are trying to quit is also a constraining option – one that, if taken, is likely to result in the impairment of autonomy rather than in its enhancement. Since broadening a person's options might only involve adding autonomy-*impairing* constraining options to his set, the fact that adding the option to sell their kidneys broadens their option set does not show that this could not lead to their autonomy being impaired. Thus, unless Radcliffe Richards can show that the addition of the option to sell a kidney is *not* an autonomy-impairing constraining option, her objection to the anti-market argument from irresistible offers is incomplete.

As well as failing to recognize the possibility that broadening a person's choices might compromise their autonomy through only introducing autonomy-impairing constraining options, Radcliffe Richards's response to the argument from irresistible offers also glosses over its theoretical sophistication. Both the arguments from economic coercion and from economic necessity fell prey to the objection that a person will not suffer impaired autonomy by their economic situation because it is not an intentional agent, and so it cannot exercise control over them in the way that the proponents of these arguments envisage. The argument from irresistible offers, however, is *not* vulnerable to this objection because it posits that the autonomy of the kidney vendor is impaired through the actions of another agent (namely, the person who is offering to buy the kidney). From this, it appears that the autonomy of the desperate vendor is impaired in the same way as the autonomy of the victim of coercion: that when a person agrees to sell their kidney as a result of an irresistible offer to purchase it they would decide *not to resist* the offer, just as the compliant victim of coercion would decide *not to resist* the coercer. Moreover, when the desperate kidney vendor A sells to the person B making the irresistible offer, A *will perform the action* that B *intends* A to perform, just as when the victim of coercion complies with the coercer's threats. Thus, it seems that just as the compliant victim of coercion suffers from impaired autonomy with respect to his actions, so too does the person who succumbs to an irresistible offer for his kidney because they decide not to resist and so relinquish control over their actions to the person making the offer (the coercer). Hence, although the above account of how coercion impairs autonomy shows that the anti-market arguments from economic coercion and economic necessity are mistaken, accepting this (ideologically neutral) account does not lead to a *pro*-market conclusion, for it appears to show that the *anti*-market argument from irresistible offers is actually correct.

This, however, is illusory. In the above account I argued that if the compliant victim of coercion failed to resist the demands of the coercer they would suffer impaired autonomy with respect to the coerced acts because it would then be the coercer, and not the victim, who was directing the performance of them. The crucial part of this account is that the victim of coercion suffered from impaired autonomy *because they did not resist the coercer* and so acted under the coercer's direction. The victim was thus passive, rather than active, with respect to the coerced actions, and so was not autonomous with respect to them.[15] Proponents of the anti-market argument from irresistible offers trade on this aspect of how coercion impairs autonomy by claiming that desperate kidney vendors likewise *fail to resist* the purchaser's offer, and so their actions are subject to outside direction rather than to their own. Thus, the proponents conclude, the desperate kidney vendor who accepts an irresistible offer is passive with respect to their actions.

For the argument from irresistible desires to be parallel to the above account of how coercion undermines autonomy, then, its proponents must establish that the desperate kidney vendor failed to resist the purchaser's offer, and in so doing ceded control over their acts. This is easy to do if the vendor is moved to act by a *genuinely irresistible* offer (that is, one that they could not resist accepting even if they wanted to), for then the claim that they were unable to resist the purchaser's offer is true by definition. If this is so, the kidney vendor would not be autonomous with respect to either their effective first-order desire or their consequent action because they would merely be a passive bystander to the operation of this desire. However, it is highly doubtful that most kidney vendors (if any) would be moved by genuinely irresistible desires in the same way, for example, that a sufferer from Tourette's Syndrome is moved by an irresistible desire to swear. Since the desire to sell a kidney is thus not (typically) a desire that its possessor *must* satisfy whether they want to or not, it is simply not true to claim, as R.A. Sells does, that since 'the financial benefits have such an impact on the life of the donor and his family as to be irresistible: *the element of voluntariness ... must be ... in extreme cases, abolished.*'[16]

Since the typical kidney vendor would not be motivated by a genuinely irresistible desire the proponents of the argument from irresistible offers need to provide an account of why it is that, when someone sells a kidney, they are, like victims of successful coercion, moved to act at the behest of another's will. This they cannot do. This becomes clear if we recall that in the above account of the relationship between coercion and autonomy the hallmark of a person's failure to resist being moved to act by another person is that the *default* action – that is, the action that they would perform unless they actively decide to do otherwise, and this decision is effective in moving them to act – is the action required of him by the person whom he fails to resist. Compliant victims of coercion will *fail to resist* their coercer since, as both Thalberg and Frankfurt noted, their default action is that which the coercer tells them to do.[17] Similarly, the (rare) kidney vendor who is moved to sell by a genuinely irresistible desire for the price offered for their kidney will *fail to resist* the offer made by the would-be purchaser since their default action is that which the purchaser requires them to perform to receive it. Since this is so, for it to be the case that the (typical) kidney vendor fails to resist the offer made for his kidney – and for the argument from irresistible offers to be sound – the (typical) kidney vendor's default action must be to sell to the would-be purchaser.

But this is clearly *not* the default action of the typical kidney vendor. Instead, the default action would be to remain as they are (that is, not sell a kidney) and continue about their business as before. This is not surprising, for the typical vendor would only sell a kidney after *deciding* to do so; that is, after actively deciding *not* to perform the default action of simply not selling and going about business as usual. Rather than failing to resist the magnetic pull of the price offered for one of their kidneys, and being *passively* moved to sell a kidney to the detriment of personal autonomy, the (typical) kidney vendor would instead *actively* decide to sell after weighing up what they believed to be the advantages and disadvantages of this act. It would thus be the vendor themself, and not someone else, that moves them to act. Their autonomy with respect to the vending action would thus be unimpaired by the fact that the price offered for the kidney is very attractive. The fact that, in selling, the typical kidney vendor would have performed the action that the purchaser intended them to perform does not effect this conclusion at all, for one agent's intention to control another is a necessary *but not a sufficient* condition for such control to occur. This is because the second agent must have performed the actions that the first intended him to perform as a direct result of actions that the first agent took to ensure this.

Despite its theoretical allure when it is considered in parallel with cases of genuine coercion, then, the anti-market argument from irresistible offers is just as mistaken as the two arguments from coercion and the argument from necessity that preceded it. Worse yet, this argument also has two highly counterintuitive implications that militate strongly against its acceptance. First, it seems mistakenly to show that no one can autonomously accept a highly attractive offer. After all, as Stephen Wilkinson points out, if this were true 'it would be impossible for anyone ever to consent validly [that is, autonomously] to lifesaving operations, not to mention [to accepting] lottery "jackpot" wins or large salaries; the mere fact that a proposal is tremendously attractive clearly doesn't mean that it can't be validly and voluntarily accepted by the offeree.'[18] Second, if the argument from irresistible offers were correct, proponents of a current market in human kidneys could readily avoid its implications by restricting the price that could be paid for a kidney so that it was no more attractive to would-be kidney vendors than the other means of making money that were open to them. But it is surely wrong to hold that one can protect the autonomy of destitute people by removing from them the opportunity to escape their poverty.

Conclusion

In this chapter I have argued that the major autonomy-based anti-market arguments are all mistaken. I have not yet, however, offered a complete defence of the view that respect for personal autonomy requires that persons be allowed to participate in a current market for human kidneys. I have only argued that typical vendors in such a market would not suffer from impaired autonomy with respect to their vending action – even if they sold their kidneys out of economic desperation. This is compatible with the option to sell a kidney being an autonomy-impairing constraining option – one that might be chosen autonomously but which is likely to compromise the autonomy of those choosing it. For respect for autonomy to ground the claim that a current market in human transplant kidneys is morally permissible, the option to sell must be both autonomously chosen by the typical kidney vendor, and also *not* a constraining option. Furthermore, even if a full defence of the claim that respect for autonomy supports allowing a current market for human transplant kidneys is forthcoming, it must be recognized that autonomy is not the only value that is relevant within this debate – and it might be outweighed by competing values such as respect for the market inalienability of human body parts. The first of these concerns is the subject of the next chapter; the second will be addressed in Chapters 7 and 8.

Notes

1   Radcliffe Richards, p. 382.
2   Ibid., p. 381.
3   I discuss why this claim is false – and the implications this has for the debate over whether a current market in human kidneys is morally permissible – below, and in the next chapter.
4   Dworkin (1970), p. 374. The following example is from Dworkin.
5   This is discussed in Taylor (2003), p. 151.
6   Frankfurt (1988c), p. 39.
7   One might argue that Othello's autonomy was impaired in both plays because he acted in ignorance, and so the direct source of his heteronomy in Shakespeare's version does not lie in Iago's manipulative actions as I argue here. To argue this would be to claim that a person's autonomy would be impaired whenever they acted out of ignorance. But, if ignorance *per se* impaired autonomy the scope of autonomous action would be severely (and implausibly) restricted, for almost all persons' actions are performed in conditions of imperfect knowledge. (This view would, for example, render Columbus nonautonomous with respect to his sailing to the New World, even though he was fully in control of his act of doing so.) Rather than claiming that ignorance *per se* impairs autonomy, then, one should claim that being *kept* ignorant (that is, by another agent) could impair autonomy – a claim that is in accord with the point I make above.
8   Frankfurt would not accept that Othello's autonomy in the original play was impaired, since he holds that the history of a person's desires – and hence the actions they motivate – has no bearing on whether they are autonomous with respect to them. See Frankfurt (1988a), p. 171, n. 13. This does not, however, undercut my claim (in Chapter 1) to be drawing on a characterization of personal autonomy in this volume that is broad enough to be acceptable to all. This is because the point of this discussion of Iago and Othello does not concern the nature of autonomy, but the nature of control – namely, that it is an intentionally characterized concept. And this is something that Frankfurt could accept.

9   Dworkin, Gerald (1988b), p. 68.
10 This possibility was noted by Rothman (2002), p. 1640 and Goyal et al., p. 1591.
11 Although the 'argument from economic necessity' is not explicitly distinguished from the similar (but more problematic) 'argument from economic coercion' in the literature (and so it is not easy precisely to identify which authors provide which argument), one of its clearest exponents is Scheper-Hughes, p. 1647.
12 Radcliffe Richards (1996), p. 384.
13 Interestingly, Dworkin acknowledged the existence of constraining options in his essay 'Is More Choice Better Than Less?' (pp. 68–9) but he failed to recognize the implications of this for his own pro-market argument. Dworkin did not use the term 'constraining option,' although his claim that increasing a person's choices might in some cases decrease the possibility of their being able to exercise their autonomy is a clear acknowledgement that certain options are constraining for the individuals who choose them.
14 J.S. Mill (1978), p. 101.
15 The metaphor of the heteronomous person being 'passive' is borrowed from Frankfurt (1988b), pp. 58–9.
16 Sells, R.A. (1991), p. 20 (emphasis added).
17 Thalberg, p. 124; Frankfurt (1988c), p. 43.
18 Wilkinson (2003), p. 119.

Chapter 4
Constraining Options and Kidney Markets

In the previous chapter I argued that the major autonomy-based arguments against the moral acceptability of a current market in human kidneys are all mistaken. However, I also noted that this does not mean that one who values personal autonomy should necessarily hold that such a market is morally permissible. The claim that the typical kidney vendor would be autonomous with respect to the sale of one of their kidneys is perfectly compatible with the claim that the option to sell a kidney is an autonomy-impairing *constraining option*, one that, if chosen and acted upon, is likely to impair their future autonomy, or the autonomy of other members of their group. Furthermore, two innovative arguments have been developed to show that the option to sell a kidney in a current market *is* a constraining option which would have either (or both) of these deleterious effects. Paul Hughes argues that selling a kidney is likely to compromise the autonomy of the person who does so, and T.L. Zutlevics argues that allowing the poor to have this option is likely to reduce the possibility that their autonomy will be promoted in the future through the provision of aid.[1] To show that respect for autonomy supports the institution of, rather than the continued prohibition of, a current market in human kidneys, then, I must show that the option to sell a kidney is not an autonomy-impairing constraining option of either of these sorts.

Hughes's Argument

Paul Hughes's anti-market argument is based on the recognition that removing barriers to one's ability to exercise personal autonomy in certain ways need not be required by respect for that autonomy because the possession of certain 'constraining options' might lead to the autonomy of those who possess them becoming impaired. In the last chapter I briefly discussed such constraining options and gave two examples: Mill's option to sell oneself into slavery, and an addict's option to take the drug to which he was addicted. To illustrate further what constitutes a constraining option Hughes cites 'the legal option of refraining from pressing charges against one's assailant.'[2] Although this option is held to enhance its possessors' control over their lives, Hughes notes that out of fear of their assailants some persons refuse to press charges; a refusal that condemns them to the possibility of yet more abuse at the hands of the original perpetrators. The option not to press charges is thus constraining because it locks some persons who choose it into a continued cycle of autonomy-compromising abuse that could have been broken (and their autonomy restored) had this option not been open to them.[3]

Having established the possibility of constraining options Hughes draws on a neo-Marxist account of exploitation to argue that the option to sell one's organs is such an option. On this account a person is exploited when their background set of options is constricted in such a way so as to force them to perform the action that the exploiter requires (for example, to work in the exploiter's factory or to sell him a kidney).[4] If a person is faced with such a constricted range of options, Hughes argues, then anything that 'presupposes and/or reinforces' this situation will perpetuate the impairment of their autonomy.[5] So, if a person is provided with an addition to their choice-set that, if chosen, would be likely to result in their remaining in their present autonomy-impairing circumstances, their possession of that new option might perpetuate the impairment of their autonomy.

To show that the option to sell one's organs in a current market is an autonomy-impairing constraining option of this sort Hughes notes that it will typically be the poor who would be the vendors in such a market. From this, he infers that for a current market in human organs to exist 'it is necessary that there be poor people and that we allow them to participate in such a market.'[6] Hughes then concludes that the introduction of a current market in human organs *presupposes* that some persons live in autonomy-impairing economic circumstances. And if a system that 'presupposes and/or reinforces' a person's presence within an autonomy-impairing situation perpetuates the impairment of their autonomy, then the introduction of a current market for human organs would be likely only to impair further potential vendors' autonomy.

Responses to Hughes

It is plausible to hold that if a system presupposes and/or reinforces an autonomy-impairing situation, then that system is itself autonomy impairing. However, this neo-Marxist claim cannot be used to object to the introduction of a current market for human kidneys, as such a market neither presupposes nor reinforces the autonomy-impairing situation of the poor in the way required for it to be an autonomy-impairing system. To show this I must first distinguish between two senses in which the introduction of a system B 'presupposes' the existence of a situation A. In the first sense a system B presupposes the existence of a situation A if B is introduced to alleviate A, such that, some time after B is introduced, A might cease to exist. In the second sense a system B presupposes the existence of a situation A if B is introduced in the belief that A exists, *and* situation A and system B are mutually reinforcing and will continue to coexist. Hughes cannot be using the first sense of 'presuppose' in his argument because he denies that a current market for human organs would alleviate the autonomy-impairing economic situation of the poor. Instead, he is using the second sense of 'presuppose.' Here, a current market for human organs would presuppose the autonomy-impairing situation of the poor if it is introduced in the belief that there are poor persons who live in such a situation, *and* that the introduction of this market both depends on their being in this situation and contributes to their continued existence within it.

Stakes and Kidneys

The sense of 'presuppose' that Hughes is using thus has two aspects: (i) that a system B is introduced in the belief that there exists a certain situation A, and (ii) that A and B are mutually reinforcing and will continue to coexist. But, since this is so, the claim that a system B is likely to be autonomy impairing if its introduction *presupposes* the existence of an autonomy-impairing situation A plays no role in Hughes's argument against a current market in human kidneys. If the sense of 'presuppose' that Hughes is using is understood as an *inclusive* conjunction (that is, aspects (i) *and* (ii) must *both* be true for B to presuppose A), then the introduction of a current market for human kidneys will not presuppose (in this sense) that there are persons who live in autonomy-impairing economic circumstances. This is because, as I will show below, aspect (i) of this sense of 'presuppose' is false in this context. The sense of 'presuppose' that Hughes is using must thus be understood as an *exclusive* conjunction – that is, that *either* aspect (i) *or* aspect (ii) must be true for B to presuppose A. In this case, the claim that a current market for human kidneys *presupposes* that there are persons who live in autonomy-impairing economic circumstances is – given the falsity of (i), which I will demonstrate below – not distinct from the claim that the introduction of such a market will be likely to *reinforce* the autonomy-impairing situation of the poor. Hughes's claim that (in this context) a market for kidneys presupposes the autonomy-impairing situation of the poor thus rests entirely on the truth of (ii): that a market for human kidneys and the autonomy-impairing circumstances of the poor are mutually reinforcing and would continue to coexist. Provided that I can show that (i) is false, then, to refute Hughes's claim that selling a kidney would be an autonomy-impairing constraining option, I need only show that a person who chooses such an option is not likely to have their position within their autonomy-impairing economic circumstances reinforced.

It is not difficult to show that the first aspect of the sense of 'presuppose' that Hughes uses is false. In the context of this discussion this is the claim that for a current market in human kidneys to be introduced it is necessary that there are 'poor people and that we allow them to participate' in it. This claim is false because all the proponents of such a market need presuppose is that some persons would be willing to purchase kidneys, that others (of any economic standing) would be willing to sell them and that the vendor and the purchaser would be able to agree on a price. Of course, there is no doubt that almost all the vendors in such a market would be drawn from the ranks of the desperate poor, and so more kidneys would be sold if there were poor people and they were allowed to participate in this market. But this point concerns the differential volume of trade that would take place in a current market for human kidneys with the participation of the poor, rather than the feasibility of such a market.

Since the first aspect of 'presuppose' that Hughes uses is false, his anti-market argument rests, as I noted above, on the truth of (ii). Hughes's account of what it is for the introduction of a market to 'presuppose' that there are persons in an autonomy-impairing economic situation is thus simply that such a market would reinforce these persons' presence in this autonomy-impairing situation. This being so, to show that Hughes is mistaken I need only show that the introduction of such a market would *not* reinforce their presence within this. At first sight, this seems fairly easy to do. Rather than reinforcing the typical kidney vendor's position within his autonomy-impairing economic circumstances there is evidence that allowing persons to sell their kidneys would provide them with a way to *transcend* those circumstances through the opportunity to acquire capital that they could use to raise themselves out of poverty, and even start businesses – as, for example, in the Philippines and in India (see Chapter 2).

However, despite the fact that some people do sell their kidneys to raise money to escape impoverishment, the view that allowing a current market in human transplant kidneys would free the poor from the shackles of poverty is a pro-market fantasy worthy only of Horatio Alger – or, more charitably, of those unaware of the evidence.[7] A more realistic picture of the likely effects that allowing persons to sell their kidneys would have on their economic status was provided in a February 2001 study conducted in Chennai (formerly Madras), in the state of Tamil Nadu in southern India, of 305 people who illegally sold their kidneys. This study demonstrated that the sale of a kidney to raise money for education or to start a business is a very rare phenomenon indeed. Instead, the study showed that the majority of kidney vendors (60 per cent) sold their kidneys to pay off debts or to meet immediate expenses, such as paying for food (22 per cent). Only 11 per cent of the kidney vendors surveyed were able to retain any of the money received from the sale as cash or a cash equivalent (such as jewellery or investment); and only 1 per cent used it to start a business. The remainder of the people surveyed used the money for marriage or future marriage.[8] The results of the Chennai study are supported by similar anecdotal evidence from Sanjay Kumar, who has noted that the Chennai suburban slum colony Villivakkam is so full of poor people who have sold a kidney that it has become internationally known as 'kidney-vakkam.'[9]

Rather than helping the poor escape from their autonomy-impairing circumstances, then, allowing them to sell their kidneys might only enable them to continue to live in poverty – perhaps to sell other non-vital body parts in future. Therefore, it seems that Hughes's claim is correct: that a current market in human kidneys *reinforces* the continued existence of the poor in their autonomy-impairing economic conditions, and so is an autonomy-impairing system. Yet this conclusion should not be accepted too readily, as, just as with the two senses of the term 'presuppose,' there are at least two distinct senses of the term 'reinforce' that Hughes could be using here. In the first sense of the term ('reinforce$_a$') a system will reinforce$_a$ a person's position within autonomy-impairing economic circumstances if, and only if, its introduction will ensure that they are likely to remain within these circumstances (that is, their chances of escape have not been improved). In the second sense ('reinforce$_b$') a system will reinforce$_b$ a person's position within their autonomy-impairing situation if, and only if, its introduction will make it *less* likely that they will be able to escape from this situation in the future.

The evidence from both Chennai and Villivakkam shows that the sale of a kidney is not likely to enhance the economic status of the typical vendor. Since this is so, the present current market for human transplant kidneys *does* reinforce$_a$ the situation of the average vendor because, even after selling a kidney they are likely to remain within their autonomy-impairing economic circumstances. However, this fact is unobjectionable to defenders of autonomy, as reinforcing$_a$ a person's position within their autonomy-impairing circumstances does not lead to any *additional* impairment of autonomy that they would have avoided had the reinforcing$_a$ system not been introduced. Moreover, reinforcing$_a$ a person's position within his autonomy-impairing situation might even *enhance* their ability to exercise autonomy. For example, if the only way a person could pay for certain necessities without which they would die (such as food or medical treatment) was by selling a kidney this sale would reinforce$_a$ their situation within autonomy-impairing economic circumstances. However, since it would do so by keeping them alive, reinforcing$_a$ a person's presence within their autonomy-impairing situation would *maintain* their ability to exercise autonomy, rather than impair it. Thus, since reinforcing$_a$ a person's presence within their autonomy-impairing economic circumstances would be unobjectionable to a defender of autonomy, Hughes cannot be using this sense of 'reinforce' when he writes that a system that will 'presuppose and/or reinforce' an autonomy-impairing situation will itself be autonomy impairing.

From this, it appears that the second sense of the term 'reinforce' is more appropriate for Hughes's purposes.[10] For Hughes, then, an autonomy-impairing constraining option is one that, if chosen, is likely to reinforce$_b$ a person's position within their autonomy-impairing economic circumstances (that is, makes it less likely that they would escape them). Is the sale of a kidney likely to reinforce$_b$ a person's position within autonomy-impairing economic circumstances? It is not. To see this, recall that the evidence from both Chennai and Villivakkam suggests that the typical kidney vendor would sell a kidney to pay off debts. But this does not show that they are now *less* likely to be able to escape their autonomy-impairing economic circumstances. Indeed, if the typical kidney vendor is able to free themselves from debt they are *more* likely to escape from poverty than before, when

they were locked into using meagre earnings to make
payments on high-interest loans with little chance of ever
repaying the capital.[11] Since this is so, the option to sell a
kidney does *not* reinforce$_b$ the typical vendor's position
within autonomy-impairing economic circumstances – and so
Hughes appears mistaken to claim that the option to sell is an
autonomy-impairing constraining option.

Kidney Sales, Aid and Group-affecting Constraining Options

In arguing that selling one's kidneys is not an autonomy-
impairing constraining option of the sort that Hughes
envisages I implied that this option would be the best that
was available to many of the desperate poor, insofar as it
would enable them to secure enough money to pay for food,
medical care or to escape debt.[12] T.L. Zutlevics, however,
argues that this implication is false, contending that the best
option available to the destitute is to be the recipients of
aid.[13] Zutlevics argues that it is important to recognize this
because we would then also see how allowing the poor to sell
their organs in a current market would provide them with an
option that is constraining for them *as a group*.

Zutlevics is right that to recognize that holding that the
best option for the poor is to be the recipients of aid is the key
to developing the argument that providing them with the
option to sell their organs is to provide a potentially
constraining option for them as a group. However, she is
wrong to argue that this undermines autonomy-based pro-
market arguments. This aid-based response to the pro-market
argument is caught on the horns of a dilemma. On one hand,
if the poor do not receive sufficient aid to enable them to
escape from their poverty then the proponents of current
markets in human organs seem right to hold that the best
option that the poor *actually* have might be to sell an organ.
On the other hand, if sufficient aid is provided to enable the
poor to escape their economic deprivation it is unlikely that
persons would wish to participate as vendors in a current
market for human organs, and so there would be no need to
prohibit this. (And, of course, it would be 'paternalist in the

extreme' to prohibit those few persons who, for reasons of their own, wish to sell their organs from doing so.)[14] Since this is so, then, it appears that a current market for human organs should be allowed whether aid is forthcoming or not.

Yet Zutlevics has a way out of this dilemma, arguing that allowing the poor of impoverished countries to be vendors in a current market in human organs now might lead to less aid coming to them in the future because it is likely that there would be a flow of organs from impoverished non-Western countries to the affluent West. This, she continues, would provide Western countries with a reason not to provide aid to the impoverished countries from which they are purchasing transplant organs as it would rescue those citizens from the economic desperation that leads them to sell their organs. So, Zutlevics concludes, a current market for human organs should be prohibited on the grounds that allowing the poor of non-Western countries to sell their organs to the West is likely to reinforce their presence in their autonomy-impairing economic situation through providing the West with a disincentive to supply them with the aid that they require to escape it.

At first sight, this argument is persuasive. Like Hughes, Zutlevics argues that the option to sell one's organs is likely to be an autonomy-impairing constraining option.[15] Unlike Hughes, however, Zutlevics does not claim that it is likely to be an autonomy-impairing constraining option *for the person who chooses it*. Instead, she contends that the possession by the poor of the option to sell their organs is likely to reduce their overall degree of autonomy *as a group* – even if such sales might enhance the individual autonomy of the vendors. Moreover, Zutlevics also provides an account of why allowing such sales would reinforce the autonomy-impairing social conditions in which the poor find themselves. Before moving to criticize Zutlevics's argument I should note that she is not against allowing current markets in human organs *per se*, but only against any market whose existence might provide a reason for the affluent to curtail provision of aid to the needy. Therefore, she does not oppose a current market in human organs in which the poor are only allowed to sell to their fellow poor, nor a market in which only the non-impoverished are allowed to sell their organs.

This last point leads directly to the first criticism of Zutlevics's argument. In 'Markets and Morals' Dworkin explicitly addressed arguments opposing a current market in human organs that, like Zutlevics's, focused on the possibility that such markets might lead to the exploitation of the poor. Dworkin rhetorically asks whether one would be more or less inclined to favour organ sales if individuals whose average income was less than 80 per cent of median family income were prohibited from selling their organs – a move that would effectively remove persons in the lower 40 per cent of income distribution from the market.[16] Here, Dworkin is attempting to draw out the intuition that such a move would be considered objectionable, prohibiting, as it would, those who would be most likely to benefit from the sale of their organs from doing so. Zutlevics has a ready response to this objection. Dworkin's rhetorical response to anti-market arguments such as hers is based on the view that restricting the class of vendors to exclude the poor is of no benefit to them. As Zutlevics has persuasively argued, however, this might not be true, for such a restriction might serve to eliminate one reason that the affluent might have to refuse aid to the poor. Rather than focusing on the short-term disadvantages that such a restriction might impose upon those poor individuals who would have otherwise sold their organs, one should instead focus on the long-term benefits that it might have for the poor *as a class*. Once one refocuses in this way such a restriction might not appear as objectionable as Dworkin holds it to be.

Provided that one accepts Zutlevics's consequentialist approach to moral reasoning, her argument is defensible against Dworkin's objection. However, it is not so readily defended against the challenge that its basic premise is mistaken. Zutlevics holds that the *possibility* that the amount of autonomy-enhancing aid that is sent to the impoverished countries of the world would decrease if current markets in human organs were allowed is high enough to justify their prohibition. This premise is a speculative one – and there are several factors that undermine its plausibility. The affluent countries of the West might wish the poorer countries to attain wealth and financial stability to provide additional markets for Western goods. Furthermore, they might wish to aid them to avoid the possible political instability that their economic deprivation might generate, and that might subsequently adversely affect Western interests in the international arena. Similarly (and especially in the wake of the September 11th terrorist attacks on New York City and Washington DC and the subsequent war in Iraq) Western countries might be motivated to provide aid to developing countries simply to dampen anti-Western sentiment.

Of course these considerations are, like Zutlevics's own premise, speculative, and so although they militate against a too-ready acceptance of it, they do not decisively refute it. However, empirical evidence suggests that Western countries would be unlikely to refuse aid to impoverished countries in order to maintain them as suppliers of transplant organs for Western citizens. As stated in Chapter 1, when it became known that Turkish nationals were selling their kidneys for transplantation to persons in Britain the resulting public outcry was largely responsible for the Human Organ Transplants Act of 1989 that prohibited this trade.[17] Although it would be unwise to generalize from such an isolated example, it does seem to show that Western countries are unlikely to form their foreign-aid policies with a view to securing a cheap supply of commercial transplant organs for a subset of their citizens, since any such desire is likely to be outweighed by the desire to avoid the opprobrium of their own citizens and of the international community.

Given both the speculative considerations outlined above and the British government's actual reaction to the public opposition to the international trade in human organs there are good reasons to reject Zutlevics's claim that such a trade would encourage Western countries to withhold aid from those impoverished countries that would become net suppliers of cheap transplant organs. And since this claim provided the basic premise for her argument that allowing the poor to sell their organs would only provide them with a constraining option that, if chosen, would be likely to diminish their autonomy as a group, these considerations provide good reasons for rejecting her arguments.

Chennai Revisited

So far, it seems that selling a kidney in a current market for transplant kidneys is neither a constraining option of the sort that would be likely adversely to affect the individual who pursued it, nor a group-affecting constraining option. In this case, and since (as I argued in the previous chapter) the typical vendor will not suffer from a diminution in autonomy with respect to his selling, it seems that Dworkin is right, and that respect for autonomy mandates that persons – even the desperate poor – be allowed to sell their kidneys if they so choose.

Yet this pro-market conclusion might have been reached too quickly. I argued against Hughes, above, that even though the Chennai study of kidney vendors showed that most did not enjoy enhanced autonomy through such sales, it did not show that selling a kidney is an autonomy-impairing constraining option. This, I argued, was because the study did not show that the typical vendor's position within the autonomy-impairing economic circumstances would be reinforced$_b$ (that is, in the sense of 'reinforce' ascribed to Hughes) as a result of the sale. But this argument overlooks two important points that were also brought out in this study. First, 'many of the participants reported a worsening of their economic status' since the sale of their kidneys, with 'the average family income ... [declining] ... from $660 at the time of nephrectomy to $420 at the time of the survey, a decrease of one third.' (The poverty line in Tamil Nadu is $538 a year for an average-sized family.) This decline in economic status is especially noteworthy since per capita income in Tamil Nadu 'has increased by 10% over the last 5 years and by 37% over the last 10 years after adjusting for inflation,' and 'the proportion of people living below the poverty line has declined by more than 50% since 1988.' Second, when the vendors in this survey rated their health status before and after the sale of their kidney using a five-point Likert scale ranging from 'excellent' to 'poor,' 38 per cent of them reported a 1- to 2-point decline, and 48 per cent reported a 3- to 4-point decline. (The five-point Likert scale is used to measure persons' attitudes. For example, it could ask persons to note their health status, the top category being 'excellent,' descending to 'good,' 'average,' 'below average' and 'poor.') Furthermore, 50 per cent of the vendors reported that they suffered from persistent pain at the nephrectomy site and 33 per cent reported long-term back pain. When the decline in health and in economic status are viewed together it is difficult not to conclude that the worsening of the economic status of the majority of the vendors is due to the decline in their health status suffered as a direct result of selling their kidneys. This hypothesis is especially compelling once one realizes that 60 per cent of the women in the Chennai study and 95 per cent of the men worked as either street vendors or labourers, and so would be more likely to be unable to work – or unable to work as much – if their health declined.[18]

Since this survey indicates that both the health and the economic standing of the typical kidney vendor are likely to suffer a dramatic decline post-nephrectomy with no real prospect of improvement, it appears that Hughes is right, and that for the typical vendor choosing to sell a kidney will only serve to reinforce[b] their position within autonomy-under-mining economic circumstances. Given the decline in health and economic status vendors are less likely to be able to afford food, household expenses and rent after the nephrec-tomy than before it. And since these were the most common debts that the Chennai vendors sold their kidneys to pay off, it is likely that they would slide back into the indebtedness that they sold a kidney to escape.[19] Thus, the Chennai survey seems to indicate that respect for autonomy does indeed support the continued prohibition of current markets in human kidneys.

An Initial Pro-market Response to Chennai – and its Rebuttal

Yet all is not lost for those who hold that respect for autonomy requires that persons be allowed to sell their

kidneys in a current market for them, for it is not so obvious
that the Chennai survey shows that allowing the desperate
poor to sell their kidneys would reinforce$_b$ their impoverished
status. Recall that to claim that a system would reinforce$_b$ a
person's position within their autonomy-impairing poverty is
to claim that it will make it less likely that they will be able to
escape that poverty. It is not clear, however, that selling a
kidney will render a desperate person *less* likely to escape
poverty than before, for even prior to the sale the average
poor person in Chennai or Villivakkam would have almost
no chance of escaping their impoverished situation. This
being so, although the sale of a kidney might render such a
person worse off than they were prior to it (which could
ground a well-being-based objection to such sales) this does
not mean that they are therefore any *less likely* to escape
poverty than before. To illustrate this point more forcefully,
imagine a man trapped in a deep pit by a cruel tormentor.
Owing to the width of the pit all this man can do is move
around a little, and owing to its depth all of his attempts to
escape will be futile. To further distress him his tormenter
deliberately builds a high wall all around the edge badly so
that chunks of brick occasionally fall into the pit, injuring his
prisoner. However, the fact that his tormentor has built this
wall does not make it *less* likely that the man will escape from
his autonomy-impairing situation because there was no
likelihood that he would escape to begin with. Similarly,
insofar as the typical kidney vendor from Villivakkam or
Chennai has no hope of escaping their autonomy-impairing
economic situation, the placing of additional impediments
(for example, the option to sell a kidney, knowing the likely
effects that such a sale would have) would not make escape
less likely. They could not escape it prior to the sale, and
cannot escape it afterwards. Therefore, allowing people the
option to sell will not be allowing them an option that, if
chosen, would make it less likely that they would escape their
poverty, for the likelihood of effecting such an escape would
be same both before and after the sale. The option to sell a
kidney would thus not reinforce$_b$ the position of the typical
kidney vendor within their autonomy-impairing economic
circumstances.

But this seems an odd response for a defender of current markets in human kidneys to make to the Chennai survey because it seems to miss the point. Even though the typical vendor's sale of a kidney will not reinforce$_b$ their impoverished position the evidence from Chennai and Villivakkam suggests that the sale reinforces the impairment of the impoverished vendor's autonomy in a third way that has not yet been considered. In this third sense ('reinforce$_c$') a system will reinforce$_c$ a person's presence within an autonomy-impairing situation if it provides them only with an option that, if chosen, would make it likely that they will be less able to exercise autonomy than prior to this choice.[20] It is clear that the kidney trade as currently practised in Chennai and Villivakkam does reinforce$_c$ the autonomy-impairing plight of the average vendor, for their post-nephrectomy decline in health eliminates the possibility of their pursuing certain options that were available prior to the nephrectomy that they would have chosen to pursue. For example, a person who is physically incapacitated as a result of a nephrectomy will be less able to perform the physical labour that he could prior to surgery, and so their options for employment will be diminished. Moreover, their income is also likely to drop, and, consequently, their range of options will be curtailed yet further. Since this is so, Hughes is correct that allowing persons the option to sell a kidney will only be to allow them an autonomy-impairing constraining option. Respect for autonomy and concern for human well-being thus require that the black market trade in human kidneys as currently practised in Chennai and Villivakkam be stopped.[21]

Black Markets and Legal Markets

However, this does not mean that all trade in human body parts should be prohibited. In fact, rather than supporting the continued prohibition of a current market in human transplant kidneys *per se*, the evidence from Chennai and Villivakkam supports the *legalization* of this market. As we have seen, selling a kidney in the black market is a constraining option for the individual vendors, as it is likely

that their ability to exercise autonomy post-nephrectomy will
be limited both by declining health and economic status. As
the authors of the Chennai survey took care to note, however,
the persistent pain and decline in health that the vendors in
the survey reported have 'not been reported in previous long-
term follow-up of volunteer donors in developed countries.'[22]
There are two possible reasons for this. First, volunteer
donors in developed countries are more likely to be healthier
at the time of their nephrectomy. This will hasten their
recovery from surgery and limit their post-nephrectomy pain
and subsequent decline in health. Second, volunteer donors in
developed countries will receive adequate post-operative
care, such as a 4–12 week recuperation period, adequate
analgesia and extended follow-up medical examinations.[23]
By contrast, accounts are legion of the desperate kidney
vendors of Villivakkam and Chennai simply being dumped
back on the streets immediately after surgery and left to fend
for themselves.[24]

To ensure that selling a kidney is *not* a constraining option
for the individual who chooses it, steps must be taken to
ensure that those who sell their kidneys are sufficiently
healthy to undergo a nephrectomy with minimal risk, and
that they receive adequate post-operative care. The best way
to achieve these aims would be to legalize and regulate a
current market for human kidneys. In such a market a kidney
purchaser (whether a transplant clinic, the end user or an
agent) might only be allowed to purchase kidneys from
persons who meet specified minimal health conditions, and
would be required to provide specified post-operative care to
the vendors as part of their contract. The purchasers would
also have to secure the vendors' informed consent to the sale.
This would require them to inform the vendors of the medical
procedures and risks involved, and also enable the potential
vendors to receive advice from persons who had previously
sold their kidneys in the regulated market.

In addition to these benefits that regulating a current
market for human kidneys would have for the vendors when
compared with its unregulated, black market alternative it
would also provide them with particular financial benefits.
Currently, fraud is endemic within the black market.

Although the amount promised to the vendors interviewed in the Chennai survey was between $450 and $6280, the amounts they actually received varied from between $450 and $2660, with the typical vendor receiving on average one third less than promised.[25] Since these transactions were illegal those involved have no recourse against those who defrauded them. Legalizing the market for human kidneys would enable persons defrauded in this way to recover (or, at least, to have a chance to recover) the amount of the contracted fee for their kidneys that was withheld from them. It would also serve as a deterrent to fraud, for persons who committed this could be prosecuted both criminally and civilly.[26] Thus, insofar as such removing the legal prohibitions that currently stand in the way of persons participating in a regulated current market for human kidneys would provide would-be vendors with a non-constraining option that they would wish to pursue, the removal of these legal sanctions is morally required by respect for autonomy.

Conclusion

In the last chapter I argued that persons who sell their kidneys out of desperation would still be autonomous with respect to their vending actions. In this chapter I argued that choosing the option to sell a kidney within a regulated current market is not likely to impair the autonomy of either the individual or the autonomy of other members of their group. As such, the option to sell a kidney is not likely to be a constraining option for the individual vendor, as argued by Hughes, or a group constraining option, as claimed by Zutlevics. Furthermore, even though the study of kidney sales in Chennai and the evidence from Villivakkam shows that the option to sell a kidney in those markets is likely to be an autonomy-impairing constraining option for the individual vendor, to conclude that this supports the prohibition of current markets in human kidneys *per se* would be to misconstrue the evidence.[27] That the sale of a kidney is an autonomy-impairing constraining option in a black market in human transplant kidneys does not show that it would also be a constraining option in a legal and regulated current market because, in the latter, safeguards would be imposed to protect the vendors from both the diminutions in well-being and the autonomy-impairing abuse to which vendors in the black market are subject.

Respect for autonomy, then, supports the view that a legal, regulated, current market in human kidneys is morally permissible. Moreover, if persons who sell their kidneys in such a market are required to give their informed consent to the transaction (as I argue in the next chapter) they would sell with knowledge of the associated risks and benefits. When coupled with the plausible view that persons are likely to be the best judges of what is in their own interests, this shows that such sales would be likely to enhance the well-being of the vendors, this providing additional support for the view that such markets are morally permissible. This pro-market conclusion can be further supported by arguing that the sale of a kidney would impair a person's autonomy and well-being less (or enhance it more) than would many other activities that are currently (and justly) free from paternalistic interference – and so, if these activities are morally permissible, kidney selling is also. I address this and related issues in the next two chapters.

Notes

1 Zutlevics (2001a) pp. 297–302; Hughes, 'Exploitation, Autonomy, and the Case for Organ Sales,' pp. 89–95
2 Hughes (1998), p. 92. For a fuller discussion of this, see Hughes (1999).
3 Hughes (1998), p. 92.
4 As Hughes puts it, exploitation 'is not just what happens when a worker labors in a factory for a wage, it's what happens to make that happen.' Ibid.
5 It is not clear how poverty would impair autonomy in the way that Hughes and Zutlevics assume in their arguments, although it is clear that poverty can reduce the instrumental *value* of personal autonomy by restricting the ways in which one can exercise it to achieve one's goals. Perhaps the view is that poverty impairs a person's ability to reflect on their desires, values and goals (either by denying them educational opportu-

nities, or simply because it is difficult to reflect in this way when struggling to survive), and that this will preclude the reflective acceptance of their effective desires that is required for them to be autonomous with respect to them. However, since Hughes's and Zutlevics's arguments fail for reasons other than the possible falsity of their views concerning the relationship between autonomy and poverty, I will not challenge this premise here.

6 Hughes (1998), p. 94.

7 The US clergyman who wrote 'poor boy makes good' adventure stories. See Taylor (2002), p. 280. Goyal et al.'s study had not been published when this article was written.

8 Goyal et al. (2002), pp. 1589–93, especially 1591. Kidney sales are prohibited in India under parliamentary (federal) legislation (Transplantation of Human Organs Act, 1994), which bans the trafficking in human organs in any form and prescribes up to seven years' imprisonment for offenders. This law was initially applicable in Union Territories and the states of Himachal Pradesh, Maharashtra and Goa. Other states were given the option to adopt the parliamentary law or to enact their own law, and all have now adopted it with minor, procedural modifications. I thank R.R. Kishore, who served as the Member-Secretary of the Drafting Committee for this Act, for providing me with this information in personal correspondence.

9 Kumar, Sanjay (1994), cited by Zutlevics (2001a), p. 300.

10 I will argue below that Hughes is not committed to the claim that an autonomy-impairing constraining option is one that would reinforce$_b$ a person's position within their autonomy-impairing situation. However, this characterization of his view of a constraining option is not only compatible with his views, but attributing this view to him here does not adversely affect his argument.

11 The Indian news magazine *Frontline* reports that many power-loom workers in the Namakkal district sell their kidneys to try to escape being indebted to moneylenders who charge interest rates of between 50 and 60 per cent. Staff writer (1997), 'One Kidney Communities,' *Frontline*, **14** (25), 13–16 December.

12 The view that the sale of a kidney is likely to be the best option available to many destitute people is explicitly argued for in Radcliffe Richards et al., p. 1951. Cited by Zutlevics (2001a), p. 300. This point is also discussed in Margaret Jane Radin (1996), pp. 123–30.

13 Zutlevics (2001a), p. 300.

14 Dworkin (1994), p. 157.

15 Although Zutlevics does not use the term 'constraining option' it is clear that she believes it to be one, for she holds that the possession of it by the poor is likely to reinforce their presence

within their autonomy-compromising economic circumstances. Zutlevics (2001a), p. 299.

16 Dworkin (1994), p. 157.

17 See also Tadd, G.V. (1991). The relevant section of the Human Organ Transplants Act is 1(1)(a), under which it is *inter alia* 'an offence to make or receive any payment for the supply of, or offer to supply, an organ removed from a living person which is intended to be transplanted into another individual whether in Great Britain or elsewhere.'

18 Goyal et al., pp. 1590–92.

19 Indeed, this is often the case. See Rothman (2002), p. 1640.

20 As I noted in Chapter 2, this does not mean that such a person is less autonomous, for they still direct their own actions as much as before. It only means that their autonomy is less instrumentally valuable to them than it was prior to the sale of the kidney because their range of action is curtailed.

21 In fact, this objection to black markets in human kidneys would be better couched in terms of vendor well-being.

22 Goyal et al. (2002), p. 1592, where the authors cite Saran, R. et al. (1997).

23 Such medical care for kidney donors (or, here, vendors) is suggested in Working Party of the British Transplantation Society and the Renal Association (2000), *United Kingdom Guidelines for Living Donor Kidney Transplantation*. In part, these guidelines were developed from a survey of 28 UK and Irish transplant centres that reported their policies on the long-term follow-up of living kidney donors. See Lumsdaine, J.A. et al. (1999).

24 See Swami, Praveen (2003).

25 Goyal et al. (2002), p. 1591.

26 In case it is not already obvious from my endorsement of *regulating* a current market in human transplant kidneys, my endorsement of legalizing such a market on the grounds that this would make it easier for persons defrauded by the purchasers of their kidneys legally to pursue them should further indicate that the pro-market argument I am presenting here is not a purely libertarian one. As James Child (1994) has persuasively argued, libertarianism cannot sustain a fraud standard.

27 This point is made by Brody, Baruch (1993).

Chapter 5
A Moral Case for Market Regulation

In the previous chapter I argued that both respect for autonomy and concern for human well-being morally justify a current market in human transplant kidneys. And, as the evidence from Villivakkam and Chennai makes clear, concern for these two values also requires that such a market must be regulated. Moreover, such regulation must go beyond merely protecting the vendors from fraud.[1] As the evidence from India shows, even if the vendors are not defrauded, their autonomy and well-being might still be compromised if they do not receive adequate post-operative care. At first sight, then, it might appear that anyone concerned with either the autonomy or the well-being of the vendors in a current market for human kidneys would require such a market to be regulated so that vendors would receive medical care to protect both their autonomy and their well-being. As I will discuss below, however, this pro-regulation argument is too weak to satisfy a person who holds personal autonomy or personal well-being (or both) to be of great moral value. This is because such a person is committed to holding that *even if* an *unregulated* current market for human transplant kidneys would not diminish the autonomy of the vendors, and would increase their well-being, the actions of the purchasers would still (in certain circumstances) need to be regulated.

Before arguing that a regulated current market in human transplant kidneys is morally required by either respect for personal autonomy or concern for human well-being (or both), I must make three important points. First, in keeping with my general approach in this volume the pro-regulation argument that I develop here is a *conditional* argument directed at persons who hold personal autonomy or human well-being (or both) to be of great moral value. That is, this argument is of the form '*If* one holds autonomy and/or well-being to be of great moral value, *then* one must hold that this type of market regulation is morally required.' Moreover, the argument in this chapter is also conditional on certain empirical claims being true, such as the claim that the regulation of wages will not adversely affect employment. Although I provide evidence for these claims, some of this evidence is highly controversial. The argument in this chapter is thus weakened to the extent that these claims transpire to be untrue. Second, this pro-regulation argument is not only applicable to a current market in human transplant kidneys, but also to any market in which persons sell their body parts or their labour. This is important because, in establishing that concern for autonomy and human well-being morally justifies certain forms of market regulation, I focus on establishing that the regulation of the market for 'sweatshop' labour is (in certain circumstances) morally required. This is not a digression from my main concern as the arguments that I use to establish that markets in labour should be regulated also justify the regulation of the kidney trade. Finally, rather than focusing my pro-regulation arguments on respect for both autonomy *and* well-being, I will instead focus solely on the question of whether such market regulation is required by respect for autonomy.[2] I have three reasons for adopting this parsimonious approach. The first is simply that developing a pro-regulation argument that is based on concern for autonomy alone will be easier than developing one based on both values. However, this does not mean that I am ignoring the value of well-being, for the following arguments can apply *mutatis mutandis* to it also. (I note during the course of my arguments where concern for autonomy and concern for well-being will lead to differing conclusions.) The second reason is that the philosophical opponents of market regulation are often motivated by the concern that such regulation would illegitimately infringe upon the autonomy of those subject to it through restricting the ways in which they can contract with each other.[3] A pro-regulation argument that is based on the value of autonomy will thus address this concern directly.[4] Third, since respect for personal autonomy is the guiding light of modern medical ethics a pro-regulation argument based on autonomy will be located firmly in the mainstream of contemporary bioethics. Again, though, anyone believing that well-being rather than autonomy should hold this privileged position can adjust the following arguments to reflect this.

A Weak Pro-regulation Argument

In Chapter 4 I accepted that the option to sell a kidney in the black markets of Chennai and Villivakkam was an autonomy-impairing constraining option because it would reinforce the poverty-induced impairment of the vendor's autonomy.[5] I then argued that the fact that the *illegal* kidney trade provides potential vendors with an autonomy-impairing constraining option does *not* show that respect for autonomy requires that the trade is itself morally impermissible. Instead, I argued, it shows that this trade should be legalized and regulated so that selling a kidney was no longer a constraining option, but one that respect for a person's autonomy should allow them to choose.

This is certainly a sound moral argument in favour of the legalization and subsequent regulation of the current markets in human transplant kidneys that presently operate illegally in both India and elsewhere. However, it is too weak to support the degree of regulation that would be required for a current market to be morally permissible. This argument *only* justifies the regulation of a current market in human transplant kidneys (or a current market in labour) in circumstances where, without such regulation, a person's autonomy *is likely* to be impaired (vis-à-vis their alternatives) if they sell one of their kidneys. Moving from the sale of kidneys to the sale of labour, this pro-regulation argument is thus compatible with allowing persons to work in *exceptionally* autonomy-impairing conditions provided that their alternatives are *even more* autonomy impairing. This view would thus not support regulating the business practices of an employer who required his employees to routinely work unpaid overtime, prohibited them from attempting to unionize, prohibited them from ever seeking employment from one of his competitors, paid them less than a living wage and required that they spend their pay only in his company's stores, *provided that* the working conditions outside his employment were even more autonomy impairing than these.

A Stronger Pro-regulation Argument

Owing to its limitations the pro-regulation argument that I developed in Chapter 4 is too weak to ground the degree of regulation that is required for a current market in human kidneys to be morally permissible, for it is compatible with allowing employment conditions (such as those outlined above) that are morally unacceptable to one who values personal autonomy highly. A stronger argument is thus needed which must not only show why kidney markets must be regulated, but also why employment practices such as those above should be prohibited even if the employees' alternative options are even more autonomy impairing.

The debate over whether to regulate autonomy-impairing labour conditions, as well as the debate over whether to allow (and then to regulate) a current market in human organs, is typically cast in terms of whether the poor should be allowed to undertake certain forms of employment (such as sweat-shop labour) or engage in certain market transactions (such as the sale of their kidneys). As such, this debate typically focuses on the question of whether it is morally permissible paternalistically to restrict the actions of the poor. This way of framing the debate places the onus firmly on proponents of regulation to explain why the activities of the poor should be restricted. Such an explanation is often hard to provide in cases where the poor will be made better off with respect to their autonomy and/or their well-being by accepting the employment, or engaging in the transactions, in question. But this is misleading because the issue here is not whether the poor should be paternalistically protected from *their own* choices, but rather whether to protect the poor from the choices of *others* – namely, those who are offering the unregulated dangerous and unpleasant employment, or offering to purchase their kidneys in an unregulated organs market.

This debate over the moral legitimacy of market regulation should thus focus on the question of whether persons who offer others unregulated autonomy-impairing employment, or offer to buy their kidneys in an unregulated market, do anything morally wrong. Of course, to answer this question one must have an account of what constitutes a moral wrong. This requirement might seem to open a Pandora's box of philosophical argument, for there is (as yet) no general agreement as to what conditions must be met for an act to be immoral. However, as I noted above, the debate over the legitimacy of the transactions in question largely turns on the issue of whether such a market is required or prohibited by respect for the autonomy of those who would participate in it. Since this is so, the answer to the question of whether persons who offer others such employment or the opportunity to sell their kidneys do anything morally wrong will be found by focusing on whether such offers evince a proper respect for the autonomy of those who accept them. Thus, insofar as such an offer evinces respect for the autonomy of the person to whom it is made, it will be (at least prima facie) morally acceptable.[6] If, however, it does not, then it will not be morally acceptable.

The Argumentative Strategy

As I noted above the central issue in the debate over whether to regulate markets (especially markets in human kidneys) is whether purchasers must be restricted to prevent them from acting immorally towards the vendors. In particular, if one holds respect for autonomy to be a central moral value one must ask whether the actions of the purchasers evince a lack of respect for the autonomy of their vendors that would justify their regulation. It is important to note that this question is *broader* than that of whether the actions of the purchasers in such markets would *impair* the autonomy of the vendors relative to the degree of autonomy they would have enjoyed without the purchasers' offers. It is possible for a person to make offers to others that, from the point of view of one who prizes autonomy, are morally impermissible because they evince a less than morally appropriate evaluation of the autonomy of the persons to whom they are made. And this could be the case even if these persons' acceptance of these offers would make them better off with respect to their autonomy if they accept them. For example, someone A who comes across a drowning person B and offers to save them if, and only if, they become A's personal slave would, if B accepts and A fulfils their promise, make B better off with respect to their enjoyment of autonomy. However, by enslaving B, A would not have responded appropriately to the value of B's autonomy.[7] Since such offers are, from the point of view of one who prizes autonomy, morally impermissible, it is possible that an employer's offer of employment, or a kidney purchaser's offer to purchase, might similarly be impermissible.

Prior to developing this line of argument I should clarify what I mean by 'a less than morally appropriate evaluation of autonomy.' At first sight, it appears that the proponents of any argument that is based upon a claim concerning the value of personal autonomy must provide some indication of its value, for otherwise they will be unable to say with certainty when a person's autonomy has been 'less than appropriately valued' in the way that they are concerned to prevent. Yet although this autonomy-based pro-regulation argument appeals to a view of the appropriate value of autonomy, given my aims in this chapter my development of this argument can progress *without* the provision of a positive account of this. My purpose in invoking the value of autonomy in this way is solely to establish that *in the eyes of those who hold autonomy to be of great moral value* certain employers and kidney purchasers impermissibly undervalue the autonomy of their employees, or kidney vendors, and so *for the defenders of autonomy* respect for autonomy justifies the regulation of markets in both labour and kidneys. As such, if I can show that at least some employees or kidney vendors would, in the eyes of the defenders of autonomy, have their autonomy less than appropriately valued by those who employ them or purchase their kidneys then I will have established that, in their view, respect for autonomy requires that these practices be prohibited by market regulation. Of course, without a positive account of the value of personal autonomy this conclusion will be limited in its practical applicability. Without such an account one could not identify all morally unacceptable market practices. Moreover, the value of autonomy is unlikely to be amenable to such precise quantification – and even if it were, there are obvious epistemological problems associated with assessing how much autonomy a person enjoys, and how much they could have enjoyed had they been treated differently. Yet these limitations do not undermine the overall thrust of this argument, which is to show that respect for autonomy justifies regulating markets in both kidneys and labour – and that there are clear (that is, non-marginal) cases where such regulation seems morally required.

Developing the Argument

The simplest way to establish that certain employment and kidney-purchasing practices evince an impermissible under-valuing of autonomy is first to identify persons whose employment conditions significantly compromise their autonomy. One must then assess whether these persons' subjection to these conditions evinces a less than appropriate evaluation of their autonomy by their employers. If so, then the regulation of the labour market will be morally justified out of respect for their autonomy, such that their employers can be required to provide them with employment conditions that would not so compromise their autonomy.

The first step of this process is not difficult to make. For example, Chinese women employed by subcontractors producing goods for American corporations are frequently required to work 70 hours a week in factories for which they are paid just pennies an hour after deductions for room and board.[8] Similarly, workers in the Chun Si Enterprise Handbag Factory in southern China were required to give up their identity papers as a condition of employment and were frequently (and illegally) fined.[9] In both cases the employees' exercise of their autonomy is significantly compromised by their working conditions, for neither the amount of time they are required to work nor the wages they are paid afford them appreciable opportunities to direct their own lives. Instead, they are merely 'wage slaves,' whose actions are primarily directed by their employers.[10] And these are not isolated cases as they appear to be typical of the autonomy-compromising working conditions of employees in the manufacturing sector in developing nations.[11]

Let us now move to establishing that subjecting employees to such conditions evinces a less than morally permissible evaluation of their autonomy. Employees are subject to poor conditions to boost their employers' profits. Employers thus value the degree to which their employees' autonomy *could* be preserved by the use of *alternative* employment practices *less* than they value the additional profits that such alternative practices would cost them if they were implemented. Of course, this alone does not show that autonomy-compromising employment practices should be considered morally unjustified by all who prize autonomy. The additional profits that the employers accrue through the use of such practices might be so high that those who value autonomy but who hold its value to be commensurable might consider the value of these *profits* to be comparable (or more than comparable) to the value of the degree of the employees' autonomy that is compromised by their employers' use of the practices in question. For *all* who prize autonomy to consider certain employment (and kidney purchasing) practices to be immoral, then, it must be the case that the amount of additional profit that these practices generate is *less* than the *lowest* value that a person who holds autonomy to be of great moral worth would accord to it.[12] Given the labour conditions that the destitute are subjected to in China and elsewhere, and the way that desperate vendors in the international black market for human transplant kidneys are typically treated, this is likely often to be the case. The additional profits that are gained by such practices are often extremely small, even when judged according to local standards of profitability. For example, according to economists Robert Pollin, James Heintz and Justine Burns even a 100 per cent increase in pay for non-supervisory apparel workers in Mexico and the United States would add only 50 cents (1.6 per cent of the retail price) to the production costs for a casual shirt sold in the United States for $32.[13] Since these workers' employers have not given them this wage increase they value the additional profits (50c per shirt) *more* than they value the additional enjoyment of autonomy that this increase would foster in their workers. Similarly, it is possible that the Chinese subcontractors mentioned above could increase their workers' wages above the current level without a significant decrease in profitability. If this is so, the fact that these employers do not increase their employees' wages shows that they value the degree of autonomy that this would have fostered in their workers less than they value the additional profits made by withholding it. They are thus placing a very low value on the degree of their employees' autonomy that they could foster with such additional pay. In other words, these employers are failing appropriately to respect the value of their employees' autonomy. To rectify this, a defender of autonomy would require that the labour markets in which these employers operate be regulated to ensure that they adopt employment practices that do not evince a less than morally permissible evaluation of their employees' autonomy. (The imposition of such regulations is thus not an attempt to change the evaluative attitude of employers towards employees' autonomy, but merely to ensure that their treatment of them does not overly compromise it.) Such regulations might require increased wages, less hazardous working conditions, optional and paid (rather than obligatory and unpaid) overtime and the option to leave their employment without repercussions.

The same argument can also be developed to show that regulating a current market in human transplant kidneys is morally required. Leaving aside the question of fraud and coercion (whose prohibition is not strictly the province of market regulation, but that of law more generally) the typical black market kidney vendor in Villivakkam or Chennai does not receive enough post-operative care to ensure that they would recover fully from the nephrectomy. Assuming that such care could be purchased in India for $2000–$3000, *not* to provide such care would be to value the difference in the degree of autonomy that vendors enjoy with it vis-à-vis that which they would enjoy without it at *less than* $2000–$3000. This would be a relatively small amount for those who are purchasing kidneys for transplant in a legal market (for example, insurance companies and government agencies). A defender of autonomy would thus require that a current market for human transplant kidneys be regulated to ensure that the vendors receive (at minimum) adequate post-operative care. Just as respect for autonomy requires regulation of the current market for labour, so too does it require regulation of the current market for human transplant kidneys.

Clarifying the Argument

Before moving to demonstrate the possible breadth of appeal of this argument, three important points must be made concerning its scope. First, it is worth repeating that this strong autonomy-based pro-regulation argument is not only of interest to those who hold autonomy to be of great moral worth. It can readily be adapted to support regulating current markets in labour and kidneys on the grounds that the purchasers in such markets would less than appropriately value some other important human good (such as well-being) without such regulation in place. Second, it is also worth repeating that this pro-regulation argument requires that even market transactions that enhance the autonomy of all parties involved might still be subject to regulation if the actions of one party (for example, the employer or the kidney purchaser) evinces a less than appropriate evaluation of the other's autonomy. The employers of the non-supervisory apparel workers in Mexico and the United States whose wages were surveyed by Pollin et al. could thus not avoid being subject to regulation by claiming that by providing this employment they were enhancing their workers' autonomy relative to the degree that they would enjoy without it. Third, this argument does not commit its proponents to advocating that *all* transactions in current markets for labour and kidneys should be regulated. Rather, the normative account of respect for autonomy on which this argument is based requires that certain market transactions (in labour or body parts) be *free* from regulation if such regulations would impair, not protect, the autonomy of the persons they affected. For example, if a sweatshop employer's profit margin is so low that regulation will cause the business to fail, and if this failure would impair both employer's and workers' autonomy, then concern for autonomy would repudiate, rather than require, the regulation of the business.

The Economic Objection to Market Regulation: Three Initial Responses

This last clarification of the scope and implications of this pro-regulation argument leads to the first objection to it: that its enforcement would undermine the economic competitiveness of manufacturers who use sweatshops, which will lead to their attempting to save costs by reducing the workforce. This economic objection is also often raised with a more 'broad picture' emphasis – namely, that regulating industries in developing countries would dull their economic competitiveness and thus slow their economic growth. In the long run, such regulation would thus result in more persons in these countries suffering autonomy-impairing poverty than if it were not imposed. Thus, this objection runs, even if such regulation does protect employee autonomy, this must be balanced against the impaired autonomy suffered by those workers whose jobs were lost through regulation, and the impaired autonomy that everybody in the country in question would suffer as a result of slower economic growth.[14]

There are three initial responses to this economic objection. The first two accept the economic analysis on which it is based: that as the price of labour rises the number of workers employed declines. Accepting this, the first response to this economic objection is simply to note that the pro-regulation argument developed above is strongest when the costs of the regulation that it would require are relatively low, and that its effectiveness diminishes as these costs rise. As such, this argument justifies regulation only to the extent that this economic objection fails to hold. This first response is important because it underscores the fact emphasized at the start of this chapter that this argument is *conditional* upon the truth of the empirical claim that market regulation is the best way to protect the autonomy (or other human good) of persons affected by it. To the extent that this empirical claim is untrue, then, the effectiveness of this argument weakens, and so those who support regulation on the basis of it would be willing to concede that, in some cases, regulation would be morally unjustified.

The second response to this economic objection moves beyond this concessionary stance to claim that accepting the economic analysis that underlies the economic objection does not mean that one has to accept that regulating industry would necessarily lead to lower employment as a result of increasing the price of labour. This is because such regulation might *also* increase workers' economic productivity. As Denis Arnold and Norman Bowie have argued (citing a wealth of empirical evidence to support their case) if employees' wages are raised so that their 'minimum daily caloric intakes ... and basic non-food needs' are met, they 'will be less likely to come to work ill ... will be absent with less frequency ... [and] ... are thus likely to be more productive and loyal.'[15] Even though regulation would result in increased labour costs, then, these might be more than offset by the increased output of the workers whose autonomy (or other human good) is thus protected.

Yet although this second response to the economic objection to market regulation moves beyond the concessionary stance adopted by the first response, it does not escape this objection's grip: there would be no need for regulation in those industries where Arnold and Bowie's claim concerning worker productivity is true. If the costs of providing good working conditions would be *more than* offset by increased productivity, companies would have an economic incentive to provide such conditions, and so regulation would be unnecessary. If the costs of providing good working conditions were *exactly* offset by the increased productivity they generate (that is, the costs and benefits to the employer of providing such benefits cancelled each other out) then companies would *still* have an incentive to provide them, to attract and retain the best employees. However, if the costs of providing such working conditions were to *outweigh* their benefits to the firm (and so regulation is *required*) the economic objection to market regulation holds once again.

Unlike these first two responses to the economic objection the third rejects its underlying economic analysis. Although the claim that if the cost of a unit of labour were to rise then, *ceteris paribus*, the quantity demanded of labour would fall is a fundamental proposition in economics, evidence shows that this correlation does not always hold true. For example, using a sample of 43 countries over the period 1993–97 Pollin et al. found that there was no statistically significant relationship between real (adjusted for inflation) wages and employment growth in the apparel industry.[16] This seems to show that the hiring decisions of multinational corporations and their subcontractors are not at all responsive to wage increases as theory would suggest. Similarly, in an extensive and influential study of the effects of minimum wage increases on employment, David Card and Alan Krueger argue that their analysis of data from the United States, Canada, the United Kingdom and Puerto Rico provides evidence against the standard view.[17] Card and Krueger's analysis of this international data is supported by their analysis of the effects of increases in the minimum wage in the United States. This latter analysis led them to conclude 'In every case [studied] ... the estimated effect of the minimum wage was either zero or positive.'[18] In all of these cases, it appears that the increase in labour costs (either directly through mandated minimum wages, or indirectly through the imposition of health and safety regulations) were passed on to consumers in the form of higher prices for the goods produced without reducing output and employment.

Card and Krueger's work has been widely and trenchantly criticized.[19] However, if they are correct, their work significantly undermines the economic objection to this argument for market regulation. This is because it suggests that imposing regulations upon sweatshops to ensure that the autonomy of the employees is respected to the greatest degree practicable would not be as economically damaging as the proponents of the economic objection to market regulation hold.

Why Regulation of Kidney Markets is Especially Immune to the Economic Objection

The above responses to the economic objection to market regulation focused on current markets in human labour rather than in human kidneys. The fourth response focuses exclusively on defending the legitimacy of regulating a current market for human kidneys on the basis that it differs in two important ways from a current market for human labour. And because of these differences, this response continues, the economic objection cannot be used to oppose the regulation of a current market in human kidneys.

The first difference between a current market for human labour and a current market for human kidneys is that the demand for kidneys is not as price sensitive as the demand for labour is believed to be. According to standard economic theory, as the price of labour rises relative to other factors of production (for example, capital or land) it will become increasingly worthwhile for employers to substitute the employment of capital and land for labour, with such substitution increasing the longer the period that labour is relatively more expensive. Since this is so, as the price of labour is increased by market regulation (for instance, by requiring the payment of a certain minimum wage, paid leave or health insurance) the quantity demanded of it will fall as it becomes increasingly worthwhile for employers to switch to other factors of production. Kidney purchasers, however, would not be subject to the same market-imposed constraints on their 'kidney budget' as labour purchasers are subject to with respect to their 'labour budget.' The reasons for this differ according to how the commercially procured kidneys are distributed. This is evident when the state is the sole purchaser of the kidneys and *also* the enforcer of the regulations that are imposed on how they are procured. Here, the state could act to ensure that the costs of regulation (both direct and indirect) are balanced against its desire to secure the requisite number of transplant kidneys, with the aim that the autonomy (or other human good) of both the vendors and the recipients be protected.

Even when the state is not the sole purchaser of commercially procured kidneys, purchasers of kidneys could still be more economically flexible than purchasers of labour. The amount that an economically rational employer would be willing to spend on labour costs would primarily be dictated by the costs of such labour relative to other means of production. The value to the potential kidney purchaser of a transplant kidney, however, would be dictated solely by how much they are willing to pay either to save the life of a person who needs a kidney, or to rescue them from the constraints of renal dialysis. Therefore as long as the price of a transplant kidney is below the price at which its potential recipient values their life or escape from dialysis, the potential recipient would be motivated to purchase one. (If the state purchases kidneys for those who lack other means to purchase the kidneys they desire their inability to pay would not diminish the demand for them.)[20] Since the price that the typical potential transplant recipient would place on their life or escape from dialysis would be high, and the price of kidneys is likely to be low (the official price of commercial human transplant kidneys is approximately $1219 in the legal, regulated market for them that operates in Iran) there is considerable leeway for raising the price of transplant kidneys through regulation.[21] This being so, although labour demand is likely to fall when its price is raised (although the various studies cited above provide reason to doubt that this occurs in all industries) the demand for human transplant kidneys would not fall when their price is raised because the budget that their potential recipients would allocate for their purchase would be much more elastic than an employer's budget for labour. Thus, even if the standard economic argument against regulating labour markets is sound, it cannot be used to oppose the regulation of a current market in human kidneys.

The second difference between a current market for labour and for kidneys lies in the fact that even if regulating labour conditions in developing countries would impose constraints on the ability of their citizens to engage in international trade, and thus on their economic development, regulating an *international* legal market in human transplant kidneys would not similarly reduce the extent to which persons in developing countries would sell their kidneys. Owing to the difference in living standards between countries, even if such a market were regulated to the degree required to ensure that the non-recipient kidney purchasers acted so as to appropriately value vendor autonomy, the price of kidneys would not increase to a level that resulted in poorer countries losing trade to richer ones. It is, for example, unlikely that a poor person in Britain or the United States would be interested in selling a kidney in a regulated market if the going rate was approximately $2000 (£1250), plus post-operative expenses.[22] By contrast, a poor person in Tamil Nadu, India *is* likely to be motivated to sell for this price, since it represents almost four years' family income.[23] Even if the market for human kidneys were regulated to enhance vendor autonomy, then, vendors in poorer countries would still have a significant comparative advantage over their rivals in more prosperous countries. In consequence, just as the kidneys that are sold in such an international trade would flow 'from East to West ... from black and brown bodies to white ones ... from poor, low status men to more affluent men,' the wealth that is used to purchase them would flow in the opposite direction: from West to East, from white bodies to black and brown ones, from more affluent persons to their poorer brethren.[24] A regulated current market in human transplant kidneys is thus more likely to aid the economic development of the world's poorer countries than impede it.

The Autonomy-based Objection to Market Regulation – and Why it is Mistaken

The economic objection to regulation thus misfires when its proponents attempt to use it against regulating an international current market in human transplant kidneys. But this does not mean that market regulation is morally justified. Some opponents of market regulation object to it on the grounds that, although it is imposed to protect autonomy, its imposition instead evinces a failure of respect for autonomy.[25]

This autonomy-based objection to the strong pro-regulation argument is based on changing the focus of the debate from whether employers or kidney purchasers may make certain offers to potential employees or vendors to whether a defender of autonomy may legitimately advocate curtailing the autonomy of these same potential employees or vendors. Proponents of this objection note that since this strong pro-regulation argument requires that persons be restricted in exercising their autonomy for their own good, it seems highly paternalistic, imposing upon the employees and vendors whose actions it restricts an evaluation of their own autonomy that they might not share. Since one who genuinely prizes autonomy should not readily countenance such interference with the autonomous decisions and actions of others, it seems that this strong pro-regulation argument is not one that a defender of autonomy can consistently make.

There is, however, a ready response to this autonomy-based objection: that, if asked, the employees and kidney vendors whose autonomy is restricted by market regulation that is required according to this strong pro-regulation argument would have agreed to have their autonomy compromised in this way. This response is, of course, that which the defenders of paternalism often invoke to justify the imposition of their views upon others, and so does not appear to be one that a defender of autonomy should readily invoke.[26] However, a defender of autonomy can legitimately claim that the market regulation that is justified by this autonomy-based argument does not impermissibly restrict the autonomy of the employees and vendors who are subject to it. The (typical) potential sweatshop employee and potential kidney vendor do not autonomously desire *simpliciter* to enter into contracts that would be prohibited in a regulated market. Instead, they only autonomously desire to enter into these contracts because of the situations that they are in. Since they would prefer not to be in these deprived situations, they would prefer not to act on their desire to enter into these contracts, as they would prefer to be in a situation where acting on this desire is not likely to be their best course of action. The implicit claim underlying this autonomy-based objection – that market regulation interferes with the potential employees' and potential vendors' autonomous pursuit of their preferences – importantly fails fully to describe their situations at hand. The prohibitions imposed by this type of market regulation thus do not prevent these persons from doing what they really want to do, as this objection to regulation implies and as some of its proponents explicitly claim.[27] Instead, the type of market regulation that would be required according to this strong pro-regulation argument would merely substitute an option that is more preferable from the point of view of the typical sweatshop employee or kidney vendor (that is, selling in a regulated market) for one that they consider to be less preferable (selling in an unregulated market). Thus, the imposition of such regulation would, from the point of view of the sweatshop employee or kidney vendor, *increase* the instrumental value of their autonomy. That is, such regulation would make it *more* likely that they will be able to use their autonomy to satisfy their own ends. The restriction of the employee's and kidney vendor's autonomy by the sort of market regulation that would be required by this argument would not conflict with the moral requirement to respect their autonomy. Instead, it seems to be required by it.

What Sort of Regulation is Required?

Since some form of market regulation is thus, *ceteris paribus*, required for a current market in human transplant kidneys to be morally permissible, what form should it take? At minimum, such a market should require that vendors give their informed consent to the sale of their kidneys, that they not be coerced into selling their kidneys by a third party and that they receive adequate post-operative care. To ensure that vendors give their informed consent the typical consequences and risks of undergoing a nephrectomy should be explained to them in terms that they can understand, so that they can comprehend the effect that such an operation is likely to have on their lives. To ensure that these explanations are accurate they should be provided not only by the staff of the transplant centre performing the operation, but also by independent healthcare professionals employed by the body responsible for ensuring that the regulations imposed upon the commercial kidney market are met. These explanations should be supplemented by discussions between prior and potential vendors, so that the former could give the latter an accurate account of what they should expect (medically, economically and socially) from the sale of their kidneys. Again, to ensure an accurate picture the potential vendor should meet not only satisfied sellers but also sellers who regret the sale of their kidneys. (These sellers should be compensated for their time by the transplant centre.) These explanations and discussions should be repeated over a period of several weeks to help to ensure that the potential vendors have time both to assimilate the information and to consider carefully whether they really want to sell their kidneys.

Transplant centres participating in a legal, regulated, current market for human kidneys should also be required to use current equipment, techniques and drugs for both vendor and recipient, operated by medical personnel who are well trained in their use. Although this requirement might seem to preclude developing countries that lack both equipment and personnel from participating in a commercial kidney trade, this would not be the case. If such countries allow persons from affluent countries to purchase transplant kidneys the trade will be lucrative enough to attract foreign investors, who would supply these centres with the requisite equipment and personnel. The transplant centres should also be required to provide adequate post-operative care to the vendors, including any additional care that might be reasonably required as a result of any unexpected medical complications that might occur as a result of their nephrectomies.[28] Such a requirement would not only protect the vendors, but would also provide an incentive to the commercial transplant centres to accept kidneys only from persons they believed would not suffer from any post-operative complications. The transplant centre should also be required to pay a guaranteed minimum price for the kidneys that they purchased.

As well as imposing such post-operative care for the protection of vendors, the transplant centres should also perform a full complement of *pre*-operative tests to ensure that the kidneys they would be purchasing are suitable for transplantation in order to protect the well-being and autonomy of the recipient, rather than that of the vendor. At minimum, this would mean testing the potential vendor's blood for all major diseases, performing HLA matching for all transplants and securing the vendor's medical history (both orally and in writing) on repeated occasions. (HLA matching checks the compatibility of the kidney donor's tissue with that of the potential recipient by testing to see how closely their human leukocyte antigens match. The closer the match the better, as then the transplanted kidney is less likely to be rejected.) Finally, if the transplant centre is not a monopsonistic purchaser it should provide potential vendors with transportation to another centre (chosen by the regulatory body overseeing the kidney trade) to enable them to compare rival offers for their kidneys. This would be required both to encourage competition between rival transplant centres and also to reassure potential vendors that they were being treated fairly.[29]

Conclusion

I argued in this chapter that respect for autonomy requires (given the truth of certain empirical claims) that current markets for both labour and human transplant kidneys be regulated. Moreover, my arguments could be adapted so that they are grounded on concern for values other than personal autonomy. However, the fact that the regulation of a current market in human transplant kidneys might be morally required by respect for autonomy (and also, *mutatis mutandis*, by other moral values such as human well-being) does not show that such a market is morally justified. Undergoing a nephrectomy is dangerous. It might thus be the case that selling a kidney is so dangerous that current markets in human transplant kidneys should be considered morally impermissible by one who prizes autonomy and/or well-being on the grounds that the risk to the vendor's future autonomy and well-being is too great. To show that a regulated current market for human transplant kidneys is morally permissible, then, I must show that the dangers associated with under-going a nephrectomy are no greater than the dangers associated with other hazardous occupations or activities that are morally permissible. I will do this in the next chapter.

Notes

1 It is possible that state regulation would not be necessary to protect participants in a legal kidney market from fraud, since this could be addressed through tort law. I thank both Damon Chetson and Mark Brady for bringing this point to my attention.

2 Recall that the type of autonomy that is of concern here is *not* the conception of autonomy that Kant developed and defended. For an argument from a Kantian perspective that favours the regulation of labour markets, see Arnold, Denis and Bowie, Norman E. (2003).

3 For example, W. Kip Viscusi writes 'Uniform standards ... deprive workers of the opportunity to select the job most appropriate to their own risk preferences. The actual ... issue involved is whether those in upper income groups ... [are justified in imposing] ... their job risk preferences on the poor.' Viscusi (1983), p. 80.

4 Libertarian philosophers often proffer this autonomy-based anti-regulation argument. Thus, if it can be shown that respect for the autonomy of the poor actually *requires* the imposition of regulation, rather than militates against it, libertarians whose views are based on respect for autonomy will have to concede that regulation of the sort I argue for here is justified. For a brief outline of the views of some such libertarians (who should be amenable to this pro-regulation argument) see Zutlevics (2001b).

5 Although see my concerns about the claim that poverty compromises autonomy in the previous chapter.

6 That an offer respects the autonomy of the person to whom it is made is not necessarily a sufficient condition for it to be morally acceptable because such an offer might be made to purchase something that should not be commodified in the way proposed. I discuss this issue in Chapters 7 and 8.

7 This person might also be blamed by someone who does not hold autonomy to be of great moral value, on the grounds that she should have saved this drowning man anyway, rather than attempted to bargain with him in this way. The point of this example in this context is, however, that a person who does hold autonomy to be of great moral value would hold that saving a person on condition that he agrees to be enslaved is morally impermissible.

8 See Kernaghan, Charles (2000), p. 2.

9 Roberts, Dexter and Bernstein, Aaron (2000). The requirement that employees give up their identity papers can only occur in states where persons are obligated to carry these. As such, this interference with employee autonomy stems not from the operation of the market, but from state intervention in the lives of its citizens. I thank Mark Brady for pointing this out to me.

10 I discuss this point further in the next chapter.

11 See, for example, Ross, Andrew (1997).

12 Persons who prize autonomy disagree as to how it should be valued, and also on what value to place on it, with some repudiating the view that autonomy is commensurable with profit. My argument here, then, is intended to be an *inclusive* autonomy-based pro-regulation argument.

13 Pollin, Heintz and Burns (2004), Table 6, p. 163.

14 This economic objection is offered by Irwin, Douglas A. (2002), p. 215 and Maitland, Ian (1997).

15 Arnold and Bowie (2003), p. 237, where they cite Bliss, C.J. and Stern, N.H. (1978a and b) to support their view.

16 Pollin et al. (2004), pp. 157–60.

17 Card, David and Krueger, Alan B. (1995).

18 Ibid., p. 389. Quoted by Arnold and Bowie (2003), p. 238.

19 See, for example, Whitman, Glen (1996).

20 I address this issue in Chapter 9.

21 This price is quoted in Zargooshi (2001a), p. 386.

22 Unless, perhaps, the would-be vendor was in Britain as an illegal immigrant and securing such a sum (or some other form of remuneration) would represent a significant benefit, as dramatized in the film *Dirty Pretty Things* (2003). There are also likely to be British citizens who need to secure such a sum quickly and have no other means of doing so.

23 Goyal et al. (2002), p. 1590.

24 This quotation is from Scheper-Hughes (2003), p. 1645.

25 This objection is applicable to the strong pro-regulation argument only when this argument is based on the value of personal autonomy.

26 And if those others inconveniently fail to agree with paternalists as to what their views are, the latter frequently have a ready response: that they would have agreed had they only been free

from their false consciousness and irrationality, or had they simply been aware of where their true best interests lay.

27 Viscusi (1983), p. 80.
28 No such post-operative care is legally required to be provided to people who sell their kidneys in Iran. (I thank Behrooz Broumand for informing me of this in conversation.) This accounts for the adverse effects on vendor well-being that occur post-operatively, and that are outlined in Zargooshi (2001b), pp. 1791–3.
29 Further regulations for current markets in human organs are discussed in Banks, Gloria J. (1995).

Chapter 6
Kidney Sales and Dangerous Employment

At the end of the last chapter I noted that although respect for autonomy and concern for personal well-being appear morally to justify both a current market for human transplant kidneys and the regulation of that market, it might be that this appearance is illusory because the sale of one's kidney might be so dangerous as to justify its paternalistic prohibition. This concern with the dangers of kidney selling does not work as an objection to the moral permissibility of a current market in human kidneys. Indeed, one of the most common arguments offered to *support* the view that such a market is morally permissible is based on the premise that the sale of a kidney would be no more dangerous than many types of activities that are morally permissible.[1] Since this is so, proponents of this pro-market argument by analogy continue, it must also be morally permissible for persons to sell their kidneys in a current market for them.[2] The response to this argument is predictable: those who morally oppose a current market in human kidneys attempt to draw disanalogies between the selling of a kidney and the pursuit of other dangerous activities to try to show that, while the latter are morally permissible, the former is not.[3]

At first sight this might appear to be a relatively straightforward debate. Either kidney sales are analogous to certain types of morally permissible activities, and are thus similarly morally permissible, or there are disanalogies that preclude this conclusion from being drawn. However, this debate is complicated both by the need to justify the moral permissibility of the activities in comparison and by the need to ensure that the analogy between kidney sales and these activities is as strong as possible. Unfortunately, those who proffer this pro-market argument by analogy frequently ignore these complications. In this chapter I will address these complications directly. Moreover, rather than relying on armchair intuitions concerning the relative dangers of kidney sales and certain types of dangerous employment, I will statistically compare the relative dangers of such activities. Finally, I will show that, insofar as there are disanalogies between the sale of a kidney and the sale of one's labour to engage in dangerous employment, these either fail to undermine the pro-market position, or else support it.

Dworkin's Pro-market Argument by Analogy

Of all the pro-market arguments based on the above analogy Gerald Dworkin's is the most prominent. Dworkin accepts that 'those who are most likely to wish to sell their organs are those whose financial situation is most desperate,' for '[t]hose who have alternative sources of income are not likely to choose an option which entails some health risk, some disfigurement, some pain and discomfort.'[4] However, he claims that even though it will typically be the desperate poor who will sell their kidneys this does not show that such sales should be banned on the grounds that they are exploitative, and hence immoral. Dworkin argues that there are many other employment opportunities open to the poor that are just as dangerous and unpleasant as selling a kidney (or perhaps even more so), and that offering these opportunities to the poor is not held to be morally impermissible. Accordingly, Dworkin claims that if a current market in human kidneys is prohibited on the grounds that it exploits the poor then this 'suggests that poor people should not be allowed to enter the army, to engage in hazardous occupations such as high-steel construction, to become paid subjects for medical experimentation.' But, Dworkin concludes, it would be 'paternalist in the extreme ... to deny poor people choices which they perceive as increasing their well-being.'[5] Thus, just as it is morally permissible to offer persons the opportunity to engage in his listed activities, so too, he argues, is it morally permissible to offer them the opportunity to sell their kidneys.

Yet although Dworkin's pro-market argument is simple, it must be clarified. In comparing the option to sell a kidney to the option of working in high-steel construction or being a paid subject of medical experimentation, Dworkin does not offer an argument that supports an *un*regulated current market in human transplant kidneys. While it is generally accepted that the poor should be allowed to seek unpleasant and dangerous employment, this acceptance often comes with caveats. For example, although most people might be willing to allow the poor to accept such employment, they might require it to meet certain basic safety standards, such as those imposed by the Health and Safety at Work Act (in Britain) or the Occupational Health and Safety Act (in the United States). Similarly, it is usually held that morality requires that persons who are thus employed be paid a certain minimum wage – a requirement that is especially germane for those dangerous or unpleasant jobs (such as sweatshop labour) where the demand for labour is lower than its supply. In appealing to the intuition that the poor should be allowed to accept dangerous and unpleasant employment, then, Dworkin's argument only supports a current market for human kidneys in which the vendors are assured of certain standards of medical care and a minimum price for their organs.[6] And so if these standards can only be ensured through regulating this market, then Dworkin's argument (and also the argument that I develop in this chapter) only supports a *regulated* market for human organs.

Why Other Activities Compared to Kidney Sales are Morally Permissible

Dworkin's pro-market argument by analogy is based on comparing the risks involved in selling one's kidney to the risks involved in other activities that it is morally permissible to provide others with the opportunity to engage in, *provided* that these activities are suitably regulated to reduce the associated risks to a morally acceptable level. Since it focuses on comparing kidney selling to employment opportunities that are *regulated* to protect those who pursue them,

Dworkin's argument (and all other similar pro-market arguments by analogy) faces two distinct objections. The first of these was encountered in the previous chapter: that respect for autonomy renders it morally impermissible to interfere with actions that persons are autonomous with respect to if such actions make those affected by them better off (for example, vis-à-vis well-being or autonomy) and do not make anyone else worse off. For example, if a person's working on an unregulated high-steel construction site would make them better off (perhaps because prior to this they were starving) it would be morally impermissible to interfere in their autonomous decision to engage in this activity. Thus, proponents of this objection conclude, insofar as Dworkin's argument by analogy supports a regulated market for human kidneys, it does not go far enough, for, in allowing such regulation, Dworkin would be allowing morally impermissible interferences with autonomy to occur. The second objection to Dworkin's argument by analogy comes from the other end of the ideological spectrum. This is that the types of dangerous employment that he considers are morally impermissible because there is not *sufficient* regulation in place to ensure that those who are currently employed in them enjoy a morally acceptable degree of protection. Thus, proponents of this second objection conclude, even if Dworkin can show that the sale of a kidney is no more dangerous than other forms of employment that are currently allowed, this does not establish that a current market in human transplant kidneys is morally permissible, for the current markets in the types of labour that he compares such a market to are morally objectionable.

Responding to the Objections

Neither of these objections is effective in undermining Dworkin's pro-market position. The first objection was met in the previous chapter. There I argued that even though a person's performance of a certain action is Pareto superior with respect to their autonomy (or some other human good), one who prizes autonomy (or the other good in question) might still be justified in prohibiting them from having the opportunity to perform this action. Moreover, if this response to the first objection is unsatisfactory to its proponents, it should be noted that this objection does not undermine the claim that a current market in human transplant kidneys is morally permissible. Instead, the proponents of this objection are committed to endorsing the moral permissibility of any unregulated kidney sales that are Pareto superior. The second objection is, as it stands, little more than an assertion rather than a principled objection to Dworkin's pro-market position. For its proponents to develop this into a principled objection they must demonstrate one of two things. They must demonstrate that a current market for human kidneys could not be regulated to secure an acceptable degree of risk imposed on the vendors, and so could not be acceptable under any circumstances. Alternatively, they must show that the requisite levels of additional regulation would lead to an increase in autonomy or well-being (or both) of those it was designed to protect that would sufficiently outweigh any consequent loss of autonomy and/or well-being that others would experience as a result of its imposition (assuming that this trade-off is legitimate). It seems unlikely that the first of these propositions is true. Moreover, given the degree of regulation that the proponents of this second objection would require, it is also unlikely that the second proposition is true. Although the second objection to Dworkin's pro-market argument by analogy has not yet been fully developed, there are already strong grounds to be sceptical of it.

The First Objection from Disanalogy

Although the pro-market argument by analogy is not vulnerable to either of the above objections, it might be vulnerable to the charge that there is a significant disanalogy between someone selling one of their kidneys and many of the other dangerous activities to which its proponents compare such sales. John Harris and Charles Erin, for example, argue that since it is morally permissible for someone to choose the dangerous job of being a firefighter, it is also morally permissible for them to choose to sell one of their kidneys – a comparison that was made earlier for the same purpose by Lori Andrews.[7] Similarly, Michael Gill and Robert Sade (and Dworkin) argue that since it is morally permissible for persons to join the military, it is also morally permissible for them to sell a kidney since the degree of danger involved in these activities is comparable.[8] Janet Radcliffe Richards (who compares the risks involved in selling a kidney to those involved with hang-gliding, rock climbing and diving from North Sea oil rigs) and Ronald Munson (who compares the risks to those associated with motorcycle racing and mountaineering) also offer versions of this argument.[9]

Unfortunately, none of these proponents of the pro-market argument by analogy recognize that the dangerous activities that they compare the sale of a kidney to are disanalogous to it in an important way. Although firefighting, soldiering, hang-gliding, rock climbing, diving, motorcycle racing and mountaineering all involve an elevated degree of danger, they are also all activities that persons choose to perform because they want to engage in these activities for their own sake.[10] By contrast, people do not (typically) choose to sell a kidney because they specifically want to sell a kidney. Instead, persons (typically) only choose to sell because this is the only way they can think of to raise money that they need.[11] Thus, while firefighters are likely to endorse their desire to be firefighters *simpliciter*, and similarly mountaineers and so on, as outlined in Chapter 2 kidney vendors are likely both to endorse their desire to sell (that is, given their situation they believe that acting on this desire would be the best thing to do) *and* to prefer to act on a desire *other than* this desire (that is, they would prefer to be in a situation where they would not perceive this desire to be the best for them to act on).

This dissimilarity between the motivational structures of, for example, a (typical) firefighter and a (typical) kidney vendor is important in two respects. First, while the typical firefighter is likely to believe that their occupation is intrinsically worthwhile (and so chose to become one at least in part for this reason), the typical kidney vendor is likely only to accord instrumental value to the sale of a kidney. This difference draws the sting of the pro-market charge that prohibiting a person from selling their kidney would, like prohibiting them from being a firefighter, be 'paternalist in the extreme.'[12] A paternalist who tried to prohibit persons from becoming firemen or kidney vendors would do so after assessing the value of their occupation to them as not being worth the associated dangers. A fireman would challenge this assessment of the relative costs and benefits of his occupation, since he would hold his occupation to be valuable in itself.[13] By contrast, a kidney vendor would not disagree to the same degree with the paternalist's assessment of the relative costs and benefits that would be involved with selling a kidney, for (unlike the firefighter) they would not consider this sale to be anything other than instrumentally valuable. The paternalist's prohibition of persons being firefighters would thus involve a *greater* imposition of alien values upon those who wished to be firefighters than a similar prohibition on kidney selling would have on those who wished to be kidney vendors.[14] Accordingly, it would be *less* paternalistic to prohibit kidney selling than it would be to prohibit people becoming firefighters. The pro-market claim that it would be just as 'paternalist in the extreme' to prohibit kidney sales as it would to prohibit firefighting, then, is overstated because it is based on a failure to recognize the difference in the degree of paternalism that is involved in the prohibition of these two activities.

As well as removing the sting of the pro-market claim of extreme paternalism, recognizing that the motivational structures of the (typical) kidney seller and firefighter differ also undermines the pro-market claim that these person's choices are morally equivalent. The fact that firefighters endorse their effective first-order desire to become firefighters *simpliciter*, while kidney vendors would prefer not to be moved by their endorsed effective first-order desire to sell a kidney, shows that the instrumental value of the kidney vendor's autonomy is *less* than the firefighter's. This is not to claim that the kidney seller is in any way less autonomous than the firefighter. Rather, this is to claim that the firefighter's satisfaction of those first-order desires that they are autonomous with respect to is likely to secure a greater increase in well-being relative to the situation prior to their satisfaction than the kidney seller. This is important. When one who places a high moral value on autonomy recognizes that the instrumental value of a person's autonomy is likely to be low (for example, the kidney vendor's) they will have to ascertain whether this imposes a moral duty upon others to raise it by improving its possessor's situation (that is, so that the satisfaction of those desires that they are autonomous with respect to would be more likely to increase their well-being). This is because if it is possible for a person significantly to raise the instrumental value of another's autonomy without sacrificing anything of comparable moral importance, in the eyes of a defender of autonomy, they must do so because not to do so would evince an illegitimately low assessment of the value of the other's autonomy.[15] Of course, whether a defender of autonomy would in any given case hold a person to be blameworthy for a failure to enhance the instrumental value of another's autonomy by failing to improve their situation will depend on what is meant by a sacrifice of 'comparable moral importance.' As I noted in a similar context in the previous chapter, however, deciding the scope of this phrase is not germane to this discussion. Instead, what *is* germane are the differing responses that a defender of autonomy will have to persons whose autonomy is likely to be of high or low instrumental value to them. If the instrumental value is likely to be low (that is, someone endorses their effective first-order desire but would prefer to be moved by another desire) then it will be an open question for a defender of autonomy as to whether this imposes any moral duties upon others to enhance this person's situation. If, however, the instrumental value of a person's autonomy is likely to be high (they endorse their effective first-order desire *simpliciter*) then a defender of autonomy will accept that there is no moral duty incumbent on others to enhance this person's situation. Hence, if there is no aid forthcoming to the prospective kidney vendor (that is, nothing has been or is being done to improve the instrumental value of their autonomy) then, whereas the firefighter chose that occupation from a situation that was morally acceptable to a defender of autonomy, it will be an open question as to whether the kidney vendor chose to sell a kidney from a situation that was similarly morally acceptable. And if the kidney vendor did *not* choose to sell a kidney from a situation that was morally acceptable to a valuer of autonomy, then the choice to sell would *not* (in the eyes of a defender of autonomy) be morally equivalent to the firefighter's choice. There would thus be important moral differences between the kidney vendor's choice to sell a kidney and the firefighter's choice of profession that undermine this pro-market argument from analogy, and that many of its proponents overlook.

Kidney Sales and Dangerous Employment

It is important to note that the conclusion of this objection to the pro-market argument by analogy is *not* that it is mistaken, but simply that those *versions* of the pro-market argument by analogy that compare kidney selling to certain dangerous activities that people choose to pursue for their own sake (for example, those versions offered above by Erin and Harris and others) are underdeveloped.[16] As such, proponents of this pro-market argument could readily concede that certain activities that they compare to kidney selling are disanalogous to it. They could then restrict themselves to comparing kidney sales to occupations and activities that are not only both morally permissible and as dangerous and as unpleasant as undergoing a nephrectomy, but that are also occupations that persons would prefer not to engage in. And many of the occupations that the proponents of this pro-market argument by analogy base it on (such as being a paid subject for medical experimentation, or a construction worker) meet all three of these criteria.[17] The groundwork is now in place to move forward with the pro-market argument by analogy.

Mortality Rates

If a current market in human kidneys were to be regulated in the way outlined in the previous chapter the sale of a kidney would be no more dangerous for the seller than the donation

of a kidney is for live donors in affluent nations. Since such
donations are morally acceptable it should not come as a
surprise to find that the dangers that are associated with them
(and so the dangers associated with the sale of a kidney in a
market regulated as I suggest) are not significant enough to
warrant their paternalistic prohibition. Studies have shown,
for example, that persons who have only one functioning
kidney do not have an increased mortality rate when
compared with persons with two.[18] One would thus be
mistaken to oppose kidney sales on the grounds that the loss
of a kidney would result in the increased likelihood that the
vendor will die of kidney failure in the long term as a result of
not having a 'spare.'[19] The risks involved in undergoing the
nephrectomy itself have also been quantified.[20] For example,
in a 1991 survey of the medical literature on deaths resulting
from nephrectomy V. Bonomini found a midrange estimate of
a 0.06 per cent likelihood of death from kidney donation, and
H.A. Gritsch et al. estimated a similar figure in 2001.[21] These
figures might, however, be high. Drawing from the data on
mortality rates of live related kidney donors in American
hospitals between 1980 and 1991 Margaret Bia et al.
estimated perioperative mortality (death within 48 hours of
application of anesthesia) to be about 0.03 per cent. A similar
figure (0.025 per cent) was discovered in J.L. Melchor's 1998
review of the medical literature, although both Melchor's
study of 134 live, unpaid, Mexican kidney donors and R.
Cortesini's report on the mortality and morbidity rates of 368
donors at his Italian hospital cited a mortality rate of zero.[22]

In the light of these figures it is clear that, at least with
respect to mortality rates, the sale of a kidney in a market
regulated as suggested in the previous chapter would be *less*
dangerous than many other hazardous occupations that it is
morally permissible for persons to engage in. For example,
commercial fishermen and merchant seamen in Britain have a
mortality rate of 0.103 and 0.0516 per cent respectively –
figures that are higher than, or comparable to, the *highest*
estimates of mortality from nephrectomy (0.06 per cent);
and considerably higher than the figure of 0.025 per cent
outlined in Melchor's review.[23] Of course, one might object
that commercial fishing and the merchant marine are

unusually dangerous occupations, practised by a relatively small proportion of the population, and so should not be taken as benchmarks of a morally acceptable level of risk. But this is a spurious objection for two reasons. First, if the risk of mortality involved in these occupations is morally acceptable, then the lesser risk of mortality involved in selling a kidney should also be acceptable. Second, both of the remarks contained within this objection apply equally to kidney selling – and so the analogy between kidney selling and these maritime occupations is especially apt. A better objection to this analogy between sea fishing, the merchant marine and kidney selling is that the first two (like firefighting) are activities whose practitioners are likely to have chosen them for their own sake, possibly owing to family or community tradition. If this is so, then the analogy between these activities and kidney selling will be weakened. Given this, rather than focusing on these maritime occupations I will instead base the pro-market argument by analogy that I develop here on comparing kidney selling to scaffolding (including staging, steeplejacking and rigging), steel erecting and roofing (including tiling, sheeting and cladding). These are all morally permissible activities that are not only dangerous and unpleasant, but which those who practise them would likely prefer not to be engaged in. Moreover, although these activities are not as dangerous as sea fishing and the merchant marine, the danger of death while working is, respectively, 0.021, 0.041 and 0.025 per cent.[24] These mortality rates are either higher than, or comparable to, the mortality rate among living kidney donors – and hence higher than, or comparable to, the mortality rate among living kidney vendors in a market that would be regulated as I suggest.

Non-fatal Harms

Since these figures show that persons employed as scaffolders, steel erectors or roofers are at greater risk of death than they would be if they sold their kidneys in a regulated market, it might seem clear that if it is morally permissible for persons to be employed in these occupations then it is also morally permissible for them to sell their kidneys. But this conclusion would be too hasty. As well as the risk of *fatal* injury both kidney selling and the dangerous occupations in comparison also carry the risk of *non*-fatal harm. The anti-market paternalist might thus claim that these non-fatal risks are so much greater in kidney selling than in these other activities that they justify the prohibition of a current market for human kidneys. To rebut this argument, and to show that the dangers of kidney selling are comparable to those of other dangerous occupations, their respective non-fatal morbidity rates must also be compared.

The potential major complications from nephrectomy in a transplant centre in the developed world (that is, the sort of centre that I suggest should be licensed to perform commercial transplants in a regulated market) include bleeding requiring reoperation, pulmonary emboli (blood clots in the lungs or blockage of the pulmonary arteries) and acute tubular necrosis (the death of tubular cells in the kidneys).[25] The potential minor complications include ileus (air introduced into the small or large intestine), superficial wound infection, urinary tract infection and pneumonia. Other complications that might arise from nephrectomy (and which might be either major or minor) include deep vein thrombosis, haematoma (the collection of blood in a soft tissue that causes a tumour to develop), herniation (the pulling apart of small sections of the abdominal wound), hypotension (high arterial blood pressure) and microalbuminuria (the urinary excretion of abnormally high amounts of albumin protein, which can indicate renal dysfunction). By comparison, the list of possible harms that might befall someone working in construction as a scaffolder, steel erector or roofer is a lengthy one. However, for the purposes at hand the major harms that can befall persons in these occupations will be taken to include only those defined as major injuries in Schedule 1 of the UK Government's Reporting of Injuries, Diseases, Dangerous Occurrences Regulations 1995 (RIDDOR 95).[26] Similarly, following RIDDOR 95 a 'minor harm' that might befall someone employed in these ways is considered to be one that causes the person so affected to be absent from work for four or more days.[27]

With these definitions of major and minor harms in place, their incidence in both kidney donation (and by implication kidney sales) and the dangerous occupations outlined above can be compared. In an early study (1986) Levey, Hou and Bush estimated that major morbidity occurs in 2–3 per cent of patients undergoing nephrectomy and minor morbidity occurs in 10–20 per cent of such patients, while Bia et al. found a 0.23 per cent likelihood of serious complications from nephrectomies performed in American hospitals between 1987 and 1992.[28] More recently, Melchor's 1998 study of 134 live, unpaid, Mexican kidney donors found only 1.3 per cent experienced any complications arising from their nephrectomies, while his literature review showed an average 1 per cent total morbidity rate from live kidney donation.[29] In 2001, however, Gritsch et al. estimated that 2 per cent of patients would experience major perioperative complications, and that 5 per cent of patients would experience minor complications.[30] (The variances between these figures are likely to reflect both improvements in medical techniques and local variations in classifying complications as major or minor.) The incidence of major morbidity arising from nephrectomy, then, varies between 0.23 and 3 per cent, and the incidence of minor morbidity from nephrectomies varies between 1 per cent and 20 per cent (or 1 per cent and 5 per cent with most recent figures). The incidence of reported injuries from the dangerous employments listed above is lower. Roofers experienced an incidence of major non-fatal injuries of 0.876 per cent in the period 2000/01, while the figures for scaffolders and steel erectors were 1.23 and 1.26 per cent respectively in the same period.[31] For construction workers in all categories the incidence of minor injuries for the years 1996/97–2000/01 was an average of 0.93 per cent.[32] Outside the construction business, the incidence of minor injuries was occasionally higher – for example, the figure for 1999/2000 in quarrying was 2.01 per cent, even though the incidence of major injuries was lower, at 0.399 per cent.[33]

It can thus be seen that whereas the risk of death from the sale of a kidney is similar to that incurred by engaging in certain dangerous occupations, someone engaging in these occupations is less likely to suffer either major or minor harm as a result than someone selling a kidney. This weakens the pro-market argument by analogy. However, it does not completely undermine it. Although one would incur more risk of harm if one sold a kidney than if one accepted work as a construction worker, the risks involved are of a very similar magnitude – between 1 and 5 per cent recent risk of minor morbidity from nephrectomy, compared with 1–2 per cent risk of minor injury in dangerous employment, and between 0.23 and 3 per cent recent risk of major morbidity from nephrectomy, compared with about 0.94 per cent risk of major injury in dangerous employment. These differences in degree of risk are thus not significant enough to justify the paternalistic prohibition of kidney sales if they would not similarly justify the paternalistic prohibition of persons taking dangerous jobs in the construction industry.

Why the Risk Differential Might Not be as Great as it Appears

The above conclusion is reinforced by four additional considerations that show that the differences in risk that are involved in selling a kidney and becoming a construction worker might not be as significant as these statistics might be taken to indicate. First, the RIDDOR 95 statistics on injury rates only cover *reported* incidences of the major and minor harms that befell workers. They are thus likely to under-represent the actual incidences of harm in these dangerous occupations, for some employers (or their representatives, such as site managers) will pressure employees not to report harmful incidents so as to avoid either lawsuits or an increase in their insurance premiums. Similarly, workers themselves might be motivated not to report incidents, either because they fear being seen as whistleblowers, or because they would not be adequately compensated for time that they did not spend working. Indeed, the UK government's Health and Safety Executive estimates that the incidence of reported injuries from the British construction industry in 1995/96 was only 43 per cent.[34] Second, the statistics for minor non-fatal injuries in construction work cover *all* types of construction

work, and not just those in the high-risk occupations focused
on above. They thus do not show if scaffolders, steel erectors
or roofers had higher incidences of minor non-fatal injuries
than other types of construction workers whose occupations
are less hazardous (for example, plasterers or painters).
Third, the United Kingdom has a far lower incidence of
work-related injuries and deaths than either the rest of the
European Union or the United States, with just 38 per cent of
the EU's average rate of minor injuries, and just 53 per cent of
the average US rate for minor injuries in 1996.[35] The risk
differential between dangerous employment and the sale of a
kidney is thus smaller in most European Union countries and
the United States than it is in Britain. Finally, the above
figures refer to the mortality and morbidity rates that are
associated with traditional open nephrectomy, which
involves cutting the back muscle and removing a portion of
the 11th or 12th rib, depending on the patient's anatomy. The
kidney is then removed through an open incision some 20–
30 cm long that begins near the stomach and wraps around
the patient's back.[36] This type of surgery is starting to be
replaced by much less invasive techniques, such as laparoscopic nephrectomy and hand-assisted laparoscopic nephrectomy. The first of these laparoscopic techniques requires only
four small incisions of less than 25 mm to be made in the
patient's abdomen, with the kidney being removed through a
small incision made below the lower abdomen. The second
procedure requires only one small incision of no more than
about 75 mm, over which a flexible, ringlike device is then
fitted. This device serves as a sterile channel and sleeve
through which the surgery is conducted, allowing the surgeon
to perform the nephrectomy with his hand placed in a gel-
filled sleeve that extends into the patient's abdomen. Because
they are much less invasive, such laparoscopic techniques
result in less post-operative pain, a shorter hospital stay and a
significantly shorter recovery time for the nephrectomy
patient.[37] With continued advances in surgical techniques,
then, it is likely that the mortality and morbidity rates for
nephrectomy patients will continue to fall. If they do, the sale
of a kidney might even become a less dangerous process than
many of the morally permissible dangerous activities to

which the proponents of the pro-market argument by analogy currently compare it.

The Moral Advantages to Kidney Selling

In addition to these four responses proponents of the pro-market argument by analogy should also note that, from the point of view of one who is concerned with human well-being and/or personal autonomy, there are also reasons to believe that the sale of a kidney is morally preferable to selling one's labour for dangerous employment. When someone sells their labour and becomes an employee they will cede a degree of control over their actions to an employer, or employer's representative (for example, the site manager). Like the victim of coercion, such a person's autonomy with respect to their actions will be compromised to the extent that the employer exercises control over their actions (for instance, by having them work in a particular part of the quarry). Furthermore, insofar as such a person is moved to accept certain employment by a desire that they would prefer not to be moved by, they are unlikely to enjoy the work as much as they would enjoy some alternative form of employment. By contrast, the sale of a kidney in a regulated market would not lead to the vendor's autonomy being compromised, and their well-being diminished, to the same extent that the sale of their labour for dangerous employment that they would prefer not to accept is likely to lead to. Unlike people who sell their services, kidney vendors do not cede any control over their actions to others (apart, perhaps, from during the recuperation period when they will be 'under doctor's orders'). Moreover, although typical vendors would similarly prefer to be moved by a desire other than the desire to sell a kidney, the sale would not require them to spend a long period of time performing actions that they would prefer not to perform, and so their well-being will suffer from a lesser degree of diminution than that of the reluctant employee. If one is concerned with paternalistically protecting autonomy and well-being, then, one should hold that the sale of labour for regulated but dangerous employment is *more* morally objectionable than is the sale of a kidney in a regulated market. And since the former is morally permissible, then the latter is also.

Objections to the Argument from Analogy

From the above discussion it appears that Dworkin is right: that since a person's risk of suffering impaired autonomy and diminished well-being as a result of selling a kidney in a regulated market is comparable to the risks that would be incurred in certain types of dangerous employment that are morally acceptable, then it seems that (*ceteris paribus*) such sales are similarly morally acceptable.

Yet it would be premature to endorse this pro-market conclusion. The above argument by analogy rests on the view that there is no morally relevant difference between the sale of a kidney and other dangerous income-generating activities that persons would prefer not to perform. (Or, where there are such differences, they can be used to show that kidney sales are morally preferable to dangerous employment.) But this view is widely contested, especially by those who claim either that the sale of a kidney is an illegitimate commodification of the human body, or that the only morally acceptable way to procure transplant organs is through altruistic donation. Since the arguments to support these two claims are both complex and important I will devote the next two chapters to examining them. There are, however, three other less complex morally relevant differences between the sale of a kidney and the sale of labour that are claimed to undermine the pro-market analogy between such sales.

Zutlevics's Argument from Social Standing

Zutlevics holds that focusing the argument by analogy on the comparative risks that are involved in selling one's kidney and selling one's labour to engage in a dangerous occupation obscures the fact that the degree of risk in an employment opportunity is not the only criterion that is used to determine whether it is morally permissible to offer it to persons. Rather, the question of whether it is morally permissible to offer certain employment opportunities to persons should be answered after considering what effects accepting such employment is likely to have on these persons' social status. Zutlevics notes that all of the dangerous occupations that the proponents of kidney markets compare them to (such as high-steel construction) are occupations that afford those who participate in them a degree of social standing.[38] Thus, she argues, unless it can be shown that the vendors in a current market for human transplant kidneys would also acquire social standing through the sale of their kidneys, the analogy between kidney selling and dangerous employment is not as strong as it might first appear – and so the pro-market argument from analogy is weaker than its proponents believe.

Zutlevics's stance against the pro-market argument by analogy gains force once it is recognized that instead of increasing their social standing by selling a kidney, vendors in some countries actually suffer from a *decrease* in social status. For example, although kidney selling now appears to have become generally socially acceptable in India and the Philippines, kidney sellers in Eastern Europe suffer from considerable social stigma.[39] In Moldova they are despised as prostitutes, while in Turkey their children are ridiculed as 'one-kidneys.'[40] Kidney vendors in Eastern Europe can also be 'excommunicated from churches, alienated from families and, if single, excluded from marriage.'[41]

Yet even if a person who sells a kidney would suffer a loss of social standing, respect for their autonomy still requires that they be allowed to sell if they so wish. If someone decides to sell a kidney in a current market that is regulated in the manner that I suggested in the previous chapter they would have discussed the implications of this sale with a person who has already sold a kidney, and who comes from a similar social and economic background. In the light of this discussion – and in the light of the other information that they would have been given to secure informed consent to the sale of the kidney – such a vendor would be autonomously deciding to trade a kidney, and a possible loss of social

standing, for the compensation on offer. Since the sale of a
kidney in a regulated current market for transplant organs is
not itself likely to impair the future autonomy of the vendor,
respect for autonomy requires that this vendor's decision be
respected – just as it requires that the decision of a person
who trades personal safety for wages to work in high-steel
construction should be respected also. Thus, even though
Zutlevics is right that the analogy between dangerous
employment and the sale of a kidney is not a perfect one,
the disanalogous aspect of these transactions that she
identifies does not seriously weaken the pro-market argument
by analogy.

Kidney Sales are Irrevocable

Robert Audi has also claimed that there is an important
disanalogy between selling a kidney and selling labour for
dangerous employment: that whereas selling one's labour is
a revocable transaction, selling one's kidney is (for all
practical purposes) not.[42] Yet although at first sight this
might appear to be a clear disanalogy between the sale of a
kidney and the sale of labour, on examination it is not clear
that this disanalogy actually holds. Once a person has
consummated the sale of their labour by having used it in
its purchaser's employ for the agreed amount of time (or
until the agreed upon project was completed) he cannot
recoup it. Strictly speaking, then, the sale of one's labour,
like the sale of one's kidney, is an irrevocable act. It is,
however, likely that Audi did not mean to use the term
'irrevocable' in this strict sense, but rather in a looser sense,
whereby the sale of some good is irrevocable if, after this
sale has been consummated, the vendor cannot (for all
practical purposes) secure a replacement of this type of
good for future sale. If Audi is using this looser sense of
the term 'irrevocable' then he is quite right to hold that the
sale of a kidney, but not the sale of labour, is irrevocable –
for whereas one can sell one's labour in the future after
one has sold it in the past, one cannot consummate the sale
of the 'spare' kidney that one was born with more than
once.

Unfortunately, Audi does not expand on how he sees this difference between selling one's kidney and selling one's labour as undermining the pro-market argument from analogy – and it is not clear how it would do so. It cannot be the case that the mere fact that the sale of a kidney is irrevocable renders this action morally impermissible. There are many acts whose consequences are irrevocable (such as, for example, undergoing elective surgery, or scattering the ashes of a cremated relative rather than establishing a permanent memorial) but whose performance is morally justified by both respect for autonomy and concern for well-being. One possible reason why this difference between the sale of a kidney and the sale of one's labour might undermine the pro-market argument by analogy has been independently offered by Henry Hansmann, who writes that the irrevocability of selling one's kidney results in 'the possibility of making a mistake in selling a kidney ... [being] ... much larger than the possibility of making a mistake in taking a job as [for example] a meatpacker.'[43] As expressed, however, this view is false. The mere fact that the consequences of a person's decision are irrevocable has no effect whatsoever on the likelihood of their making a mistaken decision. Perhaps, though, what Hansmann meant was that if a person makes a mistake when they make a decision that has irreversible consequences (for example, a kidney vendor later comes to believe that they should not have sold their kidney) then this would adversely affect them more adversely than would their making a mistaken decision whose consequences are revocable. As Hansmann himself has noted, however, this disanalogy between selling a kidney and accepting dangerous employment does not automatically lend support to an anti-market position.[44] Instead, recognizing that a person who regrets selling a kidney would be unable to rectify this situation lends further support to the view that such a market should be regulated in the ways outlined above. That is, potential kidney vendors will be required to give their informed consent to the sale of their kidney, they will have to be approved by an independent consultative panel, and they will be subject to an enforced 'cooling off' period between their initial desire to sell and the sale itself.

Yet even though it is not clear how the fact that the sale of one's kidney is irrevocable and the sale of one's labour is not is supposed to undermine the pro-market argument by analogy, it is clear how any objection to this fact could be headed off. The argument from analogy should be revised to compare the sale of a kidney to a similarly irrevocable but clearly morally permissible act, one such that those who perform it are similarly typically moved to do so by a desire that they would prefer not to be moved by. The most obvious way to revise the pro-market argument in this way is to compare the sale of a kidney to its altruistic donation to a relative. The donation of a kidney is just as irrevocable as the sale of one. The (typical) donor would prefer not to be moved to donate (that is, they would prefer that their relative did not need the kidney) and would incur similar risks to a kidney vendor in a market regulated as suggested in the previous chapter. Thus, if the altruistic donation of a kidney is not morally impermissible owing to the risks involved, then the sale of a kidney clearly cannot be morally impermissible on account of these same risks.

The Difficulties of Securing Informed Consent

Audi also claims that there is a second important disanalogy between selling one's kidney and selling one's labour: that '… the calculation of risks for sales of one's services [to engage in dangerous employment] is different and may be easier. At the very least, one can often recalculate in midstream and before withdrawal of one's services is infeasible.'[45] Audi's idea here seems to be that since it is apparently more difficult to calculate the costs and benefits of selling a kidney than it is to calculate the costs and benefits of selling one's labour, persons are more likely to make mistakes when considering whether to sell their kidneys, and so the paternalistic prohibition of kidney selling is more morally justifiable than a similar prohibition of selling one's labour.

The first response to this objection has already been outlined in response to Hansmann, above: that such difficulties simply underscore the need for a regulated market in which the vendors give their informed consent to the sale of their kidneys. Moreover, it appears that insofar as the sale of one's kidney and the sale of one's labour are disanalogous in that the costs and benefits of one are far easier to assess than the costs and benefits of the other, this disanalogy works in *favour* of the argument by analogy, and not against it. The risks involved in nephrectomy are well known, can be tailored to suit the individual vendor and, in a market for kidneys that is regulated as I suggest, would be communicated to each vendor in a way designed to ensure that they understand them. By contrast, when someone sells their labour the employer is not required to secure their informed consent to the risks that they will incur at work. As Elizabeth Anderson points out, 'Many workers in hazardous jobs ... learn about most hazards involved in their work on the job, not before entering. And many of these hazards, such as loss of fertility and increased risk of cancer, are discovered only after many years on the job.'[46] Insofar as there is a difference in the difficulty of calculating the risks involved in selling one's kidney and selling one's labour, then, it is likely to be *less* difficult to calculate the risks involved in the former exchange than the latter.

Audi is also wrong to claim that persons who sell their services can often calculate the risks before withdrawing their services becomes infeasible, whereas kidney sellers cannot. First, as Anderson noted, many serious hazards are likely to be discovered by employees only after many years, by which time they cannot avoid them by withdrawing their services. Second, it is not possible for persons to withdraw from some hazardous jobs 'midstream.' One cannot, for example, avoid many of the risks involved in commercial fishing once the ship has left port; nor, in many cases, can one withdraw from being a paid subject of medical experimentation once one has been exposed to the pharmaceutical or biological agent that is being tested. Moreover, even if it is theoretically possible for a person to withdraw from a hazardous job the costs of such exit are likely to be so considerable as to render it a practical impossibility. This is especially true if the person concerned took the job because they had no viable alternatives. And even if an exiting worker does not find themselves unemployed they might lose seniority, pension and any extra pay and vacation time accrued.[47]

Conclusion

In this chapter I have argued that the pro-market argument from analogy is correct: since it is morally permissible for a person to be employed in certain dangerous jobs, it is also morally permissible for a person to sell one of their kidneys, given that the levels of risk involved are similar. As yet, however, I have not established conclusively that a regulated market in human transplant kidneys is morally permissible. It might be the case that respect for the autonomy and concern for the well-being of those who participate in such a market as vendors would be outweighed by other moral considerations, such as the possible immorality of commodifying the human body. Alternatively, it might be the case that concern for the autonomy and the well-being of persons who need to receive a transplant kidney might lead to the conclusion that such organs should not be procured commercially, even if such procurement would respect the autonomy and well-being of the vendors. It is to these issues that I now turn.

Notes

1   This pro-market argument by analogy has two distinct forms – and two distinct conclusions – that are often confused. For a clear example of this confusion see Sells, R.A. (1993), p. 40. The first form of this argument is that since the dangerous activities that kidney selling is compared to are morally permissible, then kidney selling is morally permissible also. The second is that since these other activities are legal, then kidney selling should be legal too. In this chapter I focus only on the first of these arguments, offering a moral justification for a current market in human kidneys. I argue that the conclusion of the second form of argument should be accepted in Chapter 9.

2   This pro-market argument by analogy has been developed by Dworkin (1994), p. 157; Morden, p. 39; Feldstein, Paul J. (1999), p. 259; Hansmann, p. 73; Radcliffe Richards, pp. 385–6; Radcliffe Richards et al., p. 1951; Barnett, Andrew H., Blair,

Roger D. and Kaserman, David L. (1992), p. 375; Gill and Sade, p. 35; Harris and Erin (1994), p. 137–8; Andrews, Lori B. (1986), p. 32; Cohen, Lloyd R., p. 58; Munson, p. 121.

3   A more radical anti-market argument has been offered by B. Brecher, who argues that since kidney selling and wage labour are analogous, then given that kidney selling is to be morally condemned wage labour should be condemned also. See Brecher (1990). For a response to Brecher see Buttle, Nicholas (1991).

4   Dworkin (1994), p. 157.

5   Ibid.

6   This point was noted by Zutlevics, p. 298.

7   Harris and Erin (1994), p. 138; Andrews, Lori B., p. 32.

8   Gill and Sade, pp. 34–5, Dworkin (1994), p. 157. Gill and Sade also compare the sale of a kidney to cleaning lavatories and (rather bizarrely) to picking strawberries on the grounds that, like kidney sales, it is usually the poor (and not the rich or middle class) who perform these morally permissible occupations. These occupations, however, are not strongly analogous to the sale of a kidney as neither of them is dangerous (to my knowledge persons never die, or suffer serious injury, in strawberry picking accidents), and it is the imposition of the dangers of kidney sales on the poor that is frequently the basis for one of the moral objections to allowing them.

9   Radcliffe Richards (1996), p. 385; Munson, p. 121.

10 I write that these activities have an 'elevated' rather than a 'high' degree of danger because neither firefighting nor soldiering are as dangerous as they are perceived to be. See Roberts, Stephen (2002), p. 544.

11 That financial necessity of the primary motive for selling a kidney is documented in Goyal et al., pp. 1590–91.

12 Dworkin (1994), p. 157.

13 See Anderson, Elizabeth (1988), p. 61.

14 Perhaps persons would be prohibited from becoming firefighters where fires could be effectively fought by robots.

15 This argument is similar to that which I offered in favour of market regulation in the previous chapter. Although the phrasing of the argument here also has clear echoes of Peter Singer's views in 'Famine, Affluence, and Morality,' one need not be consequentialist to endorse this view, for a version of this argument could, *mutatis mutandis*, also be offered by a deontologist who held that persons have a duty of charity. Singer (1972), pp. 229–43.

16 In fairness it should be noted that only the version of Dworkin's argument that compares kidney selling to enlisting in the military is likely to fall prey to this objection, since (at least in peacetime) many persons join for prestige or family tradition

that (unlike Harry Feversham in A.E.W. Mason's 1902 novel *The Four Feathers*) they endorse.

17 Dworkin compares kidney selling to both of these activities; (1994), p. 157. Moreover, his comparisons also meet all of the conditions required for this analogy to be a strong one, although Zutlevics failed to recognize this, believing that Dworkin was only concerned with comparing kidney selling to other risky activities. See Zutlevics (2001a), p. 298.

18 See, for example, Narkun-Burgess, D.M. et al. (1993); Fehrman-Ekholm, I. et al. (1997). These studies reflect the mortality rates of persons who were healthy at the time of their donation. Since this is so opponents of the moral permissibility of a current market will no doubt argue that such studies cannot be used to demonstrate the safety of kidney sales by the poor, who are unlikely to be as healthy as the donors to which these studies apply. There are two immediate responses to this objection. First, since there is no equivalent data on the effects of kidney sales on the long-term health of the poor there is no evidence for or against the claim that such sales are too risky to be morally permissible. Second, even if the poor were so unhealthy that the sale of a kidney was tantamount to suicide, this would only show that the unhealthy poor should not be allowed to sell, not that such sales are morally impermissible *per se*. A third response – that even if such sales were tantamount to suicide, suicide is not necessarily immoral – could also be offered by persons who hold well-being (but not autonomy) to have intrinsic moral value.

19 This concern is voiced by Scheper-Hughes (2002a), p. 77, and by Cohen, Cynthia B. (2002), p. 51.

20 See, for example, Williams, S.L. et al. (1986); Miller, I. et al. (1985); Talseth, T. et al. (1986). I thank Joseph Shapiro for bringing these studies to my attention.

21 Bonomini, V. (1991); Gritsch, H.A. et al. (2001).

22 Melchor (1998); Cortesini (1999).

23 The statistics on mortality rates for commercial fishing and the merchant marine refer to the years 1976–95. Roberts, p. 543. This data has a 95 per cent CI (confidence interval). A confidence interval gives an estimated range of values that is likely to include an unknown population parameter, with the estimated range being calculated from a given set of sample data. A CI of 95 per cent is standard.

24 This data is drawn from HM Government (2002a), Table 16, p. 30. The data in this report has a 95 per cent CI and refers to 2000/01.

25 Information concerning the major and minor complications that might arise in conventional nephrectomy is taken from Shapiro, Joseph (2003), a thesis written for the Ethics in Society Honors Program requirements at Stanford University. Shapiro

cites Levey, A.S., Hou, S. and Bush, H.L. (1986), and an interview with Dr Oscar Salvatierra, President of the Transplantation Society, and Professor of Surgery and Pediatrics at Stanford University as the source of this information.

26 These include fractures (other than fingers, thumbs or toes), amputations, dislocations of shoulder, knee or spine, loss of sight, chemical or hot metal burns to the eye, penetrating injuries to the eye, injuries from electric shocks or burns resulting in unconsciousness or over 24 hours' admittance to hospital, unconsciousness caused by asphyxia or exposure to a biological agent, acute illness requiring medical treatment or loss of consciousness arising from absorption of any substance by inhalation or ingestion, and acute illness requiring medical treatment where there is reason to believe that this resulted from a biological agent or its toxins. HM Government (2000), Regulation 2(1) Schedule 1.

27 See HM Government (2003), p. 33. All data taken from this report has a 95 per cent CI.

28 Levey, Hou and Bush; Bia, Margaret J., Ramos, E.L., Danovitch, G.M. et al. (1995).

29 Melchor, pp. 2869–70.

30 Gritsch et al. pp. 111–29.

31 HM Government (2002a), Tables 16 and 17, pp. 30–31.

32 Ibid., Table 6, p. 24.

33 HM Government (2002b), calculated from Table A1.1b.

34 This figure is from Table 6, 'Trends in the levels of reporting of injuries, 1989/90 to 1995/96,' HM Government Statistical Service (n.d.).

35 HM Government (2002b), data from Table 1.

36 See Gritsch, H.A. and Rosenthal, J.T. (2001), pp. 146–62, esp p. 147.

37 For discussions of these two laparoscopic techniques and their advantages when compared with conventional open nephrectomy, see Schweitzer, E.J., Wilson, J., Jacobs, S. et al. (2000); Lennerling, A., Blohme, I., Ostraat, O. et al. (2001); Santos, Luiz S. et al. (2003).

38 Zutlevics (2001a), p. 298.

39 The social acceptability of kidney selling in India is noted in Chengappa, Raj (1990). Its social acceptability in the Philippines is noted in Tiong, pp. 90–93.

40 Scheper-Hughes (2003), p. 1647.

41 Scheper-Hughes (2002b).

42 Audi (1996), p. 144.

43 Hansmann, p. 73. Hansmann's view here is also subject to the same criticisms as Audi's, below.

44 Ibid., pp. 73–4.

45 Audi, p. 144.

46 Anderson, p. 61. The risks that are involved in being a paid subject for medical experimentation – one of the jobs that Dworkin compares the sale of an organ to in his version of the pro-market argument by analogy – are especially difficult to assess prior to agreeing to become such a subject, since discovering these risks is precisely the aim of this form of employment.

47 These exit costs are outlined in Anderson, p. 61. Anderson cites Nelkin, Dorothy and Brown, Michael S. (1984), pp. 59, 90–92, 180–81, who find many workers who want to leave their hazardous employment but who find these costs prohibitive.

Chapter 7

Human Dignity and the Fear of Commodification

So far, I have argued that both respect for the autonomy of potential kidney vendors and concern for their well-being supports the view that a current market in human kidneys is morally permissible. This is important, for concerns about vendor autonomy and well-being underlie many of the moral objections to a current market in human kidneys. However, that concerns about potential vendors can be laid to rest does not show that such a market is morally permissible. These moral concerns would be trumped if using a current market to procure human transplant kidneys would treat human body parts in an immoral manner, either because such treatment is immoral in itself, or because it would lead to morally objectionable consequences for the recipients of the organs thus procured.

The view that it is immoral to treat human body parts as market commodities is widespread among those who morally oppose using a current market to procure transplant kidneys. Bob Brecher, for example, holds that the purchase of human kidneys is morally objectionable because it 'represents the further commoditisation [commodification] of human beings.'[1] Similarly, Cynthia B. Cohen notes 'Commodifying the human body and its organs ... [is] viewed as contrary to our basic social values.'[2] If this view were correct, it would establish that markets in human body parts are immoral. It would also show why it is not inconsistent, as some proponents of a current market in human kidneys charge, to compensate financially the surgical staff who transplant kidneys from live donors, but to object to similar compensation for the providers of these organs. The former provide services that morally can be commodified, while the latter provide body parts that morally cannot.[3]

Unfortunately, despite its potential weight in the debate over whether markets in human kidney are morally permissible, the view that human organs should not be commodified 'is typically an emotionally charged assertion and not a reasoned argument.'[4] But this is not always the case. In this chapter and the next I will outline the most prominent arguments offered for the view that markets in human organs involve their illegitimate commodification – not to praise them, but to bury them.

The Concept of Commodification

Margaret Jane Radin has developed the clearest and most influential account of commodification, noting that there are two (related but independent) senses of 'commodification.'[5] In its narrow sense the term describes the literal buying and selling of goods and economic services. In its broad sense the term encompasses an attitude towards objects as commodities, whether or not they are actually traded in the market-place.[6] This attitude involves objectifying things, in the sense of holding them to be 'manipulable at the will of persons,' and holding them to be fungible, as 'fully interchangeable with no effect on value to the holder.'[7] It also involves holding the values of things to be commensurable, and to possess money equivalence.[8] Since the narrow sense of commodification is purely descriptive, it is its broad sense that plays the central role in the debate over whether it is morally acceptable to use a current market to procure human transplant organs. The question at hand, then, is whether it is morally acceptable to adopt this commodificatory attitude towards human organs.

Kantian Objections to the Commodification of Human Body Parts

In outlining the commodificatory attitude Radin noted that it involved objectifying that which it regards as a commodity, holding it to have the status of 'a thing in the Kantian sense of something that is manipulable at the will of persons.'[9] This is accurate, both as an account of what is involved in adopting the commodificatory attitude and as an exegesis of Immanuel Kant's view. However, Radin goes astray in her outline of Kant's view of what is included in the class of things that are 'manipulable at the will of persons.' Radin notes that, for Kant, 'only objects separable from the self are suitable for alienation,' a position that requires that an account be given of which things are not separable from the self and which are manipulable objects. She then claims that, for Kant, 'persons are essentially abstract, fungible units with identical capacity for moral reason and no concrete individuating character-istics.' Since this is so, Radin concludes, 'Kantian personhood ... facilitates conceiving of concrete personal attributes as commodified objects.'[10]

Although Radin's account of Kant's view of personhood is the conventional one it cannot be entirely correct (as Radin later acknowledges) for Kant explicitly condemns conceiving of 'concrete personal attributes' as commodifiable objects.[11] In his *Lectures on Ethics*, for example, Kant writes 'a human being is not entitled to sell his limbs for money, even if he were offered ten thousand thalers for a single finger.'[12] Similarly, in *Groundwork of the Metaphysics of Morals* he writes 'To deprive oneself of an integral part or organ (to maim oneself) – for example, *to give away or sell* a tooth to be transplanted into another's mouth, or to have oneself castrated in order to get an easier livelihood as a singer, and so forth – are ways of partially murdering oneself,' and this counts as a 'crime against one's own person.'[13] Kant's condemnation of the sale of body parts is thus clear. Unfortunately, the reasons that he provides for this con-demnation are extremely opaque. The following account of Kant's arguments against the commodification of human organs should thus be understood as a reconstruction of Kant's arguments than as an exegesis of them.

The Argument from Worth

The most well-known argument against the commodification of human body parts that can be found in Kant's work occurs immediately after his claim that a person is not entitled to sell his limbs for money. Kant writes,

> If he were so entitled [to sell his body parts] he could sell all his limbs. We can dispose of things which have no freedom but not of a being which has free will. A man who sells himself makes himself a thing, and, as he has jettisoned his person, it is open to anyone to deal with him as he pleases.[14]

There are two possible ways to interpret the argument in this passage, which I shall term the 'Argument from Worth.' The first is to view it as a slippery slope argument. Understood in this way, Kant here condemns the sale of body parts on the grounds that if a person were morally permitted to sell one body part, then by the same reasoning they should be able to sell another of them, and then another, and another. Since this continuous sale of body parts would end in the death of the vendor, accepting that it is morally acceptable to sell one's body parts is tantamount to accepting that suicide is morally permitted – a view that Kant famously rejects.[15]

When construed in this way, the Argument from Worth is beset by difficulties, the most obvious of which is the objection that Kant is mistaken to hold that suicide is immoral. If it can be shown that Kant is wrong here, then, even if he is right to claim that if a person is morally permitted to sell one of their body parts there would be no conceptual bar to their selling additional body parts until they died, this does not show that the sale of body parts is morally unacceptable. But one need not challenge Kant's views on the morality of suicide to object to this argument. As Ruth Chadwick points out, the fact that a person might think it is morally permissible to sell one body part (such as a kidney) does not commit them to thinking that it would also be morally permissible to sell another.[16]

The second way to construe the Argument from Worth eschews this understanding of it to focus on Kant's views of the value of personhood. For Kant, persons possess dignity insofar as they are capable of morality. They are thus distinguished from mere things, which have price rather than dignity; unlike things, persons cannot be replaced by something of equivalent value.[17] Moreover, for Kant, 'The body is part of the self; in its togetherness with the self it constitutes the person.'[18] Therefore, if a person sells part of their body they will be treating their person as a thing, since their body is part of their personhood, and so they will be treating their person as though it could be replaced by something of equivalent value (for example, money).[19] Selling part of oneself is thus degrading to a person. Insofar as it thus denies the person's full moral worth, then, it is immoral.

As with the first construal of the Argument from Worth one can object to it as it is outlined in this second construal by challenging the basic elements of Kant's moral philosophy that undergird it; in this case, Kant's view of the worth of persons. As with the first construal of this argument, however, one need not challenge Kant's overall moral philosophy to object to it. This is because it is not clear that Kant can consistently hold that a person's body partially constitutes personhood, such that the removal of a part of it would degrade this. Kant accepts that persons can divest themselves of body parts 'provided our motives are those of self-preservation' – such as the amputation of a diseased limb to preserve the life of the person of which it is a part.[20] Here, it seems that Kant holds that a person *can* treat part of their body as a thing *without* thereby treating themself as a thing. One might, however, attempt to defend the second construal of this argument by claiming that such a limb could be regarded as being dead, and so is no longer truly a part of the living person in the way that a person's body parts are normally constitutive of them. Thus, if one regards a diseased limb in this way, then one might well be able legitimately to treat it as a thing of which one can divest oneself. But this can at best be only a partial defence of this second construal of the Argument from Worth, for Kant *also* holds that someone can remove a *healthy* part of their body if so doing will preserve their life. In *Lectures on Ethics* he writes, 'Niebuhr relates that travelers who go to Mecca to witness Mohammedan ceremonies must allow themselves to be circumcised or be killed ... Why should I not submit to circumcision, particularly if I thereby save my life?'[21] Since Kant accepts that a person would not be acting immorally if they removed a healthy part of their body to save their life, it seems that he should also accept that a person would not be acting immorally if they (for example) sold a kidney to secure money to avoid starvation, or (to borrow Chadwick's example) to pay off loan sharks who were threatening them.[22] This undermines his claim that treating a part of one's body as a thing *entails* treating oneself as a thing, for it is clear that in some cases Kant does not believe that this is so. Moreover, since he wrote that circumcision is *particularly* acceptable if it is done to save the life of the person whose body part it is, it seems that some cases of circumcision – that is, some instances of giving up a body part – would be acceptable *even if* self-preservation were *not* the motive behind them.[23] Thus, for Kant, the class of body parts that a person could morally treat as things (that is, without thereby treating himself as a thing) is *not* coextensive with the class of body parts that need to be treated as things in order to preserve personhood through the preservation of life (for example, diseased limbs). But this renders mysterious *when* treating body parts as things is morally unacceptable for Kant (that is, when it is that a person's body parts are partially constitutive of them as a person). It also renders mysterious *why* it is that the particular cases of such treatment that are thus identified as being morally unacceptable are unacceptable. Thus, this second construal of the Argument from Worth seems unable to ground a clear case against the commodification of human body parts.

Defending the Argument – a Narrow Understanding of the Second Construal

This rejection of the second construal of the Argument from Worth might, however, have been too hasty. For Kant, something is a thing if 'something else can be put in its place as an equivalent.'[24] Given this, the second construal of the argument could be understood more narrowly than how it was understood above, as providing a rationale *not* for a general prohibition against the removal of body parts *per se*, but against the treatment of them *as if they were interchangeable*, and so possessed only the status of things. On this narrow understanding of this second construal a person is entitled to amputate an unhealthy limb or be circumcised, either to save their life or for another reason, *provided that* they do not treat their body parts as interchangeable in so doing. This dispels the mystery of both when it is that treating body parts as things is morally unacceptable for Kant, and why it is that these particular cases are morally objectionable. This more narrow understanding of the second construal of the Argument from Worth cannot, however, be used to object to the sale of body parts *per se*. This is because its proponents must accept that it is not immoral for a person to sell a body part provided that they do not view it as interchangeable in doing so. According to this narrow understanding, a person then would be morally permitted to sell an especially beautiful part of their body for display as an artwork. However, they would not be permitted to sell the same body part to be transplanted into another – and nor would they be morally permitted to *donate* a body part for this purpose.

This last point is important, for although this narrow understanding provides a clear case against the commodification of human body parts, it does so at a considerable cost in that it renders immoral the altruistic donation of body parts. This is a highly counterintuitive result which, for most participants in this debate (although not, apparently, for Kant), would count as a *reductio ad absurdum* of this argument. At the very least, then, a successful defence must be mounted both of Kant's view of the worth of persons and of the constitutive relationship that holds between personhood and body parts before this argument (and its anti-donation conclusion) can be accepted.

The Argument from Contradiction

Kant's second argument against the commodification of human body parts fares no better than the Argument from Worth. In *Lectures on Ethics* he writes,

> Man cannot dispose over himself because he is not a thing; he is not his own property; to say that he is would be self-

contradictory; for in so far as he is a person he is a Subject in whom the ownership of things can be vested, and if he were his own property, he would be a thing over which he could have ownership. But a person cannot be a property and so cannot be a thing which can be owned, for it is impossible to be a person and a thing, the proprietor and the property.

Accordingly, a man is not at his own disposal. He is not entitled to sell a limb, not even one of his teeth.[25]

Kant's view here (in what I shall term the 'Argument from Contradiction') is that something cannot be both property and proprietor of that same property, for the proprietor of property must be distinct from it. Since Kant holds that a person's body parts are partially constitutive of the person (the basis of second construal of the Argument from Worth) there is no separation between the person and their body parts in the way required for the latter to be the property of the former. Hence, a person's body parts are not objects they can dispose of, and so they should not be commodified.

The first problem with this argument was noted by Ruth Chadwick, who points out that Kant recognizes the following possible objection to his view that a person can have duties to themself:

If the I that imposes obligation is taken in the same sense as the I that is put under obligation, the concept of duty to oneself is a self-contradictory concept. For the concept of duty contains the notion of being passively constrained (I am bound). But if the duty is a duty to myself, I think of myself as binding and so as actively constraining ... hence a contradiction.[26]

Despite this, Chadwick notes that Kant goes on to assert that *nevertheless* persons have self-regarding duties. Since this is so, she argues, 'It seems open to the would-be seller of a kidney to retort as follows: if a man can both owe and be owed a duty to himself, why cannot he be both owner and property?'[27]

Chadwick's response to the Argument from Contradiction accepts Kant's view that if a person owns his body parts then the proprietor and the property will be coextensive. But, as I argued above, it seems that Kant does not really believe that a person's body parts are always partially constitutive in the way that is assumed in the Argument from Contradiction. Although Kant holds that someone's body parts cannot be treated as things since they are not separable from them as a person, he allows that a person can treat their body parts as things if it is necessary for the preservation of their life. Since such preservation encompasses not only the removal of diseased body parts, but also the divestiture of such non-essential body parts as might be required to avoid a death that is threatened for other reasons, it seems that persons can potentially treat *any* non-essential body part as a thing. This point is reinforced by Kant's discussion of circumcision, in which he implies that it would not be immoral for a person to have his foreskin removed even if this was not done to save his life. But if this is so, then any non-essential part of a person's body could legitimately be regarded as separate, and hence as a commodifiable object that can be disposed of.

Kant and the Donation of Body Parts

I have asserted that neither of the above Kantian arguments against the commodification of human body parts is satisfactory. Yet if they had been, both the Argument from Worth and the Argument from Contradiction would have rendered immoral not just the sale of human body parts, but their donation, too. As Kant explicitly recognized, to donate a body part is also to treat it as a thing. This is often overlooked by persons who invoke Kant's arguments against the sale of organs to support their anti-market positions, and yet who wish to encourage the practice of organ donation.[28] Thus, if one believes that the donation of human organs is morally permissible, one should object to the Kantian position on the sale of human body parts on the grounds that they have counterintuitive conclusions – unless one can show that while the *sale* of human body parts is contrary to the Kantian position, their *donation* is compatible with it.[29]

This latter anti-market, pro-donation approach to understanding the Kantian position has been adopted by Mario Morelli, who argues 'on a Kantian view, selling a body part is not respecting one's humanity, whereas donating an organ

may not be objectionable, at least sometimes.'[30] Morelli
writes:

> The short answer [why this is so] is, I think, that selling oneself or
> part of oneself is always treating oneself as a mere means. It is
> treating oneself as an object with a market price, and thus a
> commodity. The transaction, the selling, is done for the receipt of
> the money to be obtained ... It is not simply the giving up of a
> body part that is objectionable: it is giving it up for the reason of
> monetary gain.[31]

Since this is so, Morelli continues, the donation of a kidney
would be morally acceptable to one who adopted this
Kantian position because 'One is not using oneself as a
mere means if one donates a kidney for such beneficent
purposes.'[32] Morelli's argument rests on two distinctions.
The first is between 'treating oneself as an object with a
market price' and not treating oneself in this way. The second
distinction is between a body part that is given up 'for the
reason of monetary gain' and one that is given up for some
other reason, such as beneficence. Morelli argues that the
Kantian view would regard the former way of treating
oneself, and the former reason for giving up a body part, as
immoral, but would regard the latter way of treating oneself,
and the latter reason for giving up a body part, as morally
acceptable. Thus, claims Morelli, while proponents of the
Kantian view would condemn the sale of body parts, they
could sometimes condone their donation.

  Neither of these distinctions holds. To address Morelli's
first distinction, he seems correct to note that Kant believed
that a person should not treat their body parts as though they
were things with a price, on the grounds that they are
partially constitutive of their person and so share in its
dignity. (Although see my concerns about this construal of
Kant's view, above.) However, he is wrong to claim that if a
body part is not given a market price (that is, it is not
commodified in the narrow sense of this term) then it is not
being treated as if it had a price, for this construes the
Kantian conception of price too narrowly. As I noted above,
for Kant a thing has a price if 'something else can be put in its
place as an equivalent.' Thus, if human body parts are treated

as interchangeable then they are being treated as though they had a price in the Kantian sense, *whether or not* they are actually given a market price. Since this is so, Morelli's claim that a Kantian would morally distinguish between body parts that are donated for transplantation into another and those that are sold for the same purpose, on the grounds that the latter are being impermissibly treated as things with a price whereas the former are not, is mistaken.

Just as Morelli's first distinction evinces a mistaken understanding of Kant's views, so too does his second. Morelli holds that while Kant would morally disallow someone giving up body parts 'for the reason of monetary gain' he would permit a person to give them up for some other reason. However, as I argued above, it is not clear that Kant would condemn the selling of a body part for monetary gain if this was done to preserve the life of the person in question. Moreover, if Morelli is right and Kant would allow a person to remove a body part for beneficent reasons, then it seems that he should also allow a person to sell a body part in order to raise money to be used beneficently. And if this is so, then one cannot properly distinguish on Kantian grounds (as Morelli wishes to) between the sale of an organ and its donation.

Morelli, then, is wrong to believe that a proponent of the Kantian view would recognize a bright line between the sale of body parts and their donation, and would condemn the former while sometimes condoning the latter. Therefore, he has not rescued the Kantian position from its counterintuitive anti-donation stance. Given this, and given the serious difficulties that the Kantian arguments against the commodification of human body parts face, those who oppose current markets in human kidneys on moral grounds but who endorse the altruistic donation of these organs should look elsewhere for an argument against their commodification.

The Domino Argument or Effect

One does not, however, need to accept the Kantian views outlined above to oppose the commodification of human kidneys. Instead, one might argue that if human body parts were commodified they would lose their status as things that are 'priceless,' or 'beyond price.' If this occurs, if body parts become just another market commodity, then, one might continue, there would be no opportunity for persons to give their body parts to another as a 'pure gift' with no market price, for such a gift would be considered to be equivalent in worth to the market price of the body parts given. The elimination of this opportunity might then be considered to be immoral for consequentialist reasons. One might, for example, argue that the loss of this opportunity would compromise the autonomy of many potential donors, or that it would reduce the supply of body parts by adversely affecting donor motivation, or that the body parts that would be procured in the absence of this opportunity would be of poor quality. One might also argue that the loss of the opportunity to donate one's priceless body parts to others would undermine social cohesion and fellowship.

All of these arguments are based on the view that the commodification of kidneys would lead to their losing their status as priceless entities that cannot be secured through the market, and all have been marshalled to oppose a current market in human kidneys. They have been made famous by Richard Titmuss, who used them to argue against the commercial provision of blood in his book *The Gift Relationship*. I will not address all of these arguments in this chapter. Instead, I will focus here on the claim that underlies them – namely, that the commodification of human body parts would lead to people viewing the worth of body parts primarily in market terms, and that this would eliminate the opportunity for persons to donate a 'pure' gift of their body parts to another. This has been dubbed the 'domino argument' by Margaret Jane Radin. I will then consider the view that if this claim were true, then the commodification of human body parts would adversely affect social cohesion. I will address the other arguments, concerning autonomy and the quantity and quality of kidneys that would be procured in a current market, in the next chapter.

In Radin's view, the domino argument consists of two claims: that noncommodified versions of some things are morally preferable to their commodified equivalents, and that 'commodified and noncommodified versions of some inter-actions cannot coexist,' for the commodifed version will drive out the noncommodified version.[33] Eric Mack has pointed out that the core of the domino argument proper is the second (empirical) claim, for one can accept the first claim while remaining dubious about the second.[34] Understood in this way, the domino argument proper consists of two premises and a conclusion. The first premise is that one must think of any given good either in market terms (that is, it has a price, in the non-Kantian, colloquial sense) or in non-market terms (it is priceless). The second premise is that if there were to be a market in any given good then this good would come to be thought of in terms of its market price, even if it were also exchanged through non-market means. For example, if there were to be a market in kidneys, then my donating a kidney to a needy relative would be thought of in terms of my giving them the amount of money equivalent to its market price. These premises lead to the conclusion that if there were to be a market for a certain good then this would come to dominate the non-market transactions of that good, in that even though market and non-market transactions of that good could co-exist, they would all come to be thought of in market terms.[35] The market exchanges of that good would 'contaminate' the non-market exchanges of it and change their social meaning. This, Mack observes, results in the concern 'that actions and relations that are not appropriately perceived and evaluated in monetary terms … will come to be so perceived and evaluated.'[36] Thus, to prevent such inappropriate valuation, certain services and goods should not be commodified.

Mack Against the Domino Effect

Against the view that the domino effect is a natural result of commodification, Mack argues that market and non-market exchanges of the same good can coexist without the meaning of the latter being affected by the former. To illustrate this Mack offers two examples: his giving a nice wool sweater to his wife as a gift, and his donating a pint of his blood to a friend in hospital.[37] In both of these cases Mack asks his readers to imagine that the market price of the gift was $50. He then notes that if he holds the value of the sweater or the blood to be strictly equivalent to $50, then he would be indifferent as to whether he gave his wife the sweater or $50, and indifferent as to whether he gave his friend the blood or the $50. But he is not so indifferent. This is not, Mack notes, because he is a victim of commodity fetishism and enjoys shopping, or because he paternalistically prefers his tastes in women's sweaters to his wife's. Rather, his lack of indifference in these cases can be explained by the fact that

> what one sometimes cares about is being engaged in a certain activity or relation. One wants to please a loved one, express one's affection in a way that especially exemplifies one's sense of another individual, or to stand by a friend in a personal way that directly responds to what he has undergone.[38]

In such cases, then, the exchanges of goods are understood by those participating in them as being expressive of the relationships that they are in. Owing to the importance of these relationships to these participants, the social meanings of these exchanges are given wholly by these relationships, uninfluenced by the fact that what is being exchanged is a market commodity. Mack's point here is not simply that the market mode of evaluation *is* conceptually distinct from its non-market equivalent, such that this conceptual compartmentalization provides a barrier to market exchanges of a certain good, leading to its being seen merely as a commodity with a market price.[39] Instead, Mack's point is that *it is natural* for humans to recognize the distinction between these different modes of evaluation. It is the naturalness of this distinction that explains why it is so easy to see that Mack would not be indifferent to giving his wife a sweater or his friend the blood that he needs, rather than giving them the cash equivalent of these gifts. Our natural tendency as humans to compartmentalize these different modes of evaluation also explains why it is that when neoclassical economists write of, for example, love, marriage and the desire for children in terms of market interactions this, as Radin notes, 'seems very strange to many people.'[40] Given humans' natural tendency to make this distinction the market is not as imperialistic as the domino argument suggests, for there are certain areas of human interaction where its influence is unfelt. Thus, it need *not* be the case that a current market for human kidneys would lead to a situation in which all exchanges of kidneys would be understood primarily in market terms; a situation in which the gift of a kidney would be inappropriately perceived and evaluated in monetary terms.

Why the Scope of Mack's Argument is Too Narrow

Yet although Mack's response to the domino argument appears decisive, its scope might be narrower than it first appears. In support of his view that the market is not as imperialistic as the domino argument suggests Mack utilizes examples of persons who exchange goods and who are involved in close personal relationships. In these relationships 'giving comes naturally,' for, in David Archard's words, '[W]hat it is to be another's friend or lover is just that one wants to please them or stand by them.'[41] Archard accepts that Mack is right to note that 'monetary values will not contaminate the exchanges between persons in such relationships,' for these relationships 'are impermeable to monetary understandings.'[42] But this, Archard argues, is not true of social relationships between persons who do not know each other, and who are related only insofar as they are members of the same society. Such relationships are vulnerable to having any exchanges that take place between their participants being understood in purely monetary terms if what is being exchanged is commodified, for they are not defined in non-market terms. Unlike the personal relationships of the sort that Mack focuses on, then, there is nothing in the nature of such relationships that makes any exchanges that take place within them impervious to a market understanding. Since this is so, a further argument based on the domino effect could be constructed. The first premise of this argument is that these impersonal social relationships are morally important. (For example, it is claimed that it is morally important that strangers behave altruistically towards each other.) The second is that these relationships would be weakened or undermined if the exchanges that took place within them were understood in purely monetary terms. If these two premises are true, then there is reason not to expand the market realm through the commodification of things that are both exchanged in these relationships, and that are currently uncommodified.

Commodification and the Meanings of Exchanges

Archard's criticism that Mack's argument is based on an over-rapid generalization, from personal relationships that are invulnerable to market imperialism to social relationships that are not so invulnerable, is certainly correct. However, recognizing this should not lead one to dismiss Mack's views concerning the domino argument and its implications for the proper realm of the market. This is because there are two questions here that are still to be resolved. Is it true that the commodification of a certain good would alter the meaning of exchanges of that good between persons who exchange it within an impersonal social relationship, such that a 'pure' gift between such persons is no longer possible? And, if so, does this matter?

The answer to the first question is less than dogmatic: it depends on the persons involved in the exchange. Although Archard is right to criticize Mack for generalizing too much from his examples of exchanges made within intimate relationships, Mack is right that many non-market exchanges between persons who only have an impersonal social relationship are invulnerable to the domino argument. Just as Mack would not accomplish what he set out to do if he gave his wife $50 instead of the sweater he bought her, so too would some persons who donate their kidneys in a situation where kidneys can also be bought fail to achieve their ends merely by donating the cash equivalent of their kidneys. This claim is not, moreover, merely speculative, for the world is replete with examples of persons donating their time and their body parts who are not indifferent between these donations and the giving of their cash equivalents. A lawyer who works pro bono for the poor, a bioethicist who donates time to consult with local hospitals and a person who donates blood to strangers where this could be bought are all unlikely to view their gifts as having the same meaning as the donation of their market values.

Mack, then, is right that the realm of exchanges that are invulnerable to market imperialism is larger than the proponents of the domino argument explicitly recognize, since how persons view the exchanges that they participate in (and hence what type of exchanges these are) is coloured by their motivations for engaging in them. But, since this is so, then he should accept that for some people (that is, those who desire to exchange a noncommodifed good) the commodification of a good that was previously uncommodified *would* colour the nature of their exchanges of it in the way that proponents of the domino argument envisage. For such persons, the meaning of the donation of a kidney in a situation where these are traded would be different from that of the same donation in a situation where they were not. Thus, whereas in the latter case these persons would regard their donation as being priceless, in the former case they would be indifferent between the donation of a kidney and the donation of its cash equivalent.

Commodification and Fellowship

This last point leads to the second question posed above: does it matter if, for some, the commodification of a certain good (here, human transplant kidneys) entails that they cannot give this good as a pure gift? Richard Titmuss thought that it did, on the grounds that 'The social relations set up by gift-exchange are amongst the most powerful forces which bind a social group together.' For Titmuss, since such a 'sense of community attachment' was of great moral importance, it should be strengthened through public policy that facilitates such giving – and so any expansion of the market that would work against this should be opposed.[43]

Yet even if one accepts Titmuss's views concerning the moral importance of social fellowship, it is not clear that commodification would undermine this, even if it precluded some (but not all) persons from giving 'pure' gifts. Imagine the case of someone who would be motivated to gift a certain good only if it were 'pure,' and who would not consider it a pure gift if it were of a commodified good. If the good this person was interested in giving were to be commodified, they would not give it. However, if they were *generally* altruistic, this would not affect their future altruism in general; it would just preclude them from performing this particular altruistic act. Their 'sense of community attachment' is unlikely to be weakened. If, however, the person were only interested in acting altruistically on *this* occasion, they would lose their sole chance to be altruistic. But their sense of community attachment would not be affected by the commodification of the good they wished to give, either. This person was not generally inclined to be altruistic before this good was commodified, and they are not generally inclined to be altruistic after this occurred.

These examples cast considerable doubt on the view that the expansion of commodification would undermine persons' sense of community. Perhaps, one might argue, requiring persons to be altruistic would habituate them into behaving this way. This might be true. However, it is difficult to see how this is applicable to debates over the commodification of human body parts such as blood and kidneys, since these are goods that persons are unlikely to consider donating unless they are *already* strongly inclined to act altruistically. Such donations would thus only occur after such habituation has successfully taken place, and not as part of the habituating process. Without further arguments to establish a relationship between the expansion of the realm of the market and a decline in social fellowship, then, the concern that 'the commercialization of ... donor relationships represses ... [person's] ... expression of altruism, [and] erodes ... [their] ... sense of community' seems unfounded.[44]

Conclusion

I have argued in this chapter that the Kantian objections to the commodification of the human body are unpersuasive, that the market is not as imperialistic as advocates of the domino argument suggest and that worries that the expansion of commodification would lead to a weaker 'sense of community' are misplaced. However, I have also conceded that, for some persons at least, the commodification of previously uncommodified goods would alter the social meaning of exchanges of these goods. This is an important concession, for it allows opponents of a current market in human kidneys to argue that the market's alteration of kidneys from priceless goods to items with a market price would compromise the autonomy of at least some potential donors, and reduce the number and quality of organs procured. I will now consider these arguments.

Notes

1   Brecher (1990), p. 122. See also Brecher (1991), p. 99.
2   Cohen (2002), pp. 53–4.
3   The concern that it is unjust to compensate the surgical staff but not the donor was expressed by Smith II, George (1993). Cited in Price, David (2000), p. 413.
4   Manga p. 325. Manga was not specifically referring to the articles cited above.
5   The independence of these two senses of commodification is noted by Wilkinson, Stephen (2000), p. 191.
6   Radin (1996), pp. 12, 13.
7   Ibid., p. 118.
8   Ibid.
9   Ibid.
10 Ibid., pp. 34, 35.
11 In Radin (2001) the author accepts that her exegesis of Kant's view in *Contested Commodities* (1996) is not entirely correct; p. 307.
12 Immanuel Kant (1930), p. 124.
13 Kant (2003), p. 177 (emphasis added).
14 Kant (1930), p. 124
15 Ibid., pp. 124, 148–54. See also (2003), pp. 176–8 and (2001), p. 38.
16 Chadwick (1989), p. 132.

17   Kant (2001), p. 42.
18   Kant (1930), p. 166.
19   Charles Fried has a similar objection to the sale of human tissue: 'What is disturbing ... about selling human tissue is that the seller treats his body as a foreign object ... It is thus not the sale itself which is disturbing, but the treatment of the body as a separate, separable entity.' Fried (1978), p. 142.
20   Kant (1930), p. 149.
21   Ibid., p. 116.
22   Chadwick, p. 134.
23   One could argue that Kant's focus is on organs that are necessary for the proper functioning of the human body, and that since a foreskin is not so necessary any discussion of Kant's views concerning circumcision are peripheral to his arguments against the removal of body parts. But this overlooks the fact that a foreskin *is* functional, serving to prevent the glans from injury and becoming keratinized.
24   Kant (2001), p. 42.
25   Kant (1930), p. 165.
26   Kant (2003), p. 173.
27   Chadwick, p. 133.
28   See Gerrand, Nicole (1999), p. 61.
29   Gerald Dworkin objects to Fried's argument against the sale of human tissue on these grounds, arguing that it would counter-intuitively preclude the donation of human tissue. Dworkin (1994), p. 160.
30   Morelli, Mario (1999), p. 320.
31   Ibid.
32   Ibid.
33   Radin (1996), p. 95.
34   Mack, Eric (1989), p. 202.
35   This outline of the domino argument follows that of Archard, David (2002), pp. 93–4.
36   Mack, p. 209.
37   Ibid., pp. 209–10.
38   Ibid., p. 210.
39   This is how Adrian Walsh construes Mack's position, in Walsh (2001), p. 541. Drawing on this construal of Mack's view Walsh claims that Mack's error in criticizing the domino effect was to 'assume that conceptual irreducibility is sufficient to ensure, as a matter of sociological fact, that distinct concepts will not be conflated.' I offer a more charitable construal of Mack's view on which there is support for his 'assumption.'
40   Radin (1996), p. 1.
41   Archard, p. 100.
42   Ibid., p. 101.
43   Titmuss, p. 126.
44   Ibid., p. 264.

Chapter 8
Commodification, Altruism and Kidney Procurement

In the previous chapter I conceded that, for some persons, the commodification of previously non-market goods such as human transplant kidneys would alter the social meaning of exchanges of these goods. This concession provides the basis for three additional arguments that opponents of markets in human body parts have developed: that commodification would compromise the autonomy of some potential donors, that it would reduce the number of organs procured, and that it would reduce the quality of the organs procured, with these last two effects adversely affecting both the autonomy and the well-being of their potential recipients. These arguments are important for two reasons. First, since the publication of Richard Titmuss's *The Gift Relationship* in 1970 they have become highly influential within the debate over the moral permissibility of markets in human body parts. Second, they shift the focus of this debate from concerns about the autonomy and well-being of potential vendors to concerns about potential recipients, or those who want 'purely' to donate their kidneys in a situation where they could not be bought. Thus, even if it can be shown that allowing a market in human body parts (for example, kidneys) is required by respect for the autonomy and well-being of the would-be vendors, concern for these values might still militate against such a market if it would compromise the autonomy and well-being of both the recipients of bought body parts, and the would-be 'pure' donors.

In this chapter I will argue that none of these anti-market arguments are sound. I will argue that not only would the autonomy of the would-be pure donors fail to be compromised by the commodification of the body parts that they wished to donate, but that the prohibition of a market itself would compromise the autonomy of some persons subjected to it. I will also argue that in a regulated market the quality of the body parts that are commercially procured would be just as good (if not better) than those that would be procured through altruistic donation. The concern that the commercial procurement of body parts would adversely affect the autonomy and well-being of their recipients is thus misplaced. If one is concerned with personal autonomy and human well-being, then, one should support, rather than condemn, the claim that a regulated current market in human kidneys is morally permissible.

Organs Should Only be Procured Through Altruistic Donation

The standard view is that human body parts for transplantation should only be procured through their altruistic donation and not through commercial means. The United Kingdom's General Medical Council, for example, has declared that 'any donation of organs must be made altruistically, as a gift,'[1] while the World Medical Association avows that the 'The expression of compassionate concern for others suffering from ill health and disability through *voluntary altruistic giving* is a fundamental value for organ and tissue donation.'[2] Similarly, the Transplantation Society holds that 'It must be established by the patient and transplant team alike that the motives of the donor are *altruistic* ...'[3] while the British medical journal *The Lancet* has opined 'that altruism is a fundamental principle behind organ donation ... '[4] This professional emphasis on the necessity of altruistic donation is also a recurrent theme in discussions of the ethics of organ procurement. P.J. Morris and R.A. Sells, for example, boldly state 'The only circumstances where a kidney may be removed ethically from a living donor is when *it is a gift* to the recipient.'[5] Similarly, both Siminoff and Chillag, and Cameron and Hoffenberg, recognize that at the heart of many anti-markets arguments lies the view that 'the entire organ donation system' is, and should be, based on 'the ethic of voluntarism and altruism,'[6] in which 'organs are priceless and should be donated for altruistic reasons.'[7]

Although the view of altruistic donation appears straight-forward, it requires clarification. According to its proponents the altruistic motive that leads a person to provide a body part for transplant must have as its object the performance of an altruistic act for its recipient. Therefore, it is morally impermissible for a person to sell a body part *even if* the vendor was motivated by altruism where this altruism was directed at a person *other than* the recipient of that body part. The provision of an organ must thus be motivated by *direct* altruism (that is, altruism directed towards the recipient of the body part) and not by *indirect* altruism directed towards the well-being of someone other the recipient. Proponents of this view would thus condemn a person such as, for example, the Turkish father who wanted to sell a kidney to purchase medical care for his four-year-old daughter.[8] On the standard view, then, being moved to provide a kidney to another out of altruism (which could include the altruistic sale) is not enough for one's act to be morally permissible. One must be motivated by a certain *type* of altruism.

Direct Altruism Protects Donor Autonomy

The first argument for the view that transplant organs should only be procured through direct altruism can be drawn directly from Titmuss's *The Gift Relationship*, in which he argued that the British system of procuring blood for medical use through altruistic donation alone was superior to the commercial system used in America. In part, Titmuss argued, this was because the British system provided more freedom to its donors (and potential donors) than its American counter-part for ' ... private market systems in the United States and other countries ... deprive men of their freedom to choose to give or not to give ... '[9] Unfortunately, Titmuss did not explain why. This unclarity in his view is compounded by the fact that the most obvious construal of his position (that is, that commercial systems 'deprive men of their freedom to choose to give or not to give,' and so reduce their opportunities for exercising autonomy) is clearly false.[10] However, rather than understanding Titmuss's claim to be that if the option of selling blood was added to the option of donating blood then this would deprive persons of the option to donate (which is false), it should instead be understood as claiming that if the option to sell was added to the option of donating this would deprive persons of the option *to donate blood in a situation where this cannot be bought*. As Peter Singer puts it,

> The right that Titmuss sees threatened is not a simple right to give, but the right to give 'in non-material as well as material ways.' This means not merely the right to give money for some commodity that can be bought or sold for a certain amount of money, but the right to give something that cannot be bought, that has no cash value, and must be given freely if it is to be obtained at all. This right, if it is a right—it would be better to say, this freedom—really is incompatible with the freedom to sell, and we cannot avoid denying one of those freedoms when we grant the other.[11]

Singer's construal of Titmuss's argument against the commercial procurement of blood can be readily altered to oppose the commercial procurement of kidneys, since the introduction of a commercial system of kidney procurement would similarly eliminate the option to donate a kidney in a situation where kidneys cannot be bought. Since this is so, the introduction of a commercial system of organ procurement would, on the Titmuss–Singer view, result in persons being less free than they were prior to this, insofar as they can no longer give 'priceless' (uncommodified) kidneys. This argument thus concludes that concern for the freedom of potential donors requires the prohibition of a commercial system of kidney procurement.

Although this argument is couched in terms of the potential donor's freedom to donate a priceless kidney, it could equally well be couched in terms of donor autonomy. To say that a person's being less free to act as they wish is simply to say that their ability to exercise autonomy as they wish is diminished. Couching the argument in these terms, then, the introduction of a current market for human kidneys would appear to restrict the ability of those persons who wished to give a priceless kidney to exercise their autonomy as they wished.[12]

Responses to the Titmuss–Singer Argument

This Titmuss–Singer argument from donor autonomy focuses on the effect that the introduction of a new option into people's choice-sets (that is, to sell a kidney) would have on the ability of persons with certain *particular* preference structures (namely, to give a kidney in a situation where this could not be bought) to exercise their autonomy. However, given that the debate over whether to introduce a current market for human kidneys is concerned with the effects that this would have on the ability of *all* persons who are affected by this market to exercise their autonomy, this focus is misguided. This inquiry into the effects that such a market would have on the autonomy of those affected by it should take a broader approach. It should focus on whether it is morally permissible to introduce the option to sell a kidney into the choice-set that is possessed by many *different* persons with *different* preference structures, where this choice-set currently only contains the option to donate their kidneys.

Thus it is evident that a defender of autonomy should decide whether to introduce the option to sell a kidney into persons' choice-sets on the basis of whether this is required out of respect for the autonomy of those who would be affected by this, or whether respect for autonomy requires that this market be prohibited. This inquiry can be broken down further into two separate (but related) questions. First, is the introduction of such a market required by concern for the *instrumental* value of the autonomy that is enjoyed by those persons it would affect, or does this concern support its continued prohibition? Second, is the introduction of such a market required by respect for the *intrinsic* value of these persons' autonomy, or does such respect support continued prohibition?[13]

Prohibition and the Instrumental Value of Personal Autonomy

Those concerned with the first of these questions will focus on one simple issue: whether the introduction of a current market for human kidneys would lead to a greater or lesser number of persons being free to exercise their autonomy in the way that, given their situations, they would prefer to than were able to prior to this. And it seems evident that such a market would lead to more persons being free to exercise their autonomy in the way they wished, given their situations. If persons were allowed to sell their kidneys in a regulated current market they would lose the option altruistically to give away a kidney in a situation where kidneys cannot be bought. However, they would now have an option (to sell) that they were previously denied, *as well as* the option altruistically to give away the money secured through this sale, *and* the option altruistically to give away a kidney that has a certain determinate price. By contrast, if persons were prohibited from selling their kidneys, they would be denied all three of the options outlined above, and would only have the single option altruistically to give away a kidney in a situation where one cannot be bought. Allowing persons to sell their kidneys in a regulated market, then, would provide them with more ways to exercise their autonomy (where these ways are not autonomy-compromising constraining options) than would prohibiting them from doing this. Since this is so, it is likely that the instrumental value of the autonomy of those individuals whose decisions would be affected by this change would increase overall.

As it stands, however, this response to the Titmuss–Singer position is not yet complete. That persons would have more options to exercise their autonomy if they were able to sell their kidneys does not show that they would be better off vis-à-vis exercising that autonomy. It might be that their options *after* the introduction of such a market *would not* be options they would wish to pursue, whereas the option they *lost* after such a market was introduced (that is, to donate a priceless kidney) *would* have been one that some would have wanted to pursue. If so, then the introduction of the option to sell would have diminished, rather than increased, the instrumental value of their autonomy. While this is a legitimate concern, the evidence from both Iran and India indicates that it is likely to be unfounded. This evidence suggests that more persons would wish to exercise their autonomy in one (or more) of the three ways that a current market in human transplant kidneys would allow than would prefer to exercise it by altruistically donating a kidney in a situation where such cannot be bought. It thus seems that allowing a current market in human transplant kidneys would be to allow more persons to exercise their autonomy as they see fit than would this market's prohibition. Therefore, if one respects personal autonomy, one should hold that a current market for human kidneys is morally required.[14]

Prohibition and the Intrinsic Value of Personal Autonomy

The second response to the Titmuss–Singer argument focuses on the *actual* degree of autonomy that persons would respectively possess under a market and a non-market regime, rather than the degree to which their autonomy would be instrumentally valuable to them under these regimes. The proponents of this response argue that prohibiting kidney sales would compromise the autonomy of those who wish to sell their kidneys, but who would be prevented from doing so. Moreover, they argue, allowing persons to sell their kidneys *would not* compromise the autonomy of those who wish altruistically to make a 'pure' kidney donation. If these two claims are true, then respect for the intrinsic value of personal autonomy requires that a current market for human kidneys should be introduced into a situation where it is absent.

The argument for the two claims that provide the basis for this second response to the Titmuss–Singer position is straightforward. If a person is prohibited from selling one of their kidneys, and this prohibition is effective in preventing them from doing so, then they will have been *coerced* into not selling. This would-be vendor would have decided not to resist the penalties they were threatened with to enforce the prohibition on kidney sales. They would thus have ceded a degree of control over a subset of their actions (that is, those relating to the sale or retention of the kidney) to those threatening them (the state) in order to exercise control over this subset of their actions through such threats. This would-be kidney vendor's autonomy with respect to this subset of their actions would thus be compromised (as I maintained in Chapter 3) because someone else would be exerting control over whether or not they sold one of their kidneys.

Allowing a current market in human kidneys *would not*, however, compromise the autonomy of persons who would want altruistically to donate their kidneys in a situation where such cannot be bought. The introduction of such a market does not entail that the persons who introduce it do so with the intention of controlling the behaviour of those who want altruistically to donate a priceless kidney. As I argued in Chapter 3, for one person to influence another's behaviour in such a way that the first compromises the second's autonomy by usurping control over their actions, the first person must *intend* to usurp such control. Since persons who introduce a current market for human kidneys would *not* intend to control the actions of would-be 'pure' donors they would not exert control over the latter's actions by introducing such a market. Unlike the would-be kidney *sellers* in a situation where kidney markets were prohibited, then, the would-be pure *donors* in a market situation would retain full control over their actions, and so their autonomy would not be impaired. Instead, the introduction of a market for human kidneys would simply place them in a situation where they could no longer exercise their autonomy to satisfy one of their desires. They would thus only suffer from a diminution in the *instrumental* value of their autonomy if a market was introduced, and *not* from any compromise in their autonomy *per se*.

The prohibition of a current market in human kidneys would compromise the autonomy of some persons affected by it, whereas the introduction of a market would not. One who holds personal autonomy to be of intrinsic value, then, could object to such prohibition on the grounds that the instrumental value of the autonomy of would-be pure donors cannot be protected in this way if this would result in potential vendors suffering from impaired autonomy *simpliciter*, rather than just a diminution in its instrumental value.

A Commercial System Would Lead to Fewer Kidneys Being Procured

It seems, then, that irrespective of whether one holds personal autonomy to be intrinsically or instrumentally valuable, one has reason to reject the Titmuss–Singer anti-market argument from donor autonomy. Respect for personal autonomy thus still provides prima facie support for a current market for human transplant kidneys. However, when all things are considered, respect for autonomy might militate against the view that such a market is morally impermissible. If the introduction of such a market would result in fewer kidneys being procured, then more persons will die while waiting to receive a transplant organ than do under the current, altruistic procurement system. Since a person's death will (obviously) lead to loss of autonomy, then if the number of kidneys procured falls because of the introduction of a market, defenders of autonomy will have to determine if this loss of autonomy suffered by potential *recipients* is offset by the need to respect the autonomy of the potential *vendors*.[15] If it is not, defenders of autonomy should consider a current market for human kidneys to be morally impermissible.[16] A similar calculation will also have to be made by those who are primarily concerned with the value of human well-being.[17]

The concern that the introduction of a commercial system of organ procurement would lead to a decrease in the total number of organs procured is expressed by many of those who are morally opposed to using a current market to procure human kidneys. Their reasoning is that under a commercial system those persons who would have altruistically donated their organs (either pre- or post-mortem) would now refuse to do so, and that the consequent diminution in the number of organs procured through altruism would not be offset by the additional numbers procured through payment.[18] This worry is expressed by G.M. Abouna et al., who write that 'Paid organ donation ... will drown all voluntary donation by the public ... by accepting paid organ transplantation, not only will we be compromising our ethics, but we will lose the very battle which we are fighting to win, i.e., making more ... organs available.'[19] Similarly, Broyer claims that once it becomes 'possible to pay someone to donate' a kidney this will lead to 'the depreciation of voluntary free donation and its [eventual] disappearance.'[20]

At first sight the worry that paying for kidneys would diminish the total number that are procured might seem odd, for the introduction of a commercial system for procurement does not preclude persons from altruistically donating their kidneys, either pre- or post-mortem. As such, it seems that instead of diminishing the number of kidneys procured, purchasing them would only add to the number that are donated through direct altruism.[21] Yet although this is plausible, there is a considerable body of evidence to show that the introduction of payment for certain goods and services will partially 'crowd out' their procurement through direct altruism.[22] That is, there is evidence that people who will perform certain actions without payment would refuse to perform them for a low price, even if they would then agree to perform them if the price is raised enough. (Opponents of commercial procurement assume that the price offered for them would not be high enough to motivate those persons who would refuse to donate their kidneys if a commercial system was introduced to sell them.)[23] Gneezy and Rustichini, for example, have shown that when children who voluntarily collect for charity from house to house are paid a small amount of money for doing this the intensity of their work declines, although it increases again when the payment is subsequently increased.[24] Similarly, Upton reports the results of a study in which a payment of $10 for a pint of blood was offered to two groups of persons: those who had *regularly* given blood through direct altruism, and those who had *occasionally* given blood through direct altruism. The offer of payment substantially reduced the donation rates of the first group, while it slightly increased donations of the second group – a result that seems to bear out the anti-market view that commercial incentives will crowd out altruistic motives.[25]

The crowding out of direct altruism by economic incentives is thus a real phenomenon. Moreover, there is considerable evidence that economic incentives do significantly crowd out the direct altruistic donation of kidneys. For example, Abouna found that 50 per cent of Kuwaitis who purchased a kidney outside Kuwait had a potential related donor who 'disappeared' once it was discovered that kidneys could be purchased elsewhere.[26] Similarly, Ghods et al. found that out of 180 transplant patients at the Hashemi-Nejad Hospital in Iran 81 per cent had a potential related donor that they did not use.[27] This experience is especially instructive in demonstrating how a commercial system for organ procurement can crowd out altruistic donation. In 1986–87 the number of kidneys procured from living persons unrelated to the recipients was zero. In 1988, a system of payment for kidneys from living non-related 'donors' (that is, vendors) was introduced. In 1991–92 almost 73 per cent of all kidneys procured in the Hashemi-Nejad Hospital were from living non-related 'donors' (vendors).[28] Since the total number of kidneys procured at this hospital was almost the same during these periods it is clear that the number of organs transplanted in this hospital that were procured through direct altruistic donation fell considerably after this commercial system for kidney procurement was introduced.[29]

On reflection, that a commercial system for kidney procurement crowds out a significant number of direct altruistic donations by living donors is not surprising. Prior to the introduction of a commercial system the best chance that someone who needed a transplant had to secure one would be through the direct altruism of a relative. Since kidneys could not be bought, relatives might be willing to donate, as they would be giving the 'priceless gift of life' to the recipient. Once it is possible to purchase kidneys, however, this formerly priceless gift now has a price tag – and relatives might believe that its commercial value would not be worth the opportunity costs they would have to incur to donate. Moreover, once kidneys can be commercially procured those who need them might not wish to ask a relative to donate. Lawrence Cohen, for example, heard kidney recipients in India ask, 'Why should I put a family member I care about at risk by asking him or her to donate an organ when I can just buy one?'[30] Yet despite these reasons for the crowding out of altruistic donation by a current market for human transplant kidneys some direct altruistic donation will remain. In Iran, for example, in 1992–93 27 per cent of the kidneys procured were from direct altruistic donation by living persons related to the recipients.[31] This is also not surprising, for, as Mark J. Cherry notes, many of 'the motivations supporting such donations are likely to maintain the same force regardless of the existence of a for-profit market: love, beneficence, loyalty, gratitude, guilt, or avoidance of the shame of failing to donate.'[32]

Although it is likely that some transplant kidneys would still be procured through direct altruistic donation the available evidence indicates that the introduction of a current market would significantly crowd out direct altruistic donation. But this does not show that concern for the potential recipients of transplant kidneys militates against accepting that such a market is morally permissible, as the decrease in kidneys thus procured would be more than offset by the number that would become available in a current market for them.[33] The Iranian system of paying for kidneys has, for example, resulted in more than 8400 live organs being procured from persons unrelated to their recipients between 1988 and 2000, with the waiting list for kidney transplants in that country having been eliminated by the end of 1999.[34] Similarly, during Shapiro's research into the kidney trade in India several physicians informed him that prior to 1994, when kidney sales were legal in India, there were more willing vendors than there were buyers in areas (such as Bombay and Chennai) in which the kidney trade was prevalent.[35] This anecdotal evidence of the success of commercial systems in India is supported by the fact that after the trade was prohibited there was a sharp decrease in the number of kidney transplants performed there. For example, in the state of Karnataka the number fell from 354 in 1994 to 149 in 1995 (the year after the trade in kidneys was banned), rose slightly to 160 in 1996 and then rose again to 165 in the first 10 months of 1997.[36] Several hospitals in Tamil Nadu also reported a similar decline in the number of transplants performed after the banning of the kidney trade.[37] The evidence from both Iran and India, then, suggests that the introduction of a commercial system for kidney procurement would increase rather than decrease the numbers of kidneys that become available for transplantation.

Another concern is that introducing a commercial system would lower the overall number of cadaveric kidneys procured by reducing the incentive to create a system of cadaveric organ procurement.[38] There is, however, no evidence that a current market for human kidneys would adversely affect the development and maintenance of cadaver kidney procurement programmes. Indeed, since current markets in human kidneys are so widely condemned any legislature that legalized this trade might seek to establish a programme of cadaver kidney procurement as a way to disassociate themselves from the market system, to avoid alienating those sections of their constituency that oppose such markets. Of course, one could argue that just as current markets would crowd out the donation of kidneys from live donors, so too are they likely to crowd out the donation of cadaveric kidneys. But this concern can be met by noting that a current market for human kidneys could coexist with both a *futures* market and a market for *cadaveric* kidneys. Since the introduction of these latter markets would provide persons with an incentive to agree to have their organs used for transplantation after their deaths, it is likely that the introduction of market systems for kidney procurement would increase, rather than decrease, the number of cadaveric organs that are procured.[39]

Kidneys Procured in a Current Market Would be of Inferior Quality

In addition to the above concerns that surround the possibility of commodifying human transplant kidneys there is also concern that the quality of commercially procured kidneys would be worse than that of kidneys procured through a system of direct altruistic donation. At first sight, there is plenty of evidence to support this worry. For example, of 59 Kuwaitis who had received commercial kidney transplants in India and the Philippines that Abouna studied, six died, 13 lost their grafts through post-operative complications and a further 14 experienced serious surgical complications and/or other infections.[40] Sever et al. reported similarly dire results in India when they followed the progress of 34 Turks who had received commercial transplants.[41] Patients who have purchased kidneys on the black market have also been infected with tuberculosis, and A.S. Daar has reported a 1:18 incidence of HIV infection among Arab recipients of commercially procured kidneys in Bombay.[42]

The first point to make about these dire statistics is that they cannot indicate the extent to which the commercial procurement of kidneys secures organs that are of a lower quality than those secured through direct altruism. These cases represent only a very small fraction of the total number of transplantations performed in India using commercially procured kidneys. (It is estimated that more than 2000 kidneys were bought in the metropolitan centres of India in 1991, and over 3500 in 1994.)[43] It is thus impossible to say whether these cases are representative of the quality of commercially procured kidneys.

Yet, even if it is accepted that many commercially procured transplant kidneys have been of poor quality, this does not show that a current market would procure kidneys that are of worse quality than those procured in a system that depended entirely on altruism. This is because the quality of the kidneys is not affected in any way by the motives of the persons from whom they are taken. The mere fact that a kidney has been purchased rather than altruistically donated does not in itself indicate the quality of the organ. Rather, the quality of the kidney will depend solely on whether the provider suffered from a disease that would lead to risks for the recipient.[44] To ensure that procured kidneys are of a high quality, then, procurers should be provided with extrinsic incentives to ensure that the persons from whom the kidneys are procured are not suffering from any diseases that could be transmitted to the recipients of their kidneys.

Unfortunately, such incentives are lacking for many persons who currently commercially procure transplant kidneys. As is clear from the above accounts of the poor quality of transplant kidneys, many persons who receive a poor quality kidney will have purchased it (and undergone transplant) outside their own country, which makes it difficult for them to seek legal redress if they purchase a defective kidney. Moreover, such redress might be impossible if the purchase of a transplant kidney was illegal in either the recipient's own country, or the country in which the transplant took place. Since the recipients of commercial kidneys currently have little recourse against those from whom they purchased them, then (provided that persons desperate for transplants continue to be willing to take immense risks to receive them) those who procure commercial transplant kidneys have no extrinsic incentive to ensure that their products are of good quality. Instead, insofar as ensuring that the kidneys they procure are of good quality will require them to subject the initial vendors to medical examinations, those who illegally procure these kidneys have a financial incentive not to ensure that the organs are of good quality. By contrast, those who procure transplant kidneys from altruistic donors in (for example) Western Europe and the United States have strong extrinsic incentives to ensure high quality as they would be both legally and professionally liable if they transplanted diseased organs.

The question of whether a particular system of organ procurement will secure high- or low-quality transplant kidneys thus turns on whether the persons engaged to procure the kidneys have sufficient incentive to obtain good-quality kidneys, and not on how the kidneys are procured.[45] There is thus no reason why a current market could not procure kidneys that were as good as those procured through direct altruistic donation, provided that such a market offered the procurers sufficient extrinsic incentives to secure good-quality organs.[46] And the easiest way to provide such incentives is to make those who commercially procure kidneys legally liable for any injuries sustained by the recipients as a result of any defects in the kidneys that they purchased.[47]

   The view that a commercial system of kidney procurement could secure organs just as good as those secured through direct altruistic donation is not, however, merely based on 'blind faith' in the positive effects that could be brought about by incentives. It is also supported by evidence from the commercial system that operates in Iran. According to Ahad J. Ghods, 942 transplants using kidneys from living unrelated 'donors' (that is, vendors) were performed at the Hashemi-Nejad Hospital between April 1986 and July 2001, and their survival rates during this period were approximately 92, 85 and 72 per cent at one, five and ten years post-transplant respectively.[48] These results compare favourably to patient survival rates of persons who received kidney transplants from living donors in the United States between January 1989 and December 2001 – 92.5, 85 and 74.2 per cent at one, five and ten years post-transplant.[49] Graft survival rates for patients who received kidneys from living unrelated donors (vendors) at the Hashemi-Nejad Hospital during this period were approximately 87, 63 and 43 per cent at one, five and ten years post-transplant.[50] The equivalent figures for the United States are 93.1, 77.2 and 54.4 per cent.[51]

   Although these data show that the commercially based Iranian system of kidney procurement compares favourably to the altruism-based American system, two points must be noted before continuing. First, the UNOS (United Network for Organ Sharing) figures include patient and graft survival rates for kidneys received from both living *related* and living *unrelated* donors. The figures from the Hashemi-Nejad Hospital include only living *unrelated* 'donors' (vendors). Since both patient and graft survival rates are likely to be higher for kidneys received from living related donors, and since a significant majority of living kidney donors in the United States are related to the recipients of their organs, it is only to be expected that the UNOS data presented here show higher survival rates than those from the Hashemi-Nejad Hospital.[52] Second, the difference in graft survival rates between Iran and the United States is also partly explicable by differences in the health budgets enjoyed by these two countries. Indeed, Ghods explicitly notes, 'Some patient deaths and graft losses could have been prevented if our transplant unit were not deficient with respect to laboratory facilities, scientific consulting staff, and necessary drugs.'[53] Moreover, some of the transplant patients at the Hashemi-Nejad Hospital were from small towns and rural areas where long-term post-transplant care is difficult to achieve, and patient deaths and graft losses have been higher in this subpopulation of transplant recipients.[54] Similar problems are unlikely to confront the American hospitals that participate in UNOS, and against whose success the commercial system in Iran is here measured.

The success rate of the Iranian commercial transplantation programme is thus comparable to that of altruistically based programmes within the United States. Rather than procuring defective kidneys, then, a properly regulated current market for human transplant kidneys (that is, one in which those who procure the kidneys have incentives to secure good-quality organs) would procure organs of comparable quality to those secured through direct altruistic donation.

Conclusion

In this chapter I have argued that none of the three concerns that proponents of direct altruism express about current markets in human kidneys are well founded. First, respect for autonomy requires that persons be allowed to engage in a current market for human kidneys if they so wish, even if this precludes others from noncommercially donating 'priceless' kidneys. Second, although procuring kidneys through a current market for them will lead to some altruistic donations being crowded out, the reduction in the number of kidneys donated altruistically will be more than offset by the number that are procured through the market. Finally, it is not true that a commercial system of kidney procurement will lead to a reduction in the quality of the organs procured. Instead, a well-regulated market system could provide kidneys of the same quality as those procured through a system of direct altruistic donation by live donors.

This latter point is worth emphasizing. This chapter has focused on comparing the quality of kidneys that would be procured in a commercial system to the quality of kidneys procured from live donors. However, it must be stressed that most of the kidneys that are currently procured for transplant are *cadaveric* kidneys. Medically speaking, persons with end-stage renal disease are better off receiving kidneys from live unrelated donors than they are receiving unrelated cadaveric kidneys.[55] If a current market in human transplant kidneys secures enough organs from unrelated live donors so that unrelated cadaveric kidneys are no longer needed, then, this would result in those who need transplants receiving better-quality organs than they would have done in the absence of such a market. (And, of course, absent such a market they are less likely to receive a transplant at all.) Moreover, as Andrew Love has argued, the use of a current market would make it more likely that persons in certain ethnic groups would receive a transplant kidney.[56] In the United States, organ donors are likely to be Caucasian, and so it is more difficult to secure a transplant organ that is an immunological match for an African-American patient.[57] As Nancy Scheper-Hughes notes with concern, if an organ market is instituted it is likely that many of those who would participate in it as vendors would be *non*-Caucasians.[58] However, despite her concerns about this, kidneys in such a market would not only move 'from black ... bodies to white ones,' but also *between* non-Caucasians. This would increase the supply of kidneys that would be immunological matches for patients with certain ethnic backgrounds. A current market would thus be of greater comparable benefit to non-Caucasian patients than to their Caucasian counterparts because, for medical reasons, without such a market the former group would have even less chance of securing a transplant kidney than the latter.

Once again, then, it is clear that both respect for autonomy and concern for human well-being (here, of the kidney recipient) support the view that a current market for human transplant kidneys is morally permissible. However, this does not automatically support the claim that it should be legalized, for there might be reasons of public policy not to take this further step. This will be the subject of my concluding chapter.

Notes

1   *General Medical Council Supplement News Review* (1992), December, point 3.
2   World Medical Association (2000), section C.4 (emphasis added).
3   Transplantation Society Council (1986).
4   Editorial (2000), 'Altruism and confidentiality in organ donation,' *The Lancet*, 355, p. 765.
5   Morris, P.J. and Sells, R.A. (1998), p. 229 (emphasis added).
6   Siminoff, L.A. and Chillag, K. (1999), p. 34.
7   Cameron J. and Hoffenberg, R. (1999), p. 726. Cited by Wilkinson (2003), p. 109, who notes (p. 233, n. 34) that Cameron and Hoffenberg merely cite this position; they do not support it.
8   This case was reported in Ballantyne, A. and Howard, J. (1989).
9   Titmuss, p. 307. A similar point is made by Margaret Jane Radin, when she writes that commodifying objects (for example, kidneys) that were previously uncommodified will lead to persons being unable to 'freely give of themselves to others. At best they can bestow commodities ... ' Radin (1987), p. 1907.
10 This was noted by Arrow, Kenneth J. (1972), pp. 349–50. Walter Block similarly criticizes Radin's Titmussesque claim cited above. See Block (1999), p. 66.
11 Singer, Peter (1976), pp. 185–6.
12 None of the following responses to this argument rest on construing it in terms of autonomy rather than in terms of freedom.
13 Not every defender of autonomy will ask both of these questions, for there is no consensus as to whether personal autonomy should be valued intrinsically or instrumentally—or through some combination of these two approaches to its evaluation. The persons whose decisions would be affected by this change would, in this context, be those who would now decide not to donate a priceless kidney, those who would now decide to sell and those who would now decide to donate a kidney of a certain value.
14 This argument is conditional upon persons having certain motivations. As such, it is not a decisive objection to the Titmuss–Singer position for all possible worlds in which the debate over the moral permissibility of kidney markets could take place – although the evidence indicates that it is a decisive objection in *our* world.

15 The answer to this question for any given defender of autonomy will depend, in part, on whether they value autonomy primarily instrumentally or intrinsically.

16 Critics of market systems for procuring kidneys do not often focus on the loss of autonomy that the introduction of a current market would result in if it is true that fewer kidneys would be procured under such a system. However, one such autonomy-based anti-market argument can be drawn from Titmuss, pp. 308–309. See Plant, Raymond (1977), p. 168 for an outline of this understanding of Titmuss's argument.

17 One need not adopt such consequentialist reasoning to oppose a current market on the grounds that it will result in fewer kidneys being procured than in a system that relies on direct altruistic donation. One could, for example, hold that human life is sacred, and so that no matter how much more vendor autonomy and well-being there might be if such a market was introduced, if this would result in fewer kidneys being procured, and more potential recipients dying as a result, then such a market is objectionable.

18 This concern is most famously expressed by Titmuss with respect to the commercial procurement of blood. See Titmuss, p. 263.

19 Abouna, G.M. et al. (1991), p. 169, writing specifically of payment for cadaver organs.

20 Broyer, M. (1991), p. 199.

21 This response is implicit in Kenneth Arrow's remarks regarding Titmuss's version of this worry. See Arrow, pp. 349–51, 361. See also Barnett, Blair and Kaserman (1992), p. 374 and (2002), p. 91.

22 For an overview of this literature see Frey, Bruno and Jegen, R. (2001).

23 This assumption is not implausible if one understands those persons who would refuse to donate their kidneys if others were being paid for them to be from affluent countries, and those selling their kidneys to be from poorer countries. In this situation the prices paid for the kidneys would likely be too low to provide a significant incentive to members of the former group.

24 Gneezy, U. and Rustichini, A. (2000).

25 Upton, W (1973), cited by Hansmann, p. 68, n. 23. This result is compatible with the view that more blood would be procured overall if payment were made for it.

26 Abouna, G.M. (1993), p. 2311.

27 Ghods, A.J., Savaj, S. and Khosravani, P. (2000).

28 Broumand, B. (1997) and Zargooshi (2001a). Broumand states that this figure remained stable in 1992–93, when 70 per cent of all procured kidneys were from unrelated 'donors.' Although Broumand does not explicitly state that an unrelated living

kidney donor should be understood to be a vendor, that this is so is clear from his remarks in this paper. He has also confirmed this in personal conversation.

29   Joseph Shapiro notes that the constancy of the number of transplants performed might be because the programme at this hospital was working at capacity. See Shapiro (2003), p. 58. That the number of kidney transplants at this one hospital did not increase after a commercial system for organ procurement was introduced is thus compatible with it being the case that the overall number of kidney transplants performed in Iran rose as a result of the introduction of the commercial system.

30   Cohen, Lawrence (1999), p. 161.

31   Broumand, Table 1, p. 1831.

32   Cherry (2000b), p. 341.

33   It is thus untrue that the use of markets to procure human transplant organs 'will probably be ineffective, perhaps even counterproductive (in reducing donations and perhaps even the number of organs available for transplantation … ' Childress, J.F. (1992), p. 2145. When Childress expressed these concerns it would have been difficult to secure the data that I present below on the number of organs being sold in India and Iran, and so his worry was, at the time, legitimate.

34   Ghods, A.J. (2002), p. 224.

35   Shapiro, p. 59.

36   Staff writer (1997), 'Kidneys still for sale,' *The Hindu*, **14** (25), 13–26 December.

37   Ibid. For example, Dr R. Ravichandran of the Vijaya Health Centre, Chennai, reported a 25–30 per cent drop in the number of transplants performed there and at the Malar Hospital after kidney sales were banned, while Dr K.C. Reddy of Willingdon Hospital reported a 40 per cent drop.

38   See, for example, Broyer, p. 199.

39   Claims concerning the effects that commercial systems of kidney procurement would have on the number of cadaveric kidneys procured are largely speculative, owing to the limited availability of evidence. Some empirical support for the view that a futures market in human organs would increase supply is given by Adams, Frank A., Barnett, A. H. and Kaserman, David L. (1999), whose survey of Auburn University (Alabama) students that showed that in 1996 the market clearing price for cadavers for use as organ providers would be $1000. Adams et al., however, are clear that these results should not be taken as conclusive. Moreover, Margaret Bryne and Peter Thompson charge that surveys such as this should be discounted. Byrne and Thompson (2001). When retrieving organs healthcare professionals will ask the relatives of the potential provider if they agree to the harvesting of the organs. If the relatives know that the deceased was given a reward to register as a donor, it is

likely, Bryne and Thompson argue, that they will discount the deceased's expressed wish to have their organs retrieved on the grounds that this might not be these persons' 'real' desire. One response to this criticism would simply be to have enforceable contracts for organ retrieval, irrespective of relatives' views – or else the relatives could 'buy out' the company retrieving the organs. In the absence of any real markets in cadaveric organs, however, such debates remain speculative.

40   Abouna (1990), p. 918.

41   Sever, M.S. et al. (1994).

42   Daar, A.S. (1991). See also Abouna et al., p. 165 and Chugh, Kirpal S. and Jha, Vivekanand (1996), p. 1183.

43   Chugh and Jha, p. 1183, where the authors cite Kandela, P. (1991), p. 1534 as their source for the 1991 figure.

44   This point opposing Titmuss's argument against the commercial procurement of blood was quoted in Kessel, Reuben (1976), p. 190.

45   Unfortunately, the incentives that are in place for procurers of human body parts in the noncommercial systems of the United States and Western Europe do not always ensure that these systems procure the safest parts that are available. For example, when it became clear in late 1982 that a new disease (HIV) might be spreading through blood products, the blood banks that operated through voluntary donation 'played down the extent of the risk ... claimed that the evidence did not show conclusively that HIV was a blood-borne disease, and ... refused to screen out potentially infected donors. By contrast, the plasma companies [who procured plasma commercially] accepted that there was a good chance that HIV was being transmitted by their products, they moved very quickly to switch the source of their supply, and introduced new methods to inactivate viruses in plasma derivatives.' Healy, Kieran (1999), p. 537. This is because, Healy argues, whereas the commercial plasma companies were concerned to protect the recipients of their products (their markets) blood banks were concerned about their suppliers, since these were more valuable to them than the recipients of their products. Unfortunately, however, the male homosexual community was a significant source of blood for the blood banks – as well as being a significant vector for HIV transmission. Thus, in this situation the incentives that the blood banks responded to (that is, to avoid alienating a significant portion of their suppliers) resulted in their blood being of lower quality than that procured commercially. For further discussion of this, see ibid., pp. 529–58; Shearmur, Jeremy (forthcoming), *Living With Markets* and (2001), p. 32.

46   Diseases contracted as a result of commercially procured kidney transplants (for example, HIV, hepatitis C) can be

detected in the initial vendor prior to the purchase of the organ. Commercial procurers of organs thus do not have to rely on vendors to tell the truth about their health status. For an outline of the screening procedures that kidney vendors would be subjected to in a commercial system where procurers were liable for the quality of the organs (and which altruistic donors undergo) see Rosenthal, J. Thomas and Danovitch, Gabriel M. (1996), pp. 97–9.

47   This idea was suggested by Kessel in response to Titmuss's claim that a commercial blood supply would be of worse quality than a donated supply. Kessel, pp. 144–6. See also Stewart, Robert M. (1984), pp. 233–5.

48   Although (like B. Broumand, his colleague at the hospital), Ghods does not explicitly state that an unrelated living donor should be understood to be a vendor, this is clear from his remarks in this paper. Ghods (2002), p. 225, Fig. 4. The more accurate (and higher) numbers in his article refer to patient and graft survival rates of kidneys taken from both related and unrelated vendors, calculated using the Kaplan–Meier method.

49   Data from United Network for Organ Sharing (UNOS), current to 1 August 2003. I thank Denise Tripp of UNOS for providing me with the annual data from which I calculated these average survival rates.

50   Ghods, p. 225, Fig. 4 (see note 48 above).

51   Data provided by UNOS, current to 1 August 2003.

52   The best graft survival rates at five years accord to kidneys transplanted from siblings, and the worst to kidneys from living unrelated donors. See HHS/HRSA/OSP/DOT and UNOS (2003), Chapter 6, 'Living donor kidney graft survival'. The overall numbers of living unrelated donors rose from 6 per cent to 24 per cent from 1992 to 2001. Ibid., Chapter 3, 'Living donor characteristics'. See also Ghods, p. 225, Fig. 4 and p. 226, Fig. 5.

53   Ghods, p. 226.

54   Ibid.

55   See, for example, Cecka, J.M. (1999).

56   Love (1997), pp. 179–80.

57   Perez, Luis M. et al. (1988), pp. 553–7. Cited by Love, p. 180, n. 98. See also Pruviance, Susan M. (1993).

58   Scheper-Hughes (2003), p. 1645.

Chapter 9
Conclusion

In this volume I have sought to establish that if one holds personal autonomy and/or human well-being to be morally valuable then one should morally favour the use of a regulated current market to procure human kidneys for transplantation. There remains, however, the further question of whether it would be morally permissible to use a market mechanism to distribute, as well as to procure, these kidneys. Moreover, even if it is moral to use markets both to procure and to distribute human transplant kidneys, this does not show that these markets should be legalized. One might, for example, hold that while there is nothing morally objectionable about using a market for procurement or distribution, such a market should not be legalized because it would be so prone to abuse that its benefits would be outweighed by its disadvantages.

I will address both of these issues in this concluding chapter. I argue that not only is it morally acceptable to use a current market (regulated in the ways I suggest) both to procure and to distribute human transplant kidneys – but that such a market should be legalized, too.

The Objection from Fairness

Although I have argued in this volume that if one values personal autonomy or human well-being (or both) then one should morally favour the use of a current market to *procure* human transplant kidneys, I have left it an open question as to whether market mechanisms should also be used to *distribute* the organs thus procured. I initially restricted the scope of my argument in this way to avoid the objection that any market in medical resources would be immoral because it would be unfair, insofar as the rich and the middle class would be able to secure the means necessary to save or improve their lives, whereas the poor would not.

Any argument that is offered in favour of using markets to distribute human transplant kidneys will be faced immediately with what I shall term the 'Objection from Fairness' that I noted above. This objection expresses a common concern about the morality of using market mechanisms to distribute human transplant kidneys. After all, no one wants to see the poor (or, and apparently worse yet, the *children* of the poor, such as Tiny Tim) die simply because they (or their parents) cannot afford to buy the transplant kidney that they so desperately need. Yet despite the rhetorical force of this objection it should not be accepted because it rests on three assumptions, two of which are false. The first is that there would be fewer kidneys available for transplant than there would be persons in medical need of them. The second is that the individuals who medically need transplant kidneys (or their friends, relatives or insurance companies) would purchase them directly from vendors, or from agents who would act as kidney brokers between the vendors and the potential recipients. Taken together, these two assumptions naturally lead to the view that if a current market were to be used to distribute transplant kidneys those who need them would bid against each other to secure them. When this view is combined with a third assumption – that the desires of those who are rich or middle class to secure transplant kidneys would be at least as strong as the same desires of those who are poor – it seems clear that in a current market for distribution with more persons in medical need of kidneys than there are kidneys available, the poor will be least likely to receive them, for they would frequently be outbid by wealthier persons. This being so, proponents of the Objection from Fairness conclude, since it is morally objectionable that the poor die simply because they are poor, while the wealthy live simply because they are wealthy, the use of a current market to distribute human transplant kidneys would be morally objectionable, since such a market would lead to this immoral result.

The third of these assumptions is innocuous. Unless one (rather bizarrely) assumes that the rich and middle class are so jaded or beset by fashionable ennui that they no longer have any will to live, it is plausible to assume that their desires to secure transplant kidneys are as strong as the same desires of the poor. The two assumptions that accompany it, however, are demonstrably mistaken. First, the Iranian experience of using a current market to procure human transplant kidneys suggests that under such a system there will be no medical shortage of kidneys, and so everyone who medically needs one will be able to secure one. Of course, that this assumption is mistaken does not show that the Objection from Fairness is misguided. A proponent of this objection could respond by noting that even though there are *potentially* enough kidneys available, whether everyone who medically needs a kidney would *actually* receive one under a system of market distribution will depend on whether everyone could *afford* to buy one. And, such a proponent of this objection could note, not everyone who so needed a kidney could afford to buy one. Thus, even though the first assumption that undergirds this objection might be mistaken, this objection still holds.

This defence of the Objection from Fairness leads directly to the reason why the second assumption that it is based upon should be rejected: that if a current market were used to distribute transplant kidneys persons (or those concerned with their health) would purchase them themselves. This is a perfectly natural assumption to make, especially since some supporters of markets in human kidneys have focused on such direct purchases, and this is how the black market now operates.[1] However, were a current market for human transplant kidneys to be legalized it is unlikely that most (if any) kidney purchases would be made by individuals. Instead, they would be made by insurance companies on behalf of their clients, or by the state for persons who qualified for state assistance. This last point must be emphasized. Under current law in both the United States and Britain persons who meet certain economic and health criteria are entitled to have virtually all of their expenses for dialysis and transplantation covered by (in Britain) the National Health Service,[2] or (in the United States) by Medicaid or Medicare.[3] If a market system were to be used to distribute human transplant kidneys, and if the state acted as a kidney purchaser in such a system, poverty would not preclude the poor from securing kidneys that they needed. Even though they might not be able to afford the kidneys and they might not be covered by private health insurance plans that would purchase the organs for them, they could have the kidneys they medically needed purchased for them by the state. And since this is so, the Objection from Fairness fails.[4]

A Partial Defence of the Assumption that the State Should Provide Healthcare

In Chapter 6 I noted that proponents of the pro-market argument from analogy had to show that the dangerous and unpleasant activities that they compared to kidney selling were themselves morally permissible for this argument to be sound. Yet in the above response to the Objection from Fairness I simply *assumed* that state provision of healthcare was morally legitimate. Given the context of this assumption, however, it is a legitimate one to make. The Objection from Fairness arises from a moral viewpoint in which certain resources (such as healthcare) should be available to persons irrespective of their ability to pay for them. The proponents of this objection would thus accept that some level of resource redistribution by the state is morally justified to ensure that all persons have access to these resources. Since this is so, they would share the assumption that my above response was based upon – namely, that it is morally legitimate for the state to provide healthcare to those who need it.

Of course, persons other than proponents of this objection do not share this assumption. (Many libertarians, for example, would emphatically deny it.[5]) Yet insofar as those who reject it do so because they reject the view that certain resources should be available to all irrespective of their ability to pay, they would also – and for the same reason – reject the Objection from Fairness. Since this is so, adopting the assumption that it is morally legitimate for the state to provide healthcare resources to those who need them is a legitimate argumentative strategy in this context. If a person opposes the use of a market mechanism to distribute transplant kidneys on the grounds that such a method is unfair, they will accept the assumption that certain resources should be available to all regardless of their ability to pay, and thus accept that the state provision of healthcare to those who need it but cannot pay for it is morally permissible. And, since this is so, that person should accept that the Objection from Fairness fails as an objection to the institution of a market mechanism for the distribution of human transplant kidneys in any state that provides healthcare to those who need it but cannot pay. If, however, a person rejects the assumption that certain resources should be available to all regardless of ability to pay, they would not consider it morally objectionable that some persons go without the resources that they need to live (for example, transplant kidneys). This person would thus reject the Objection from Fairness, since they reject the moral viewpoint from which it arose. Thus, whether or not one accepts the assumption on which my response to the Objection from Fairness was based, one should accept that this objection fails to show that the use of a market mechanism to distribute human transplant kidneys is morally impermissible.[6] Yet this argumentative strategy is not merely persuasive. It also shows that whether or not it is legitimate for the state to provide healthcare to those who need it but cannot pay for it, it is legitimate for a market mechanism in which the state acts as a purchaser to be used to distribute human transplant kidneys.

Market or Monopsony?

However, showing that the Objection from Fairness is mistaken is not a sufficient reason to endorse the use of a market mechanism to distribute as well as procure human transplant kidneys. Once one recognizes that the state would (and, perhaps, should) act as a purchaser for transplant kidneys one might suggest that a state monopsony should be

established, in which *only* the state could legitimately
purchase transplant kidneys and then distribute them
according to 'some ... fair principle' to those who required
them.[7] (Alternatively, one might suggest that a non-state
monopsony be established for the same purpose. The
ownership of the monopsony is, however, irrelevant to the
arguments below.) Such a monopsony would be immune to
the Objection from Fairness if it adhered to a fair principle of
distribution. However, both concern for the well-being and
respect for the autonomy of the potential recipients of the
transplant kidneys, provide reason morally to prefer a
competitive market for the distribution of transplant kidneys
to a state monopsony.

If a competitive market were used to procure and distribute
transplant kidneys, the primary purchasers would be the state
and insurance companies (on behalf of their clients). Since it
is typically cheaper to provide someone with a kidney
transplant than it is to keep them on dialysis insurance
companies would have an economic incentive to provide
transplants for their clients – and to provide them as quickly
as possible. This would, in turn, provide a political incentive
for the state to attempt to ensure that its transplant
programme would keep pace (at least to some extent) with
its private sector rival, as it would be politically disadvanta-
geous for those in charge of this aspect of the public sector for
it to be significantly and noticeably inferior to its private
sector rival. If, however, a state monopsony were to be
instantiated, it would not be subject to such comparison, and
so the political incentive to provide an efficient transplant
service would not be as strong.

Allowing the private sector to compete with the public
sector in the provision of transplant kidneys would thus work
to enhance the well-being of persons who would rely on the
latter to provide transplant kidneys for them. Such competition is also required by respect for the autonomy of some of
the potential kidney recipients. As I argued in Chapter 8,
prohibiting persons from performing an action that they
would otherwise have performed compromises their autonomy by coercing them into refraining from acting in the way
they desired. Respect for autonomy thus requires that persons

be allowed to sell their kidneys to private procurement
agencies or other individuals, or to buy privately the
transplant kidneys they need. Moreover, the instrumental
value of some of the potential kidney recipients' autonomy
would also be enhanced if they could choose between
securing a transplant kidney from the public or the private
sectors, for they would now be able to exercise their
autonomy to secure a kidney from the type of provider they
preferred.

An International Kidney Market

The above arguments against the Objection from Fairness
have proceeded on the implicit assumption that providing
kidney transplants would be cheaper overall than providing
dialysis, otherwise it is unlikely that the state would be
motivated to buy kidneys for its citizens, for it would have a
financial incentive only to provide them with dialysis. Since,
medically speaking, most persons with end-stage renal disease
would be better off receiving a transplanted kidney than
undergoing dialysis, if transplants were not cheaper than
dialysis the Objection from Fairness would rise again.[8] This is
because under such conditions even if the state were to act as
the payer of last resort for healthcare it would be likely that
the rich would receive transplants and the poor would not.

Under the current situation in which all transplant kidneys
are donated the assumption that transplants are cheaper than
dialysis is correct.[9] This assumption becomes less plausible in
a situation where kidneys are procured in a current market,
since then transplantation costs must also take into account
the cost of the kidneys purchased for transplant. Thus, since
kidney patients are typically better off receiving a kidney
transplant than they are undergoing dialysis, concern for their
well-being supports securing transplant kidneys as cheaply as
possible.

This supports the establishment of an international market
for human transplant kidneys, with kidneys being purchased
from live vendors in countries (such as India) where they are
cheapest. As I have already argued, the usual objections to

such purchases (that they are coercive, exploitative or that they provide the vendors with only a constraining option) are mistaken if they are made within a legal, regulated current market. Yet one might still object to a regulated international market in human kidneys on the grounds that it would lead to fewer kidneys being available for transplantation to citizens of the countries that are the net suppliers of kidneys within this market. This objection can be readily met, for the states in question could simply place limits on the numbers of kidneys that can be exported in any given year, and tax kidneys sold to non-citizens to subsidize a domestic transplantation programme.[10] It should also be noted that this objection to an international trade in human kidneys has a rather Marie Antoinette-esque quality about it. In the countries that would be net exporters of human transplant kidneys their availability for their own citizens is not the most pressing medical concern. Instead, the most pressing medical concerns that such countries face are far more basic, such as preventing water-borne diseases through access to safe drinking water.[11] Instead of focusing on the possibility that an international market will make it even less likely that persons in poor countries will receive a kidney transplant when they need one, then, it would be better to focus on the positive health benefits that such a trade could bring to those countries that would become kidney exporters. Their governments could tax the purchase of kidneys and use the money thus raised to (for example) provide clean drinking water for their citizens, or to improve the provision of basic medical care. Rather than worsening the plight of the poor in those countries that would be net exporters of kidneys, then, allowing a regulated international trade in human kidneys could actually improve their living standards.

Kidney Theft and the Black Market

That an international market in human transplant kidneys is morally acceptable does not, however, show that it should be legalized. There is widespread concern that allowing such markets would provide 'an inducement to commit murder,'[12] lead to 'criminal dealings in the acquisition of organs for profit' and stimulate the black market in transplant kidneys with all its attendant abuses.[13] If these concerns are well founded, then even if regulated markets in human kidneys are morally permissible there would be good public policy reasons to prohibit them.

The concern that legalizing markets in human kidneys would lead to criminal activity (such as the murder of persons for their organs) is widespread, no doubt in part owing to the urban legend in which a businessman's or tourist's kidney is stolen after he is drugged by a woman he meets in a bar.[14] The prevalence of this concern is also no doubt partly due to the fictional portrayal of organ theft in such popular works as Robin Cook's 1977 novel *Coma*, a 1991 episode of the American television programme *Law and Order* ('Sonata for Solo Organ') and films such as *The Harvest* (1993), *Central Station* (1998) and *24 Hours in London* (2000). This concern is further stimulated by well-publicized allegations of the theft of human body parts, such as that of the Turkish man who in 1989 alleged that one of his kidneys had been stolen in Britain during medical tests to secure a work permit,[15] and by both official and academic pronouncements condemning thefts that have allegedly taken place. In 1993, for example, the European Parliament adopted a resolution calling 'for action to be taken to put a stop to the mutilation and murder of fetuses, children, and adults in certain developing countries for the purposes of providing transplant organs,'[16] while the anthropologist Nancy Scheper-Hughes has reported rumours of organ stealing that are common among the poor in Brazil, Guatemala and South Africa.[17]

Yet despite the widespread belief in the existence of such modern-day Burke and Hare partnerships there is no evidence that such criminal activities actually occur.[18] The European Parliament's 1993 resolution was based on a report from the August 1992 edition of *Le Monde Diplomatique* that was later discredited.[19] Similarly, the anthropologist Mac Marshall has vigorously criticized Scheper-Hughes's major article on 'rumours' of organ theft as failing to adequately assess 'the validity of "rumor" versus "reality," ' and as failing to be sufficiently grounded 'in the rich contextualized data we still

expect from good ethnography.'[20] Rumours of organ theft
have also been investigated and dismissed by the Geneva-
based non-governmental organization Defence for Children
International, the European Community Commission, the
Division of Organ Transplantation of the US Public Health
Service, the US Federal Bureau of Investigation and the Paris-
based International Federation for Human Rights, among
other concerned official bodies.[21]

That no evidence for such thefts was found is not
surprising, for there are clear practical obstacles to this being
a viable criminal enterprise. Even assuming that the kidney
thieves were stealing organs to order, and that they ensured
that their clients were close to the location of the thefts so
that difficulties with the sale and transport of the stolen
kidneys were minimized, killing people at random to steal
their kidneys is unlikely to procure organs that would be
good matches for the criminals' clients. It is thus likely that
several murders would have to be committed to secure a
viable organ. This increase in risk would lead to an increase
in cost for the kidney thieves, and thus for their clients.
However, since there is a flourishing black market in human
kidneys procured from willing vendors, and that it is possible
to ensure a tissue match between these organs and their
would-be recipients, the prices that the kidney thieves could
viably charge would be limited by those charged by persons
operating in the 'willing vendor' sector of the black market.
Given this, the high risks involved in organ theft, and the
greater punishments imposed on organ thieves compared
with those imposed on those who purchase kidneys from live
vendors, the commercial theft of kidneys is not an economically viable activity.

Yet although there is no evidence that organ theft *currently*
takes place, one might argue that it would be *more likely to
occur* if markets for human body parts were legalized. Behind
this concern is, presumably, the view that if kidneys are
legally traded then it would be easier to dispose of those that
are *illegally* acquired, and that this would provide an
incentive to steal them. Rather than encouraging the criminal
acquisition of, and subsequent black market trade in,
transplant kidneys legalizing a regulated current market for

these organs would further discourage it. The requirement that both kidney vendors and recipients in the legal market be subject to extensive pre-nephrectomy medical tests and receive adequate post-operative care would ensure that the interests of both parties would be best served in the legal, rather than the black, market. If a legal current market both to procure and distribute transplant kidneys existed, then, it would drive down the demand for black market kidneys as the legal kidney brokers would offer a safer product. Similarly, if the kidney trade were to be legalized persons would be even less likely to be motivated to purchase kidneys with a dubious provenance from black market 'organ-leggers.'[22] This would provide an additional disincentive to potential kidney thieves. The legalization of a current market for human kidneys would require black market dealers to compete not only with each other but also with legal providers of organs for pay. Such competition would under-mine the ability of the black market traders to sell kidneys at the same prices they were charging prior to legalization. This, together with the decrease in demand for black market kidneys, would further reduce the profitability of the illegal kidney trade and thus reduce the incentives that persons currently have (that is, in a situation where the kidney trade is banned) to become organleggers.

Legalizing a current market for human transplant kidneys would also provide states in which the black market is prevalent with an incentive to eliminate it. If the kidney trade were legalized states would be able to secure tax revenues from it, both directly – by taxing vendors and/or recipients of the kidneys – and indirectly, through additional income taxes that would be gained from the increased incomes of those entrepreneurs and healthcare professionals who would profit from it. (The state could also receive additional taxes from recipients of commercial kidneys whose transplants were successful, and which thus enabled them to become more economically productive taxpayers.) Since this is so, countries with a legal trade would now have an economic incentive to eliminate the black market, for such untaxed transactions would now represent a loss of state income. The concern that legalizing a current market in human kidneys for both their procurement and distribution would stimulate the black market in transplant kidneys and encourage murder and kidney theft is thus clearly misguided, and so should pose no bar to the legalization of these markets.

Further Issues

The arguments that I have offered in this volume in favour of the moral permissibility of legalizing a regulated current market in human kidneys can be readily expanded to favour legalizing similar markets for any nonreplenishable body part whose removal would not affect the vendor's ability to live normally afterwards. They could also be expanded to justify current markets in replenishable body parts, such as blood, semen, skin or hair[23] – even if the end users of the traded body parts did not use them for therapeutic purposes. Absent arguments to the contrary, one could, for example, morally purchase human body parts for use in (or as) artworks – or even for cannibalistic purposes. Moreover, insofar as current markets are considered by the critics of markets in body parts to be the most morally objectionable of all such markets, my arguments in this volume can, *mutatis mutandis*, be used also to justify the moral permissibility of both markets in cadaveric body parts and future markets in human body parts. My arguments in this volume could also be used to show that commercial surrogate pregnancy is morally permissible.

Some of the pro-market arguments in this volume could also be modified to endorse the moral legitimacy of current markets in nonreplenishable body parts that are essential to life, such as hearts or whole livers. (Although I must stress that, as they stand, my arguments do not lead to this conclusion, and it is not my intention that they should.) However, although one might be able to construct an argument for such sales that would be satisfactory to persons who value human well-being, or who instrumentally value personal autonomy (or who value both), it is unlikely that one will be able to construct such an argument that would be convincing to persons who hold personal autonomy to be intrinsically valuable. The option to sell such parts of one's body would not just be a constraining option for the vendor, but an *eliminating* option – one that, if chosen, would altogether preclude them from the future exercise of autonomy.[24]

The arguments in this volume do not only lead to the moral questions of which body parts persons should be allowed to sell – and for what uses. They also lead to a host of public policy questions. For example, if persons can trade their kidneys, should they be allowed, like Antonio in *The Merchant of Venice*, to take out loans guaranteed by their organs?[25] Similarly, could the state count a person's organs as capital when assessing liability for taxation or eligibility for welfare payments,[26] provide the option of persons giving it their replenishable body parts (such as blood) in lieu of taxes or fines – or require that some taxes or fines be *paid* in such body parts?[27] These are interesting questions but, since they do not bear directly on the issue of whether a regulated current market for human kidneys is morally permissible, but arise out of the recognition that it is, I will leave consideration of them for another time.

Conclusion

It is now time to take stock. In this volume I have argued that the two most widely held values in contemporary bioethics – respect for personal autonomy and concern for human well-being – both support the view that a regulated, current market in human kidneys is morally permissible, and should be legalized. This is not, of course, to argue that such a market should be the only means used for the procurement of human transplant organs. Instead, it should operate alongside other means of procurement (such as altruistic donation or mandated choice) that are also ethically acceptable. Such a market would not compromise the autonomy of the poor by enabling their poverty to coerce them into selling their kidneys, or through presenting them with an autonomy-compromising constraining option. The option to sell a kidney is thus an option that respect for personal autonomy requires that persons should be allowed to pursue if they so choose. A legal, regulated, current market for human kidneys would also enhance the well-being of those who sell their kidneys by enabling them to trade their kidneys for the financial means with which to purchase items they value more. It would also enable the states that become net providers of kidneys to tax the purchasers of these organs, and then to use this income to provide better medical facilities for their countries' poor. It would also greatly benefit those persons who are currently desperately waiting for a transplant kidney, either to escape their reliance on dialysis or simply to save their lives, for a regulated current market would increase the number of transplantable organs that would be available for those who need them. It would also, as I noted in Chapter 8, be likely to increase the number of organs available for transplantation into ethnic minorities. The issues of whether a current market in human transplant kidneys is morally permissible, and, if so, if it should be legalized, are thus not only of academic interest. For every day that a current market in human organs continues to be prohibited persons will die or continue to suffer needlessly, waiting for the organs that such a market might have provided for them. Given this, persons who truly respect personal autonomy, and who are truly concerned with human well-being, should regard a market for human kidneys of the sort I advocate not just as morally permissible, but as morally *imperative*. The stakes in this debate over the permissibility of a current market for human transplant kidneys are very high indeed.

Notes

1   Kervorkian (2001).
2   According to the UK's Department of Health Renal Team, 'All children, young people, and adults likely to benefit from a kidney transplant are to receive a high quality service which supports them in managing their transplant and enables them to achieve the best possible quality of life.' DH Renal Team (2004), p. 3. In essence, this articulates one of the founding principles of the National Health Service, namely that

'individuals have equal access to services solely on the basis of clinical need and irrespective of … ability to pay.' Noted by Eaves, D (1998).

3   Noted by Barnett II, William et al. (2001), p. 375, n. 3. See also Medicare (1995) and Rettig, Richard A. (1996).

4   This point was also made by Barnett et al. (2001), pp. 375–7.

5   Although they might not deny that *individuals* have a moral responsibility to so provide for those who are less fortunate, for libertarianism is a *political* philosophy (that is, it is concerned with what the state might and might not justly do) rather than a *moral* philosophy.

6   The proponent of the Objection from Fairness would add a rider: that this argument only shows that the use of markets to distribute kidneys would not be morally impermissible in any state in which the government acted as the payer of last resort for the provision of transplant kidneys.

7   This was suggested by Harris and Erin (2002), p. 114.

8   See Wolfe, Robert A. et al. (1999).

9   Beasley et al. estimate that a kidney transplant saves almost $42 000 per patient over a 10-year period. Beasley, C.L. et al. (1997), p. 549.

10 Something similar has already occurred in South Africa, where one hospital in Cape Town kept its transplant unit solvent in the face of budget cuts through profits made from Mauritian patients. See Scheper-Hughes (2000), p. 199.

11 See Mudur, Ganapati (2003).

12 Leader (1989), 'Ask, don't pay, for kidneys,' *The Independent*, 23 January, p. 16. This worry is also articulated in Caplan (1988), p. 66.

13 Abouna et al. (1991), p. 171. This worry was also expressed by Mohamed, S.S. and Velasco, N. (1990). David Friedman writes that the possibility of organ theft is 'the best argument I know of against a *completely free market* in organs.' Friedman (2001), p. 242 (emphasis added). I am not proposing a completely free market here. However, it is unlikely that organ theft would be widespread even in such a market. As I argue below, a legal market in human organs would drive out the black market, since persons (or, perhaps, their post-mortem estates) would have recourse against vendors who sold them poor-quality kidneys in a legal market that would be lacking in a black market – and this would create a disincentive for persons to purchase from organ thieves.

14 This urban legend is outlined in Brunvand, Jan Harold (1993), pp. 149–54.

15 McKinnon, Ian and Kelsey, Tim (1989), 'Turkish peasant "duped into selling a kidney,"' *The Independent*, 18 January, p. 2.

16 Resolution of the European Parliament on prohibiting trade in transplant organs, Strasbourg, 14 September 1993.

17 Scheper-Hughes (2000), pp. 201–204. See also Fasting, Ulla et al. (1998).

18 For a systematic refutation of such rumours, see Leventhal, Todd (1994). See also section IV of Rothman, D.J. et al. (1997), and Delpin, Santiago, E.A. (1996).

19 The author of this report was Leon Schwartzenberg, who admitted that the sole information he had of the organ thefts he condemned was an article that was later discredited. See Leventhal (1994).

20 Marshall, Mac (2000), pp. 215–16.

21 See Leventhal.

22 The term 'organlegger' for a person who steals human body parts for resale to those who need transplant organs was coined by the science fiction novelist Larry Niven. Niven (1967), pp. 216–31.

23 For a discussion of which body parts one might justifiably have markets in, and why, see Cherry (2000c).

24 For a brief discussion of this issue see Brecher, B. (1994), p. 998.

25 This issue is discussed in Smith, Kevin H. (1999), pp. 127–84.

26 This second possibility is discussed by Harris and Erin (1994), pp. 144–5.

27 This last was suggested (but not argued for) by Walzer, Michael (1983), p. 93.

Bibliography

Abouna, G.M. (1993), 'Negative Impact of Trading in Human Organs on the Development of Transplantation in the Middle East,' *Transplantation Proceedings*, **25**, 2310–13.

— (1990), 'Commercialisation in Human Organs: A Middle Eastern Perspective,' *Transplantation Proceedings*, **22**, 918–21.

Abouna, G.M. et al. (1991), 'The negative impact of paid organ donation,' in Land and Dossetor, (eds), *Organ Replacement Therapy: Ethics, Justice, Commerce*, New York: Springer-Verlag, pp. 164–72.

Adams, Frank A., Barnett, A.H. and Kaserman, David L. (1999), 'Markets for Organs: The Question of Supply,' *Contemporary Economic Policy*, **17** (2), 147–55

Anderson, Elizabeth (1988), 'Values, Risks, and Market Norms,' *Philosophy and Public Affairs*, **17** (1), 54–65.

Andrews, Lori B. (1986), 'My Body, My Property,' *Hastings Center Report*, **16**, 28–38.

Andrews, Peter A. (2002), 'Renal Transplantation,' *British Medical Journal*, **324**, 2 March, 530–34.

Anon. (2003), Leader, *The Guardian*, 4 December.

Anon (2000), 'Altruism and confidentiality in organ donation,' *The Lancet*, **355**, 4 March, 765.

Anon. (1997), 'One Kidney Communities,' *Frontline*, **14** (25), 13–16 December.

Anon. (1997), 'Kidneys still for sale,' *The Hindu*, **14** (25), 13–26 December.

Anon. (1989), 'Ask, don't pay, for kidneys,' *The Independent*, 23 January, p. 16.

Archard, David (2002), 'Selling Yourself: Titmuss's Argument Against a Market in Blood,' *The Journal of Ethics*, **6** (1), 87–103.

Arnold, Denis and Bowie, Norman E. (2003), 'Sweatshops and Respect for Persons,' *Business Ethics Quarterly*, **13** (2), 221–42.

Arnold, R. et al. (2002), 'Financial incentives for cadaver organ donation: an ethical reappraisal,' *Transplantation*, **73** (8), 1361–7.

Arrow, Kenneth J. (1972), 'Gifts and Exchanges,' *Philosophy and Public Affairs*, **1** (4), 343–62.

Audi, Robert (1996), 'The Morality and Utility of Organ Transplantation,' *Utilitas*, **8** (2), 141–58.

Ballantyne, A. and Howard, J. (1989), 'Kidney deal claim alarms surgeons,' *The Guardian*, 28 January, p. 3.

Banks, Gloria J. (1995), 'Legal and Ethical Safeguards: Protection of Society's Most Vulnerable Participants in a Commercialized Organ Transplantation System,' *American Journal of Law and Medicine*, **21** (1), 45–110.

Barnett II, William, Saliba, Michael and Walker, Deborah (2001), 'A Free Market in Kidneys: Efficient and Equitable,' *The Independent Review*, **5** (3), Winter, 373–85.

Barnett, Andrew H., Blair, Roger D. and Kaserman, David L. (2002), 'A Market for Organs,' in Tabarrok, Alexander (ed.), *Entrepreneurial Economics: Bright Ideas from the Dismal Science*, Oxford: Oxford University Press, pp. 89–106.

— (1992), 'Improving Organ Donation: Compensation Versus Markets,' *Inquiry*, **29**, 372–8.

Beasley, C.L. et al. (1997), 'Living Kidney Donation: A Survey of Professional Attitudes and Practices,' *American Journal of Kidney Diseases*, **30** (4), 549–57.

Beauchamp, Tom L. (2003), 'Methods and Principles in Biomedical Ethics,' *Journal of Medical Ethics*, **29** (5), 269–74.

Beauchamp, Tom L. and Childress, James (2001), *Principles of Biomedical Ethics*, 5th edition, Oxford: Oxford University Press.

Bia, Margaret J., Ramos, E.L., Danovitch, G.M. et al. (1995), 'Evaluation of Living Renal Donors: The Current Practice of U.S. Transplant Centers,' *Transplantation*, **60** (1995), 322–7.

Bliss, C.J. and Stern, N.H. (1978a), 'Productivity, Wages, and Nutrition 1: The Theory,' *Journal of Development Economics*, 5, 331–62.

— (1978b), 'Productivity, Wages, and Nutrition 2: Some Observations,' *Journal of Development Economics*, 5, 363–98.

Block, Walter (1999), 'Market Inalienability Once Again: Reply to Radin,' *Thomas Jefferson Law Review*, 22 (1), 37–88.

Bonomini, V. (1991), 'Ethical Aspects of Living Donation,' *Transplantation Proceedings*, 23, 2498.

Bratman, Michael E. (1996), 'Identification, Decision and Treating as a Reason,' *Philosophical Topics*, 24 (2), 1–18.

Brecher, B (1994), 'Organs for Transplant: Donation or Payment?,' in Gillon, Raanan (ed.), *Principles of Health Care Ethics*, New York, NY: John Wiley & Sons, pp. 993–1002.

— (1991), 'Buying human kidneys: autonomy, commodity and power,' *Journal of Medical Ethics*, 17 (2), 99.

— (1990), 'The kidney trade: or, the customer is always wrong,' *Journal of Medical Ethics*, 16 (3), 120–23.

British Medical Association (2000), *Organ Donation in the 21st Century: Time for a Consolidated Approach*, London: British Medical Association.

Brody, Baruch (1993), 'Assessing Empirical Research in Bioethics,' *Theoretical Medicine*, 14, 211–19.

Broumand, B. (1997), 'Living donors: the Iran experience,' *Nephrology Dialysis Transplantation*, 12, 1830–31.

Broyer, M. (1991), 'Living Organ Donation: the Fight Against Commercialization,' in Land and Dossetor, (eds), *Organ Replacement Therapy: Ethics, Justice, Commerce*, New York, NY: Springer-Verlag, pp. 197–9.

Brunvand, Jan Harold (1993), *The Baby Train and Other Lusty Urban Legends*, New York, NY: W.W. Norton.

Byrne, Margaret and Thompson, Peter (2001), 'A positive analysis of financial incentives for cadaveric organ donation,' *Journal of Health Economics*, 20, 69–83.

Buttle, Nicholas (1991), 'Prostitutes, workers, and kidneys: Brecher on the kidney trade,' *Journal of Medical Ethics*, 17 (2), 97–8.

Cameron J. and Hoffenberg, R. (1999), 'The ethics of organ transplantation reconsidered: paid organ donation and the use of executed prisoners as donors,' *Kidney International*, 55, 724–32.

Caplan, Arthur L. (1988), 'Beg, Borrow, or Steal: The Ethics of Solid Organ Procurement,' in Mathieu, Deborah (ed.), *Organ Substitution Technology: Ethical, Legal, and Public Policy Issues*, Boulder, CO: Westview Press, pp. 59–68.

— (1984) 'Ethical and policy issues in the procurement of cadaver organs for transplantation,' *New England Journal of Medicine*, 311 (15), 981–3.

Card, David and Krueger, Alan B. (1995), *Myth and Measurement: The New Economics of the Minimum Wage*, Princeton, NJ: Princeton University Press.

Cecka, J.M. (1999), 'Results of More Than 1000 Recent Living-Unrelated Donor Transplants in the United States,' *Transplantation Proceedings*, 34 (1–2), 234.

Chadwick, Ruth (1989), 'The market for bodily parts: Kant and duties to oneself,' *Journal of Applied Philosophy* 6 (2), 129–39.

Chengappa, Raj (1990), 'The Organs Bazaar,' *India Today*, 31 July, 60–67.

Cherry, Mark J. (2000a), 'Body parts and the marketplace: insights from Thomistic Philosophy,' *Christian Bioethics*, 6 (2), 171–93.

— (2000b), 'Is a Market for Human Organs Necessarily Exploitative?,' *Public Affairs Quarterly*, 14 (4), 337–60.

— (2000c), 'Bodies and Minds in the Philosophy of Medicine: Organ Sales and the Lived Body,' in Engelhardt, Tristram H., *The Philosophy of Medicine: Framing the Field*, Dordrecht: Kluwer Academic Publishers, pp. 57–78.

Child, James W. (1994), 'Can Libertarianism Sustain a Fraud Standard?,' *Ethics*, 104 (4), 722–38.

Childress, James F. (1992), 'The Body as Property: Some Philosophical Reflections,' *Transplantation Proceedings*, 24 (5), 2143–8.

— (1989), 'Attitudes of Major Religious Traditions Toward Uses of the Human Body and Its Parts,' in Knight, Douglas A. and Paris, Peter J., (eds), *Justice and the Holy*, Atlanta, GA: Scholars Press, pp. 215–40.

Christman, John (1989), 'Introduction,' in Christman, (ed.), *The Inner Citadel: Essays on Individual Autonomy*, Oxford: Oxford University Press, pp. 3–23.

Chugh, Kirpal S. and Jha, Vivekanand (1996), 'Commerce in Transplantation in Third World Countries,' *Kidney International*, **49**, 1181–86.

Clay, Megan and Block, Walter (2002), 'A Free Market for Human Organs,' *The Journal of Social, Political and Economic Studies*, **27** (2), 227–36.

Cobden, Richard (1878), 'England, Ireland, and America,' in Mallet, Sir Louis, (ed.), *The Political Writings of Richard Cobden*, London: William Ridgway & Co.

Cohen, Cynthia B. (2002), 'Public Policy and the Sale of Human Organs,' *Kennedy Institute of Ethics Journal*, **12** (1), 47–64.

Cohen, Lawrence (1999), 'Where it Hurts: Indian Material for an Ethics of Organ Transplantation,' *Daedalus*, **128** (4), 135–65.

Cohen, Lloyd R. (1995), *Increasing the Supply of Transplant Organs*, Austin, TX: R.G. Landes Co.

Cortesini, R. (1999), 'Medical and Ethical Aspects of Living Donation,' *Transplantation Proceedings*, **25**, 2305–2306.

Council on Ethical and Judicial Affairs (1994), 'Strategies for Cadaveric Organ Procurement: Mandated Choice and Presumed Consent,' *Journal of the American Medical Association*, **272** (10), 14 September, 809–12.

— (1994/95), *Code of Medical Ethics*, American Medical Association.

Daar, A.S. (1991), 'Organ donation—World Experience—The Middle East,' *Transplantation Proceedings*, **23**, 2505–2507.

de Castro, L.D. (2003), 'Commodification and exploitation: arguments in favour of compensated organ donation,' *Journal of Medical Ethics*, **29** (3), 142–6.

Delpin, Santiago, E.A. (1996), 'Allegations of Organ Commerce in Middle America,' *Transplantation Proceedings* **28**, 3370–73.

DH Renal Team (2004), *The National Service Framework for Renal Services Part One: Dialysis and Transplantation*, London: Department of Health.

Dickens, B.M. (1990), 'Human rights and commerce in health care,' *Transplantation Proceedings*, **22**, 904–905.

Dossetor, John B. and Manickavel, V. (1992), 'Commercialization: The buying and selling of kidneys,' in Kjellstrand C.M. and Dossetor, J.B., (eds), *Ethical Problems in Dialysis and Transplantation*, Dordrecht: Kluwer Academic Publishers, pp. 61–71.

Dworkin, Gerald (1994), 'Markets and Morals: The Case for Organ Sales,' in Dworkin, Gerald, (ed.), *Morality, Harm, and the Law*, Boulder, CO: Westview Press, pp. 155–61.

— (1988a), 'The Nature of Autonomy,' in Dworkin, Gerald, (ed.), *The Theory and Practice of Autonomy*, Cambridge: Cambridge University Press, pp. 3–20.

— (1988b), 'Is More Choice Better than Less?', in Dworkin (ed.), *The Theory and Practice of Autonomy*, pp. 62–81.

— (1976), 'Autonomy and Behavior Control,' *Hastings Center Report*, **6**, 23–8.

— (1970), 'Acting Freely,' *Nous*, **4** (4), 367–85.

Eaves, D (1998), 'An examination of the concept of equity and the implications for health policy if equity is re-asserted as one of the key government objectives for the National Health Service,' *Journal of Nursing Management*, **6** (4), 215–21.

Ells, Carolyn (2001), 'Shifting the Autonomy Debate to Theory as Ideology,' *Journal of Medicine and Philosophy*, **26** (4), 417–30.

Engelhardt, Tristram H., Jr (1999), 'The Body for Fun, Beneficence, and Profit: A Variation on a Post-Modern Theme,' in Cherry, Mark, J. (ed.), *Persons and Their Bodies: Rights, Responsibilities, Relationships*, Dordrecht: Kluwer Academic Publishers, pp. 277–302.

Epstein, Richard (1997), *Mortal Peril: Our Inalienable Right to Health Care?*, Cambridge, MA: Perseus Publishing.

Erin, Charles A. and Harris, John (2003), 'An ethical market in human organs,' *Journal of Medical Ethics*, **29** (3), 137–8.

Fasting, Ulla et al. (1998), 'Children Sold for Transplants: medical and legal aspects,' *Nursing Ethics*, **5** (6), 518–26.

Fehrman-Ekholm, I. et al. (1997), 'Kidney donors live longer,' *Transplantation*, **64** (7), 976–8.

Feldstein, Paul J. (1999), *Health Policy Issues: An Economic Perspective on Health Reform*, second edition, Chicago, IL: Health Administration Press.

Finkel, Michael (2001), 'Complications,' *New York Times Magazine*, 27 May, 26–33, 40, 52, 59.

Frankfurt, Harry G. (1999a), 'The Faintest Passion,' in Frankfurt, Harry G. (ed.), *Necessity, Volition, and Love*, pp. 95–107

— (1999b), 'Autonomy, Necessity, and Love,' in Frankfurt, Harry G. (ed.), *Necessity, Volition, and Love*, Cambridge: Cambridge University Press, pp. 129–41.

— (1988a), 'Identification and Wholeheartedness,' in Frankfurt, Harry G. (ed.), *The Importance of What We Care About*, pp. 159–76.

— (1988b), 'Identification and Externality,' in Frankfurt, Harry G. (ed.), *The Importance of What We Care About*, pp. 58–68.

— (1988c), 'Coercion and Moral Responsibility,' in Frankfurt, Harry G., (ed.), *The Importance of What We Care About*, Cambridge: Cambridge University Press, pp. 26–46.

— (1988d), 'Freedom of the Will and the Concept of a Person,' in Frankfurt, Harry G. (ed.), *The Importance of What We Care About*, pp. 11–25.

Frey, Bruno and Jegen, R. (2001), 'Motivation Crowding Theory,' *Journal of Economic Surveys*, 15, 589–611.

Fried, Charles (1978), *Right and Wrong*, Cambridge, MA: Harvard University Press.

Friedlander, Michael M. (2002), 'The right to sell or buy a kidney: are we failing our patients?,' *The Lancet*, 359, 16 March, 971–3.

Friedman, David D. (2001), *Law's Order: What Economics has to do with Law and Why it Matters*, Princeton, NJ: Princeton University Press.

Frishberg, Y. et al. (1998), 'Living (unrelated) commercial renal transplantation in children,' *Journal of the American Society of Nephrology*, 9, 153–9.

Garwood-Gowers, Austen (1999), *Living Donor Organ Transplantation: Key Legal and Ethical Issues*, Aldershot: Ashgate Publishing Co.

Gaylin, Willard and Jennings, Bruce (1996), *The Perversion of Autonomy: The Proper Uses of Coercion and Constraints in a Liberal Society*, New York, NY: The Free Press.

General Medical Council Supplement News Review (1992), December.

Gerrand, Nicole (1999), 'The Misuse of Kant in the Debate about a Market for Human Body Parts,' *Journal of Applied Philosophy*, **16** (1), 59–67.

Ghods, A.J. (2002), 'Renal transplantation in Iran,' *Nephrology Dialysis Transplantation*, **17**, 222–8.

Ghods, A.J., Savaj, S. and Khosravani, P. (2000), 'Adverse Effects of a Controlled Living Unrelated Donor Renal Transplant Program on Living Related and Cadaveric Kidney Donation,' *Transplantation Proceedings*, **32**, 541.

Gill, Michael B. and Sade, Robert M. (2000), 'Paying for kidneys: The case against prohibition,' *Kennedy Institute of Ethics Journal*, **12**, 17–45.

Gneezy, U. and Rustichini, A. (2000), 'Pay Enough or Don't Pay At All,' *Quarterly Journal of Economics*, **115** (2), 791–810.

Goyal, Madhav et al. (2002), 'Economic and Health Consequences of Selling a Kidney in India,' *Journal of the American Medical Association*, **288** (13), 1589–93.

Gritsch, H.A. and Rosenthal, J.T. (2001), 'The transplant operation and its surgical complications,' in Danovitch, *Handbook of Kidney Transplantation*, pp. 146–62.

Gritsch, H.A. et al. (2001), 'Living and Cadaveric Kidney Donation,' in Danovitch, Gabriel M. (ed.), 3rd edition, *Handbook of Kidney Transplantation*, Philadelphia, PA: Lippincott Williams & Eilkins, pp. 111–29.

Hansmann, Henry (1989), 'The Economics and Ethics of Markets for Human Organs,' *Journal of Health Politics, Policy and Law*, **14** (1), 57–85.

Harvey, J. (1990), 'Paying Organ Donors,' *Journal of Medical Ethics*, **16**, 117–19.

Harris, Curtis E. and Alcorn, Stephen P. (2001), 'To Solve a Deadly Shortage: Economic incentives for human organ donation,' *Issues in Law and Medicine*, **16**, 213–33.

Harris, John and Erin, Charles A. (2002), 'An ethically defensible market in organs,' *British Medical Journal*, **325**, 20 July, 114–15.

— (1994), 'A monopsonistic market: or how to buy and sell human organs, tissues and cells ethically,' in Robinson, I. (ed.), *The Social Consequences of Life and Death Under High Technology Medicine*, Manchester: Manchester University Press, pp. 134–57.

Healy, Kieran (1999), 'The emergence of HIV in the U.S. blood supply: organizations, obligations, and the management of uncertainty,' *Theory and Society*, **28**, 529–58.

HHS/HRSA/OSP/DOT and UNOS (2003), *2002 Annual Report of the U.S. Scientific Registry of Transplant Recipients and the Organ Procurement and Transplantation Network*, Rockville, MD and Richmond, VA.

HM Government (2003), *Health and Safety Commission Statistics of Workplace Fatalities and Injuries: Construction (1996/97–2001/02)*, London: Health and Safety Executive.

— (2002a), *Health and Safety Commission Statistics, 2000/01*, London: Health and Safety Executive.

— (2002b), *Rates of Workplace Injury: Europe and the USA*, London: Health and Safety Executive, 19 November.

— (2000), *Statutory Instrument 1995 No. 3163: The Reporting of Injuries, Diseases and Dangerous Occurrences Regulations 1995*, London: HMSO.

— (no date), Government Statistical Service, *Levels and Trends in Workplace Injury: Reported Injuries and the Labour Force Survey*, London: Health and Safety Executive.

Hoffenberg, Raymond (2001), 'Acquisition of kidneys for transplantation,' in Levinsky, Norman (ed.), *Ethics and the Kidney*, Oxford: Oxford University Press, pp. 130–43.

Hughes, Paul M. (1999), 'Paternalism, Battered Women and the Law,' *Journal of Social Philosophy*, **30** (1), 18–28.

— (1998), 'Exploitation, Autonomy, and the Case for Organ Sales,' *International Journal of Applied Philosophy*, **12** (1), 89–95.

Irwin, Douglas A. (2002), *Free Trade Under Fire*, Princeton, NJ: Princeton University Press.

Jeffries, David E. (1998), 'The Body as Commodity: The Use of Markets to Cure the Organ Deficit,' *Indiana Journal of Global Legal Studies*, **5** (2), 621–58.

John Paul II, Pope (2001), 'Address to the International Congress on Transplants,' *The National Catholic Bioethics Quarterly*, **1** (1), Spring, 89–92.

Joralemon, Donald and Cox, Phil (2003), 'Body Values: The Case Against Compensating for Transplant Organs,' *Hastings Center Report*, **33**, 27–33.

Kandela, P. (1991), 'India: Kidney bazaar,' *The Lancet*, **337**, 22 June, 1534.

Kant, Immanuel (2003), *The Metaphysics of Morals*, ed. Gregor, Mary, Cambridge: Cambridge University Press (first published 1797).

— (2001), *Groundwork of the Metaphysics of Morals*, ed. Gregor, Mary, Cambridge: Cambridge University Press (first published 1785).

— (1930), *Lectures on Ethics*, trans. Infield, Louis, New York, NY: The Century Co.

Kennedy, I. et al. (1998), 'The case for presumed consent in organ donation,' *The Lancet*, **351**, 1650–52.

Kernaghan, Charles (2000), *Made in China: The Role of U.S. Companies in Denying Human and Worker Rights*, New York, NY: National Labor Committee.

Kervorkian, Jack (2001), 'Solve The Organ Shortage: Let The Bidding Begin!,' *American Journal of Forensic Psychiatry*, **22** (2), 7–15.

Kessel, Reuben (1977), 'Ethical and Economic Aspects of Government Intervention in the Medical Care Market,' in Dworkin, Gerald, Bermant, Gordon and Brown, Peter G. (eds), *Markets and Morals*, New York, NY: John Wiley & Sons, pp. 137–48.

— (1976), 'Transfused Blood, Serum Hepatitis and the Coase Theorem,' in Johnson, David B. (ed.), *Blood Policy: Issues and Alternatives*, Washington, DC: American Enterprise Institute for Public Policy Research, 183–207.

Kumar, Sanjay, (1994), 'Curbing trade in human organs in India,' *The Lancet*, **344**, 2 July, 48–9.

Lennerling, A., Blohme, I., Ostraat, O., et al. (2001), 'Laparoscopic or open surgery for living donor nephrectomy,' *Nephrology Dialysis Transplantation*, 16, 383–6.

Leventhal, Todd (1994), 'The "Baby Parts" Myth: The Anatomy of a Rumour,' report for the United States Information Agency, May.

Levey, A.S., Hou, S. and Bush, H.L. (1986), 'Kidney Transplantation from Unrelated Living Donors: Time to Reclaim a Discarded Opportunity,' *New England Journal of Medicine*, 314, 914–16.

Love, Andrew J. (1997), 'Replacing Our Current System of Organ Procurement with a Futures Market: Will Organ Supply Be Maximized?,' *Jurimetrics Journal*, 37 (2), 167–86.

Lumsdaine, J.A. et al. (1999), 'Live kidney donor assessment in the UK and Ireland,' *British Journal of Surgery*, 86, 877–81.

Lysaght, M.J. and Mason, J. (2000), 'The Case for Financial Incentives to Encourage Organ Donation,' *ASAIO Journal*, 46 (3), 235–56.

Mack, Eric (1989), 'Dominos and the Fear of Commodification,' in John W. Chapman, John W. and Pennock, Roland J. (eds), *Markets and Justice: Nomos XXXI*, New York, NY: New York University Press, pp. 198–225.

Mackler, Aaron L. (2001), 'Respecting Bodies and Saving Lives: Jewish Perspectives on Organ Donation and Transplantation,' *Cambridge Quarterly of Healthcare Ethics*, 10, 420–29.

Maitland, Ian (1997), 'The Great Non-Debate Over International Sweatshops,' *British Academy of Management Conference Proceedings*, September, 240–65.

Manga, Pranlal (1987), 'A Commercial Market for Organs? Why Not,' *Bioethics*, 1 (4), 321–38.

Marshall, Mac (2000), 'Comment on Nancy Scheper-Hughes, "Global Traffic in Human Organs,"' *Current Anthropology*, 41 (2), 215–16.

Marshall, Patricia A., Thomasma, David C. and Daar, Abdallah S. (1996), 'Marketing Human Organs: The autonomy paradox,' *Theoretical Medicine*, 17, 1–18.

Martyn, Susan, et al. (1988), 'Required Request for Organ Donation: Moral Clinical, and Legal Problems,' *Hastings Center Report*, **18**, April/May, 27–34.

McConnell, Terence C. (2000), *Inalienable Rights: The Limits of Consent in Medicine and Law*, Oxford: Oxford University Press.

McKinnon, Ian and Kelsey, Tim (1989), 'Turkish peasant "duped into selling a kidney,"' *The Independent*, 18 January, p. 2.

Medicare (1995), *Medicare Coverage of Kidney Dialysis and Transplantation Services: A Supplement to your Medicare Handbook*, Washington, DC: Government Printing Office, Pub. No. HCFA 594 B.

Mehlman, M.J. (1991), 'Presumed consent to organ donation: A reevaluation,' *Health Matrix*, **1** (1), 31–66.

Meinkoff, Jerry (1999), 'Organ Swapping,' *Hastings Center Report*, **29**, 28–33.

Melchor, J.L. (1998), 'Living Donors in Kidney Transplantation: Five-year Follow-up,' *Transplantation Proceedings*, **30**, 2869–70.

Menzel, P.T. (1991), 'The moral duty to contribute and its implications for organ procurement policy,' *Transplantation Proceedings*, **24**, 2175–8.

Mill, J.S. (1978), *On Liberty*, ed. Rapaport, Elizabeth, Indianapolis, IN: Hackett Publishing Co., Inc.

Miller, I. et al. (1985), 'Impact of Renal Donation: Long-term Clinical and Biochemical Follow-Up of Living Donors in a Single Center,' *American Journal of Medicine*, **79**, 201–208.

Mohamed, S.S. and Velasco, N. (1990), 'Kidneys for sale,' *The Lancet*, **336**, 1384.

Morden, Michael (1988), 'Cyclosporine as an Ethical Catalyst: Recent Issues in Kidney Transplantation,' *Public Affairs Quarterly*, **2** (4), 31–45.

Morelli, Mario (1999), 'Commerce in Organs: A Kantian Critique,' *Journal of Social Philosophy*, **30** (2), 315–24.

Morris, P.J. and Sells, R.A. (1998), 'Paying for Organs from Living Donors,' in Caplan and Coelho (eds), *The Ethics of Organ Transplants: The Current Debate*, Amherst, NY: Prometheus Books, pp. 229–30.

Mudur, Ganapati (2003), 'India's burden of waterborne diseases is underestimated,' *British Medical Journal*, **326**, 1284.

Munson, Ronald (2002), *Raising the Dead: Organ Transplants, Ethics, and Society*, Oxford: Oxford University Press.

Munzer, Stephen R. (1994), 'An Uneasy Case Against Property Rights in Body Parts,' *Social Philosophy & Policy*, **11** (2), 259–86.

Narkun-Burgess, D.M. et al. (1993), 'Forty-five year follow-up after uninephrectomy,' *Kidney International*, **43** (5), 1110–15.

National Conference of Catholic Bishops (1995), *Ethical and Religious Directives for Catholic Health Care Services*, Washington, DC: US Catholic Conference.

Nelkin, Dorothy and Brown, Michael S. (1984), *Workers at Risk*, Chicago, IL: University of Chicago Press.

Nelson, Mark T. (1991), 'The Morality of a Free Market for Transplant Organs,' *Public Affairs Quarterly*, **5** (1), 63–79.

Niven, Larry (1967), 'The Jigsaw Man,' in Ellison, Harlan, (ed.), *Dangerous Visions*, London: Doubleday, pp. 216–31.

Nuffield Council on Bioethics (1995), *Human Tissue: Ethical and Legal Issues*, London.

Oswald, Andrew (2001), 'Economics that Matters: Using the Tax System to Solve the Shortage of Human Organs,' *Kyklos*, **54**, 579–81.

Pattison, Shaun D. (2003), 'Paying Living Organ Providers,' *Web Journal of Current Legal Issues*, **3**, accessed on 21 January 2004 at: http://webjcli.ncl.ac.uk/2003/issue3/pattinson3.html.

Pena, J.R., Pena, R. and da Costa, A. Gomes (1991), 'Presumed Consent and Cadaver Organ Donation,' in Land W. and Dossetor, J.B. (eds), *Organ Replacement Therapy: Ethics, Justice, Commerce*, London: Springer-Verlag, pp. 277–9.

Perez, Luis M. et al. (1988), 'Organ Donation in Three Major American Cities with Large Latino and Black Populations,' *Transplantation*, **46** (4), 553–7.

Perry, Clifton (1980), 'Human Organs and the Open Market,' *Ethics*, **91**, 63–71.

Pius XII, Pope (1960) 'Tissue Transplantation,' in The Monks of Solesmes, (eds and trans.), *The Human Body: Papal Teachings*, Boston: St Paul Editions, pp. 373–84.

Plant, Raymond (1977), 'Gifts, exchanges and the political economy of health care, Part I: Should blood be bought and sold?,' *Journal of Medical Ethics*, **3** (4), 166–73.

Pollin, Robert, Heintz, James and Burns, Justine (2004), 'Global Apparel Production and Sweatshop Labor: Can Raising Prices Finance Living Wages?,' *Cambridge Journal of Economies*, **28** (2), 153–71.

Price, David (2000), *Legal and Ethical Aspects of Organ Transplantation*, Cambridge: Cambridge University Press.

Pruviance, Susan M. (1993), 'Kidney Transplantation Policy: Race and Distributive Justice,' *Business and Professional Ethics Journal*, **12** (2), 19–37.

Radcliffe Richards, Janet (1996) 'Nepharious Goings On: Kidney sales and moral arguments,' *The Journal of Medicine and Philosophy*, **21** (1996), 375–416.

Radcliffe Richards, J. et al. (1998) 'The case for allowing kidney sales', *The Lancet*, **351**, 27 June, 1950–51.

Radin, Margaret Jane (2001), 'Response: Persistent Perplexities,' *Kennedy Institute of Ethics Journal*, **11** (3), 305–15.

— (1996), *Contested Commodities*, Cambridge, MA: Harvard University Press.

— (1987), 'Market Inalienability,' *Harvard Law Review*, **100**, 1849–1937.

Ram, Vidya (2002), 'International Traffic in Human Organs,' *Frontline*, **19** (7), 30 March–12 April.

Reddy, K.C. (1993), 'Should Paid Organ Donation be Banned in India? To Buy or Let Die!,' *National Medical Journal of India*, **6** (3), 137–9.

Rettig, Richard A. (1996), 'The Social Contract and the Treatment of Permanent Kidney Failure,' *Journal of the American Medical Association*, **275** (14), 1123–6.

Roberts, Dexter and Bernstein, Aaron (2000), 'A Life of Fines and Beatings,' *Business Week*, 2 October.

Roberts, Stephen (2002), 'Hazardous occupations in Great Britain,' *The Lancet*, **360**, 17 August, 543–4.

Rosenthal, J. Thomas and Danovitch, Gabriel M. (1996), 'Live-Related and Cadaveric Kidney Donation,' in Danovitch, Gabriel M., *Handbook of Kidney Transplantation*, second edition, Boston: Little, Brown and Company, Inc., pp. 95–108.

Ross, Andrew (1997), *No Sweat: Fashion, Free Trade and the Rights of Garment Workers*, London: Verso.

Rothman, David J., (2002), 'Ethical and Social Consequences of Selling a Kidney,' *Journal of the American Medical Association*, **288** (13), 1640–41.

— (1998), 'The International Organ Traffic,' *The New York Review of Books*, **45** (5), 26 March, 14–16.

Rothman, D.J. et al. (1997), 'The Bellagio Task Force Report on Transplantation, Bodily Integrity, and the International Traffic in Organs,' *Transplantation Proceedings*, **29**, 2739–45.

Santos, Luiz S. et al. (2003), 'Hand-assisted laparoscopic nephrectomy in living donor,' *International Brazilian Journal of Urology*, **29** (1), 11–17.

Saran, R. et al. (1997), 'Long-term follow-up of kidney donors: a longitudinal study,' *Nephrology Dialysis Transplantation*, **12**, 1615–21.

Savulescu, J. (2003), 'Is the sale of body parts wrong?,' *Journal of Medical Ethics*, **29** (3), 138–9.

Scheper-Hughes, Nancy (2003) 'Keeping an eye on the global traffic in human organs,' *The Lancet*, **361**, 10 May, 1645–8.

— (2002a), 'The Ends of the Body: Commodity Fetishism and the Global Traffic in Organs,' *SAIS Review*, **22** (1), 61–80.

— (2002b), 'Organ markets must be shut, not legalized,' *The National Post*, 8 April, p. A16.

— (2000), 'The Global Traffic in Human Organs,' *Current Anthropology*, **41** (2), 191–224.

Schneider, Carl (1998), *The Practice of Autonomy: Patients, Doctors and Medical Decisions*, Oxford: Oxford University Press.

Schweitzer, E.J., Wilson, J., Jacobs, S. et al. (2000), 'Increased rates of donation with laparoscopic donor nephrectomy,' *Annals of Surgery*, **232**, 392–400

Schwindt, R. and Vining, A. (1986), 'Proposal for a Future Delivery Market for Transplant Organs,' *Journal of Health, Politics, Policy and Law*, **11** (3), 483–500.

Scott, Russell (1981), *The Body as Property*, London: Viking Press.

Sells, R.A. (1993), 'Consent for Organ Donation: What Are the Ethical Principles?,' *Transplantation Proceedings*, **25** (1), 39–41.

— (1991), 'Voluntarism of consent,' in Land and Dossestor (eds), *Organ Replacement Therapy: Ethics, Justice, Commerce*, New York: Springer-Verlag, pp. 18–24.

Sever, M.S. et al. (1994), 'Living unrelated (paid) kidney transplantation in third-world countries: High risk of complications besides the ethical problem,' *Nephrology, Dialysis, Transplantation*, **9**, 350–54.

Shapiro, Joseph (2003), *The Ethics and Efficacy of Banning Human Kidney Sales* (unpublished MS).

Shearmur, Jeremy (forthcoming), *Living With Markets*, London: Routledge.

— (2001), 'Trust, Titmuss, and Blood,' *Economic Affairs*, **21** (1), 29–33.

Siegel-Itzkovich, Judy (2003), 'Israel considers paying people for donating a kidney,' *British Medical Journal*, **326**, 18 January, 126.

Siminoff, Laura A. and Mercer, Mary Beth (2001), 'Public Policy, Public Opinion, and Consent for Organ Donation,' *Cambridge Quarterly of Healthcare Ethics*, **10**, 377–86.

Siminoff, L.A. and Chillag, K. (1999), 'The fallacy of the "gift of life" and its implications for transplant recipients and donor families,' *Hastings Center Report*, **29**, 34–41.

Singer, Peter (1976), 'Freedoms and Utilities in the Distribution of Health Care,' in Veatch, Robert M. and Branson, Roy, (eds), *Ethics and Health Policy*, Cambridge, MA: Ballinger Publishing Company, pp. 175–93.

— (1972), 'Famine, Affluence, and Morality,' *Philosophy and Public Affairs*, **1**, 229–43.

Smith II, George (1993), 'Market and Non-Market Mechanisms for Procuring Human and Cadaveric Organs: When the Price is Right,' *Medical Law International*, **1**, 17.

Smith, Janet, (1997), 'The Pre-Eminence of Autonomy in Bioethics,' in Oderberg, David S. and Laing, Jacqueline A. (eds), *Human Lives: Critical Essays on Consequentialist Bioethics*, New York, NY: St Martin's Press, Inc., pp. 182–95.

Smith, Kevin H. (1999), 'Security Interests in Human Materials,' *Hofstra Law Review*, **28** (1), 127–84.

Spital, Aaron (1998), 'Mandated Choice for Organ Donation: Time to Give It a Try,' in Caplan, Arthur L. and Coelho, Daniel H. (eds), *The Ethics of Organ Transplants: The Current Debate*, Amherst, NY: Prometheus Books, pp. 147–53.

Stempsey, William E., S.J. (2002), 'Organ Markets and Human Dignity: On Selling Your Body and Soul,' *Christian Bioethics*, **6** (2), 195–204.

Stewart, Robert M. (1984), 'Morality and the Market in Blood,' *Journal of Applied Philosophy*, **1** (2), 227–37.

Swami, Praveen (2003), 'Punjab's Kidney Industry,' *Frontline*, **20** (3), 1–14 February.

Tadd, G.V. (1991), 'The Market for Bodily Parts: a Response to Ruth Chadwick,' *Journal of Applied Philosophy*, **8** (1), 95–102.

Talseth, T. et al. (1986), 'Long-term Blood Pressure and Renal Function in Kidney Donors,' *Kidney International*, **29**, 1072–6.

Taylor, James Stacey (2005), 'Introduction,' in Taylor, James Stacey (ed.), *Personal Autonomy: New Essays on Personal Autonomy and its Role in Contemporary Moral Philosophy*, Cambridge: Cambridge University Press, pp. 1–29.

— (2003), 'Autonomy, Duress, and Coercion,' *Social Philosophy & Policy*, **20** (2), 127–55.

— (2002), 'Autonomy, Constraining Options, and Organ Sales,' *Journal of Applied Philosophy*, **19** (3), 273–85.

Thalberg, Irving (1989), 'Hierarchical Analyses of Unfree Action,' in Christman, John, (ed.), *The Inner Citadel: Essays on Individual Autonomy*, Oxford: Oxford University Press, pp. 123–36.

Tiong, Danilo C. (2001), 'Human Organ Transplants,' in Alora, Angeles Tan and Lumitao, Josephine M. (eds), *Beyond a Western Bioethics: Voices from the Developing*

World, Washington, DC: Georgetown University Press, pp. 89–93.

Titmuss, Richard (1997), *The Gift Relationship: From Human Blood to Social Policy*, ed. with new chapters by Oakley, Ann and Ashton, John, New York: The New Press (first published 1970).

The Transplantation Society Council (1986), 'Commercialization in transplantation: The problem and some guidelines for practice,' *Transplantation*, **41**, 1–3.

Trebilcock, Michael J. (1993), *The Limits of Freedom of Contract*, Cambridge, MA: Harvard University Press.

UNESCO (1989), *Human Rights Aspects of Traffic in Body Parts and Human Fetuses for Research and/or Therapeutic Purposes*, Geneva.

United States Task Force on Organ Transplantation (1986), *Organ Transplantation: Issues and Recommendations*, US Department of Health and Human Services, Washington, DC: US Government Printing Office.

Upton, W. (1973), 'Altruism, Attribution, and Intrinsic Motivation in the Recruitment of Blood Donors,' in American Red Cross (ed.), *Selected Readings in Donor Motivation and Recruitment*, vol. 3, Washington, DC: American Red Cross.

Veatch, R.M. (1991), 'Routine inquiry about organ donation—an alternative to presumed consent,' *New England Journal of Medicine*, **325**, 1246–9.

Veatch, R.M. and Pitt, J.B. (1998), 'The Myth of Presumed Consent,' in Caplan, Arthur L. and Coelho, Daniel H. (eds.), *The Ethics of Organ Transplants: The Current Debate*, Amherst, NY: Prometheus Books, pp. 173–82.

Velasco, N. (1998), 'Letter,' *The Lancet*, **352**, 8 August, 483.

Viscusi, W. Kip (1983), *Risk By Choice: Regulating Health and Safety in the Workplace*, Cambridge, MA: Harvard University Press.

Walsh, Adrian (2001), 'Are Market Norms and Intrinsic Valuation Mutually Exclusive?,' *Australasian Journal of Philosophy*, **79** (4), 525–43.

Walzer, Michael (1983), *Spheres of Justice: A Defense of Pluralism and Equality*, New York, NY: Basic Books, Inc.

Whitman, Glen (1996), 'Myth, Measurement, and the Minimum Wage: Sound and Fury Signifying What?,' *Critical Review*, **10** (4), 607–19.

Wilkinson, Stephen (2003), *Bodies for Sale: Ethics and Exploitation in the Human Body Trade*, London: Routledge.

— (2000), 'Commodification Arguments for the Legal Prohibition of Organ Sale,' *Health Care Analysis*, **8** (2), 189–201.

Wilkinson, Stephen and Garrard, Eve (1996), 'Bodily integrity and the sale of human organs,' *Journal of Medical Ethics*, **22** (6), 334–9.

Williams, S.L. et al. (1986), 'Long-Term Renal Function in Kidney Donors: a Comparison of Donors and their Siblings,' *Annals of Internal Medicine*, **105**, 1–8.

Wolfe, Robert A. et al. (1999), 'Comparison of Mortality in All Patients on Dialysis, Patients on Dialysis Awaiting Transplantation, and Recipients of a First Cadaveric Transplant,' *New England Journal of Medicine*, **341** (23), 1725–30.

Working Party of the British Transplantation Society and the Renal Association (2000), *United Kingdom Guidelines for Living Donor Kidney Transplantation*, London.

World Health Organization (1992), *A Report on Developments under the Auspices of WHO (1987–1991)*, Geneva: WHO.

World Medical Association (2000), *Statement on Human Organ and Tissue Donation and Transplantation*, adopted by the 52nd WMA General Assembly, Edinburgh, October.

Zargooshi, Javaad (2001a), 'Iranian kidney donors: motivations and relations with the recipients,' *The Journal of Urology*, **165**, 386–92.

— (2001b), 'Quality of Life of Iranian Kidney "Donors,"' *The Journal of Urology*, **166**, 1790–99.

Zutlevics, T.L. (2001a), 'Markets and the Needy: Organ Sales or Aid?,' *Journal of Applied Philosophy*, **18** (3), 297–302.

— (2001b), 'Libertarianism and Personal Autonomy,' *Southern Journal of Philosophy*, **39** (3), 461–71.

Index